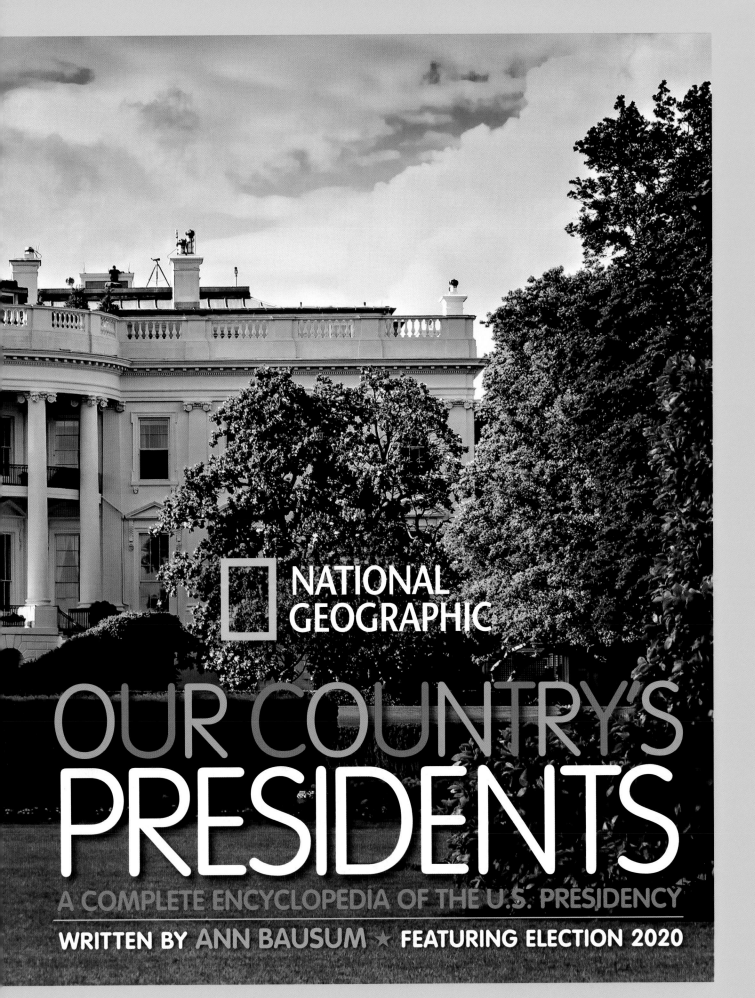

NATIONAL
GEOGRAPHIC

OUR COUNTRY'S
PRESIDENTS

A COMPLETE ENCYCLOPEDIA OF THE U.S. PRESIDENCY

WRITTEN BY ANN BAUSUM ★ FEATURING ELECTION 2020

CONTENTS

Although the presidents and their history may seem to literally be set in stone (here, Mount Rushmore), these figures are the subject of ongoing study and reflection.

The Oval Office serves as the command center for a presidency. Each Chief Executive usually redecorates the space to suit individual tastes for such items as carpet, draperies, and furniture. The so-called Resolute desk (center) was presented to President Rutherford B. Hayes in 1880 by Great Britain's Queen Victoria. It was placed in various locations around the White House until the 1960s, when John F. Kennedy began to use it in the Oval Office. Most presidents have done the same since.

FOREWORD
BY JOHN DICKERSON

When the 11th president, James K. Polk, walked into a room, his wife worried that people would not recognize him. So she asked the band to play "Hail to the Chief." Now we always notice the president—streets are cleared to make way for the eight-ton, armor-plated presidential limousine; planes veer off course to give Air Force One a straight flight path; and adults cheer or jeer a president as wildly as if the Super Bowl game were on the line. The president is the most famous person in the United States and arguably the most influential politician in the most powerful country on the planet.

It was not meant to be this way. In the summer of 1787 when the framers drew the blueprint for the job, they imagined a limited office. The president would serve as commander in chief of the armed forces and ensure that the laws were faithfully executed, but would share power with the legislative and judicial branches. After winning a revolution against a British king, the Founders were determined to guard against the rise of an American version of a monarchy.

For the new country's first 150 years, the limited design held. Congress, as well as state and local governments, had more sway over American life than the president. As the United States grew in the 20th century, however, the speed of communication and commerce required faster, centralized action from government. Presidents stepped in to meet those demands. Americans turned to President Franklin D. Roosevelt to steer the country out of the economic collapse of the Great Depression and have turned to his successors for domestic solutions ever since. The Second World War expanded the president's role as commander in chief. The Cold War and the fight against terrorism have continued that trend.

From the start, Americans have expected the president's character to match their lofty aspirations for the country. The first president, George Washington, knew that how he behaved would guide the behavior of those who held the job after him. Honest Abe Lincoln modeled himself after Washington and added his reputation for truth-telling to the virtues expected of the office. This emotional connection between the president and what is best about the country explains why Americans turn to the Chief Executive for uplift and unity. Not every president has fulfilled the duties of the office—or even recognized that they exist. But the American presidency has remained resilient over its 230 years, helping to build a prosperous nation, which at its best has aimed to be a beacon for liberty and equality for the entire world.

John Dickerson

John Dickerson is a correspondent for *60 Minutes* and the author of *The Hardest Job in the World: The American Presidency*.

ABOUT THE PRESIDENCY
AN INTRODUCTION

O n February 4, 1789, a few dozen men held simultaneous meetings in the various United States. By unanimous vote they selected George Washington to be the nation's first president. These electors hoped Washington would head an unbroken chain of capable national leaders. America's experiment in democracy had begun, but no one knew if it would endure.

Eleven years later the nation's second president, John Adams, moved into the still unfinished home that is known today as the White House. "May none but Honest and Wise Men ever rule under this Roof," he wrote. Those who followed him to the presidency have tried to honor his hopes, and so will the men and women who become president in the future.

Each president takes a short oath of office: "I do solemnly swear that I will faithfully execute the Office of President of the United States, and will to the best of my Ability, preserve, protect and defend the Constitution of the United States."

Each person must meet a simple list of qualifications in order to seek the presidency: He or she must be born as a U.S. citizen, be at least 35 years old, and have lived in the country for at least 14 years. Each candidate strives to represent the best hopes of fellow citizens for meeting the nation's needs.

Places change over time. The 1790 census counted not even four million people in the United States, including more than half a million enslaved people. Women, African Americans, Native Americans, and many poor white males had not yet won the right to vote. Over the years, transportation advanced from horse power to steam power to jet power. Inventors, scientists, and explorers changed the landscape with factories, technologies, and discoveries. The United States grew from a tentative experiment in democracy into a world superpower.

U.S. presidents helped shape this evolving nation. Some, such as Thomas Jefferson, transformed the country's geography and outlook with their visions for change. Others, such as Abraham Lincoln, led the nation through critical periods of national and world history. Many left a personal stamp

George Washington (above, far right) was sworn in as the nation's first president on April 30, 1789. The ceremony took place at Federal Hall in New York City, the first seat of national government for the new republic.

Abraham Lincoln, who won the four-way race of 1860 with a plurality of votes (less than 50 percent), spent his presidency trying to unite a divided nation.

"Ask not what your country can do for you—ask what you can do for your country." This challenge in John F. Kennedy's Inaugural Address of 1961 inspired a generation of young people to undertake national public service.

Theodore Roosevelt laid the groundwork for the formation of the National Park Service in 1916 through his efforts to conserve natural lands during his presidency (above, visiting Yosemite in California, 1903).

on the outcome of the nation. Most served as good stewards; they tried to do their best work. All marked their place in the history of the nation.

U.S. presidents are a favorite topic of study for young and old alike. Presidents attract attention for different reasons, whether it's for their bold policies, as with Franklin D. Roosevelt; for their power to inspire, as with John F. Kennedy; or for their adventurousness, as with Teddy Roosevelt. Readers are curious about how presidents coped with the challenges of their eras and how they lived their personal lives.

Presidents come with funny stories (one had his clothes stolen while he was skinny-dipping), jarring facts (many of the early ones championed the cause of freedom while simultaneously holding people in bondage), and overlooked accomplishments (how they helped establish national traditions). They give us words that inspire ("Government of the people, by the people, for the people, shall not perish from the earth"—Abraham Lincoln) and words that reassure ("The only thing we have to fear is fear itself"—Franklin D. Roosevelt).

We give presidents nicknames—from Uncle Jumbo to Tricky Dick, from Honest Abe to Old Rough-and-Ready. We remember them for their extremes, their milestones, and their originality. Who was the only unmarried president? Who won the closest election? How many presidents died on the Fourth of July? How many died in office? Who was our youngest president? Who was the oldest? Which presidents are regarded by historians as our best leaders? Who might historians judge as among the worst?

Our Country's Presidents answers these questions and hundreds more. It introduces the presidents as individuals, with full disclosure of good traits as well as flaws. By viewing the presidents in full dimension, it is possible to breathe life into their historic portraits. Readers may measure their own dreams and challenges against those of their national leaders, perhaps gaining a stronger sense of self as a result.

The presidents' stories, both personal and professional, are part of the nation's story. When we understand them, they become part of our extended family history. Welcome to the stories of our country's presidents.

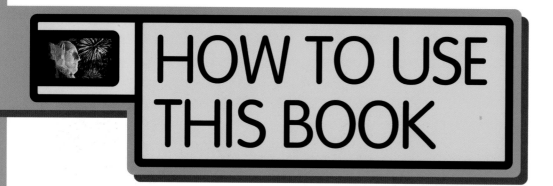

HOW TO USE THIS BOOK

You may choose to read *Our Country's Presidents* from cover to cover, just browse through the photos, or investigate one topic of interest. Knowing a bit more about how the book is organized should help you use it with greater success.

Timelines

This book presents the U.S. presidents in chronological order grouped by six historical periods. A brief essay explains the common themes shared by the presidents within these groupings, accompanied by an illustrated timeline that introduces readers to important events of the period, from wars to inventions, from explorations to protests.

Profiles

Individual essays present key elements of the history of each president, including family background, childhood, education, prepresidential careers, election highlights, important events during the presidency, and activities pursued in retirement years. The opening paragraph of each essay summarizes major points about the significance of each leader's administration. Multiple illustrations provide a visual dimension to the story. Profiles range in length from two to six pages depending on the significance of the individual. Longer essays feature notable quotes by the presidents that are highlighted in large type.

Presidential Portraits

Each presidential profile is introduced by a full-page reproduction of the leader's official portrait. These paintings are unveiled sometime after the president leaves office and are displayed throughout the White House. A different collection of presidential portraits is maintained by the nearby National Portrait Gallery.

Fact Boxes

A fact box appears on the opening spread of each profile. It features the president's signature as well as quick reference facts in categories ranging from nicknames to election opponents, from important dates to the number of states in the Union at the start of each presidency. Each box includes a list of selected landmarks to help readers make geographic connections with the lives of the presidents.

Thematic Spreads

Nearly two dozen two-page spreads are placed strategically throughout the book to explain particular themes that relate to the presidency. By reading these topical essays, you will be able to make connections between presidents. Your understanding of U.S. history and the operation of the federal government will grow, too. Some essays cover topics of human interest, such as background about the families of the presidents. Others explain how the government functions, including the workings of the Electoral College and the three branches of government. Additional thematic spreads explore how the presidents work, play, travel, stay safe, and more—even what they do after they retire from the presidency.

Reference Aids

A summary of U.S. election history introduces the reference material in the final pages of *Our Country's Presidents*. This chart shows the results of every election, including victors and major challengers. It also presents Electoral College tallies and the results of the popular voting that began in 1824. A resource guide follows with ideas for how to find out more about the presidents. Information on sources used for the book's text and photos as well as a comprehensive index conclude the book.

summary of the era

timeline

SEEKING STABILITY IN THE ATOMIC AGE

1945–1989

The challenges faced by presidents increased in complexity as the 20th century progressed. Leaders struggled to fight wars, end poverty, preserve democracy, extend equality, survive energy shortages, and heal national wounds. They led citizens through the tragedies of presidential deaths and scandals, too. Much of the era was dominated by the uneasy balance of power between the rivals of the atomic age—the United States and the Soviet Union. Presidents sought to offset the troubles of the times with hopes for a promising future.

A mushroom cloud marks the devastating impact of the atomic bomb dropped by an American aircraft on Hiroshima, Japan, on August 6, 1945. Three days later, the U.S. destroyed Nagasaki, Japan, with another atomic bomb. Soon after, Japan agreed to surrender, bringing an end to World War II. Nuclear weapons have never again been used in combat.

1946
The first programmable electronic computer weighed 30 tons and used some 18,000 bulky vacuum tubes to transfer information. By 1952 computers were calculating election results.

1957
Racial tensions mounted in Little Rock, Arkansas, after the governor ignored the 1954 Supreme Court ruling on the integration of public schools, Brown v. Board of Education.

1962
Labor advocates César Chávez and Dolores Huerta (above, during a national grape boycott) established what became the United Farm Workers union to promote safety and fair pay for migrant farm workers.

1967
Widespread protest of U.S. involvement in the Vietnam War developed during the late 1960s, particularly among young people (above, a protester fills gun barrels with flowers).

1969
On July 20, humans set foot on the moon for the first time. A series of six Apollo lunar missions carried 12 U.S. astronauts to the moon between 1969 and 1972.

1973
Some 200 members of the American Indian Movement occupied Wounded Knee on South Dakota's Pine Ridge Reservation to protest broken treaties and tribal mismanagement. Two died during the 71-day armed siege.

1981
A new technology company named Microsoft helped launch the personal computer industry with its MS-DOS operating system. It quickly became a leader in the field (above, floppy disks, 1993).

1989
Berlin citizens marked the end of the Cold War by tearing down the wall that had divided their city into separate zones. East reunited with West in a new democracy.

146   147

---

official presidential portrait

introductory summary paragraph

term of office dates

signature

fact box

ABRAHAM LINCOLN
16TH PRESIDENT OF THE UNITED STATES 1861–1865

When Abraham Lincoln was inaugurated in 1861, he became president of states that were not united. In fact, after arguing for years about slavery and states' rights, Northerners and Southerners were on the brink of civil, or internal, war. Lincoln, expressing his commitment to the highest ideals of democracy, succeeded in reuniting the country and ending slavery. He was assassinated just after the end of the Civil War in 1865.

Lincoln's humble beginnings are a schoolbook legend. He was born in a log cabin in Kentucky to parents who could neither read nor write. The sum of his schoolhouse education was about one year's time, so he taught himself by reading books he borrowed from others. When Lincoln was nine years old, his mother died. His father, a carpenter and farmer, remarried and moved his family farther west, eventually settling in Illinois. Lincoln was taller (at six feet four inches) than any other president. His high-pitched voice and thick frontier accent (saying "git" for "get" or "thar" for "there") made an odd contrast with his dignified figure and inspiring words.

Lincoln worked as a flatboat navigator, storekeeper, soldier, surveyor, and postmaster before being elected at age 25 to the Illinois Legislature in Springfield. Once there, he taught himself law, opened a law practice, and earned the nickname Honest Abe. He served one term in the U.S. House of Representatives during 1847–1849 but lost two U.S. Senate races in the 1850s. He spoke in opposition to the expansion of slavery during his famed 1858 debates with Stephen Douglas. This stance helped earn him the Republican presidential nomination two years later.

First Lady Mary Todd Lincoln

Abraham Lincoln's lifelong love of reading whenever and wherever he could begin in his youth, when books often took the place of school. Favorite reading included U.S. history, Aesop's Fables, Robinson Crusoe, the Bible, and works by Shakespeare.

Abraham Lincoln

NICKNAME
Honest Abe

BORN
Feb. 12, 1809,
near Hodgenville, KY

POLITICAL PARTY
Republican (formerly Whig)

CHIEF OPPONENTS
1st term Stephen Arnold Douglas, Northern Democrat (1813–1861); John Cabell Breckinridge, Southern Democrat (1821–1875); John Bell, Constitutional Unionist (1797–1869); and 2nd term: George Brinton McClellan, Democrat (1826–1885)

TERM OF OFFICE
March 4, 1861–April 15, 1865

AGE AT INAUGURATION
52 years old

NUMBER OF TERMS
two (cut short by assassination)

VICE PRESIDENTS
1st term Hannibal Hamlin (1809–1891); 2nd term Andrew Johnson (1808–1875)

FIRST LADY
Mary Todd Lincoln (1818–1882), wife (married Nov. 4, 1842)

CHILDREN
Robert, Edward (died young), William, Thomas (Tad)

GEOGRAPHIC SCENE
23 United States;
11 Confederate States

NEW STATES ADDED
West Virginia (1863),
Nevada (1864)

DIED
April 15, 1865,
in Washington, DC

AGE AT DEATH
56 years old

SELECTED LANDMARKS
Hodgenville, KY (birthplace); Springfield, IL (home, grave, and library); Lincoln Memorial, President's Cottage, Washington, DC; Mount Rushmore National Memorial, Keystone, SD

78   79

11

THE PRESIDENCY AND HOW IT GREW

1789–1837

The authors of the U.S. Constitution only sketched a loose outline of the presidency when they defined the federal government in 1787. They expected the first presidents to work out the details of the job in cooperation with Congress and the Supreme Court. As a result, the first officeholders helped shape the way presidents make decisions, fight wars, work with Congress, add territory to the country, entertain, and so on. The presidency became a position that could be revised and improved as needed by future presidents.

1789
Delegates wrote a new set of laws for governing the United States at the Constitutional Convention of 1787. By 1789 the Constitution was ratified, and the nation's first president was in place.

1795
The Constitution put the federal government in charge of issuing money. The $10 eagle coin was minted from 1795 to 1933. The capped figure of Liberty faced the coin.

1803
Thomas Jefferson offered to buy the Mississippi port of New Orleans. France sold it and the rest of its adjacent North American lands to the United States as the Louisiana Purchase.

1804–1806
A handful of men and Sacagawea, a Shoshone woman, helped Meriwether Lewis and William Clark explore the land between the Mississippi River and the Pacific Ocean.

In 1825 President John Quincy Adams nearly drowned in Tiber Creek (foreground). The waterway now flows through tunnels beneath the nation's capital.

1810
John Marshall served as the nation's Chief Justice longer than anyone else. His 1810 Supreme Court ruling in *Fletcher* v. *Peck* was the first to declare a state law unconstitutional.

1812–1815
Major naval battles (above, on Lake Erie) were a prominent feature of the U.S. conflict with Great Britain known as the War of 1812.

1820
Eli Whitney's 1793 invention of the cotton gin fueled the growth of the cotton industry and the expansion of slavery. By 1820 enslaved laborers were being forced to work in most southern states.

1836
When Texans battled Mexico for their independence, they suffered a crushing defeat at the Alamo in San Antonio (above). Two months later they won their independence.

GEORGE WASHINGTON
1ST PRESIDENT OF THE UNITED STATES 1789–1797

George Washington helped transform 13 British colonies into a new nation through a lifetime of public service as both a military leader and a statesman. As the first president of the United States, he set precedents, or patterns of behavior, for future presidents to follow. After his death, he was praised for being "first in war, first in peace, and first in the hearts of his countrymen."

Little is known about the early life of the man who grew up to be called the Father of His Country. Stories about his virtues—such as his honest confession of chopping down his father's cherry tree—were actually invented by an admiring "biographer" soon after Washington's death. Washington grew up in colonial Virginia. His father, a landowner and planter, died when George was 11. The youth inherited 10 enslaved persons at the time and held hundreds more in bondage during his lifetime. Washington

George Washington's legendary cherry tree confession

was educated in such subjects as reading, writing, and mathematics, but he did not attend college.

His skill with mathematics led to early work as a surveyor, or measurer and mapper of land. While still a teenager, Washington surveyed the unsettled wilderness of Virginia's Blue Ridge Mountains. He ventured farther west during his 20s—this time as a soldier. Washington fought in the French and Indian War, Great Britain's territorial dispute with France over the lands of the Ohio River Valley. His reputation spread after he published firsthand accounts of his experiences.

Washington (foreground) survived an icy crossing of the Allegheny River as a British scout in 1753. Later, he made a trustworthy president because citizens knew Washington, being childless, could not place a family heir in power to succeed him. He truly was the "Father of His Country."

NICKNAME
Father of His Country

BORN
Feb. 22, 1732, at Pope's Creek, Westmoreland County, VA

POLITICAL PARTY
Federalist

CHIEF OPPONENT
none; elected unanimously

TERM OF OFFICE
April 30, 1789–March 3, 1797

AGE AT INAUGURATION
57 years old

NUMBER OF TERMS
two

VICE PRESIDENT
John Adams (1735–1826)

FIRST LADY
Martha Dandridge Custis Washington (1731–1802), wife (married Jan. 6, 1759)

CHILDREN
none; 2 stepchildren from his wife's first marriage

GEOGRAPHIC SCENE
11 states and 2 former colonies still debating ratification of the Constitution

NEW STATES ADDED
North Carolina (1789), Rhode Island (1790), Vermont (1791), Kentucky (1792), Tennessee (1796)

DIED
Dec. 14, 1799, at Mount Vernon, VA

AGE AT DEATH
67 years old

SELECTED LANDMARKS
Pope's Creek Plantation (Wakefield), VA (birthplace); Valley Forge National Historical Park, Valley Forge, PA; Mount Vernon, VA (homestead and grave); Washington Monument, Washington, DC; Mount Rushmore National Memorial, Keystone, SD

General Washington served as commander in chief of the Continental Army throughout the Revolutionary War.

Washington struggled to keep up morale among troops wintering over at Valley Forge, Pennsylvania, in 1777–1778.

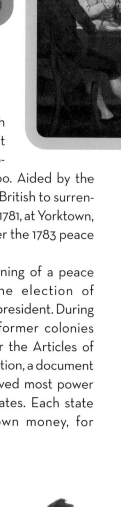

Virginians elected Washington to their colonial legislature, the House of Burgesses, when he was 26. Soon after, Washington married Martha Dandridge Custis, a wealthy widow with two young children who had inherited 84 enslaved people. Their combined household settled at Washington's estate, Mount Vernon.

As a colonial legislator, Washington spoke out against unfair aspects of British rule. Later he was one of Virginia's representatives at the First and Second Continental Congresses. These meetings led to the organization of a Continental Army to oppose the British. Washington, who attended the meetings in his military uniform, was chosen by the Continental Congress to head the Army. He was 43 years old. His selection added a prominent Southerner to a Revolutionary War movement that was led mostly by Northerners.

Washington held the Continental Army together for six years of fighting against British forces. His troops suffered significant defeats, but they won important victories in the fight for independence, too. Aided by the French, Washington finally forced the British to surrender most of their troops on October 19, 1781, at Yorktown, Virginia. He retired from the Army after the 1783 peace treaty and returned to private life.

Six years passed between the signing of a peace treaty with Great Britain and the election of Washington as president. During that time the former colonies operated under the Articles of Confederation, a document that reserved most power for the states. Each state printed its own money, for

Washington led a daring attack across the ice-filled Delaware River in 1776.

In 1787 Washington presided over the Constitutional Convention in Philadelphia. Delegates drafted a plan for a new national government with hopes that Washington would serve as the country's first president.

New York residents gave Washington a hero's welcome when he entered the city in 1783 after the end of the Revolutionary War.

example. There was no national Chief Executive. States sent representatives to a federal Congress, but this legislature did not even have the authority to collect taxes. Neither the states nor the federal government were able to repay the millions of dollars that had been spent on the Revolutionary War. The states were so poorly linked that their fate as a nation seemed in jeopardy.

In 1787 state representatives gathered in Philadelphia to try to resolve these problems. George Washington, one of Virginia's delegates at this Constitutional Convention, was selected to preside. By the time the convention ended four months later, the delegates had written the Constitution of the United States. This document outlined the basic design for a strong federal government, with two chambers of legislators, a federal court system, and a president. It continues to serve as the foundation for the United States government today.

Nine state governments were required to ratify, or approve, the document before the new federal government could form. By the next summer more than enough states had ratified the Constitution for it to take effect. Following the Constitution's directions, states chose representatives to serve as electors for the president. These members

> **"Liberty, when it begins to take root, is a plant of rapid growth."**
>
> George Washington, letter to James Madison, March 2, 1788

of the first Electoral College cast two votes apiece. All of them gave one vote—for a total of 69—to George Washington, thus making him president. John Adams received the greatest number of remaining votes and became vice president. Washington was reelected unanimously four years later, with Adams again voted in as vice president. No other president has ever been unanimously elected.

In 1789 Washington traveled to New York City, then the nation's capital, for his Inauguration. The next year the capital moved temporarily to Philadelphia. Washington brought enslaved laborers from his plantation to help staff the president's home. Although Washington helped plan a permanent national capital, his presidency ended before the federal government moved to the city later named in his honor.

President Washington set many precedents for future Chief Executives to follow. A few, like bowing in

The small size of Washington's Cabinet (left) didn't necessarily make governing any easier. The president had to contend with rival factions of advisers who disagreed about federal versus state powers, foreshadowing the development of political parties.

Washington helped lay the cornerstone of the U.S. Capitol during his first year as president.

"Many things which appear of little importance in themselves and at the beginning may have great and durable consequences."

George Washington, letter to John Adams, May 10, 1789

greeting, quickly went out of fashion. (Thomas Jefferson introduced the custom of shaking hands.) Many other precedents, such as seeking regular advice from department secretaries in Cabinet meetings, remain essential today. Washington established how the U.S. negotiates treaties, if presidential vetoes could encourage the reworking of legislation (yes), whether the Chief Justice had to be the oldest member of the Supreme Court (no), if the president could decide who would join the Cabinet (yes), and even how many terms he thought a president should serve (two). He established

speechmaking traditions, too, from his Inaugural Addresses to State of the Union messages to a farewell address upon leaving office.

Washington appointed the first federal judges, signed laws that established basic government services like banking and currency, and sought to keep the nation out of wars with Native American and European nations. During his presidency, political parties began to form despite Washington's objections. He became identified with the Federalist Party.

Martha Washington, who had joined her husband

Washington (left, in retirement at Mount Vernon) brought enslaved laborers from his household to work at his presidential residences in New York and Philadelphia. He was the first of seven early presidents with ties to Virginia—the place where, in 1619, slavery first reached the American Colonies. Each of these Virginians was linked with slavery while president, or at other times, or both.

The former president welcomed a stream of visitors to Mount Vernon, including his Revolutionary War ally the Marquis de Lafayette of France (shown here with the former first lady, right, and other family members). Washington's image has been preserved over the years on everything from postage stamps (below) to geographic landmarks. He is the only president to have a state named for him.

at winter battle camps during the Revolutionary War, left Mount Vernon again to be with him during his presidency. Lady Washington, as she was called, helped set presidential social customs.

Washington established one more tradition—attending the Inauguration of his successor—before he and his wife retired to Mount Vernon in 1797. He was not left at peace for long. In 1798 he agreed to take charge of the Army once more, this time to defend the country in case war developed with France. (It did not, and he was able to complete his service from home.)

Washington died in 1799 after a brief illness. Although he continues to be widely revered for his leadership during the country's founding, his reputation is forever tarnished by his support of slavery and his lifelong dependence upon enslaved labor. Washington left instructions for the people he had enslaved to be liberated during the years following his death, but even this gesture carries a false ring. Many of these individuals and their relatives had spent decades—even entire lifetimes—in forced service, unable to enjoy the same freedoms as the man who held them in bondage.

JOHN ADAMS
2ND PRESIDENT OF THE UNITED STATES **1797–1801**

John Adams devoted his adult life to the twin causes of creating the United States and securing its long-term survival. Adams—as the president who succeeded, or followed, George Washington—showed that the nation's most important office could peacefully survive a change of leadership. He helped his new country avoid war with France during his single term of office.

The man who became known as the Father of American Independence was born in the colony of Massachusetts. He was the son of a leather craftsman and landholder who farmed without the use of enslaved labor. Adams grew up enjoying toy boats, marbles, kites, hunting, books, and learning. He graduated from Harvard University in 1755 and took up the study of law.

Adams practiced law in Boston for 12 years and served briefly in the state

This pair of farmhouses served as the birthplaces for two U.S. presidents: John Adams and his son John Quincy Adams.

legislature of Massachusetts before becoming a delegate to the First and Second Continental Congresses. At these meetings in Philadelphia he encouraged the colonists to seek independence from Great Britain. It was Adams who suggested that George Washington command the new Continental Army, and

Adams, the nation's second president, went to school in a setting like the one pictured in this illustration. He cherished his status as a U.S. citizen, a right he earned thanks to the American Revolution. "I have not one drop of blood in my veins, but what is American," Adams observed in 1785 while serving as a diplomat in Europe.

Abigail Adams and her husband wrote hundreds of letters to each other during their marriage because John Adams was frequently away on government business. In 1776 when he was a delegate to the Continental Congress in Philadelphia, she reminded him to "remember the ladies. Be more generous and favorable to them than your ancestors." She went on to suggest that women should "not hold ourselves bound by any laws in which we have no voice or representation." It would be the 20th century before women won the right to vote in every state.

Adams (below, right) at times felt overshadowed by other significant figures of the day. He joked: "The history of our Revolution will be one continued lie from one end to the other. The essence of the whole will be that Dr. Franklin's electrical rod smote the earth and out sprang General Washington. That Franklin electrified him with his rod and thenceforward these two conducted all the policies, negotiations, legislatures, and war."

Adams coordinated the crafting of the Declaration of Independence.

Adams was overseas during much of the Revolutionary War. He represented his new country to governments in Europe. During his stay in the Netherlands, he arranged for important loans to help fund the Revolutionary War effort. Later he helped negotiate the peace treaty that ended the war with Great Britain.

After the war, Adams served as the first U.S. ambassador, or representative, to Great Britain. He returned to the United States in 1788 just as a federal government was being organized under the new U.S. Constitution. He was elected to serve as vice president to George Washington. Adams held the post for both of Washington's terms, but he found the job dull. He observed: "My country has in its wisdom contrived for me the most insignificant office that ever the invention of man contrived or his imagination

Adams is called the Father of the American Navy for establishing a permanent U.S. naval fleet. Among the ships constructed during his presidency was the U.S.S. *Philadelphia*.

The U.S.S. *Constellation* captured *L'Insurgente* of France in 1799 when the two nations were on the brink of war.

conceived." His efforts while vice president to establish flattering terms of address for the president (such as "His Highness") only earned him nasty nicknames like His Rotundity (Adams was overweight) and Bonny Johnny Adams.

Whereas Washington had become president by a unanimous vote of the Electoral College, Adams had no such luck. The Constitution originally called for all candidates to be considered for president. It directed that the runner-up, or second-place finisher, become vice president. This plan failed to anticipate the development of political parties. (A constitutional amendment in 1804 established separate votes for each office.) In 1796 Adams (a Federalist) became president by only a three-vote margin over Thomas Jefferson, a member of the rival Democratic-Republican Party, who became vice president. Tensions arose between the two men because they represented different political viewpoints. Adams was defeated by Jefferson during his bid for a second presidential term.

Adams devoted much of his presidency to avoiding war with France or Great Britain after fighting broke out in Europe over the increasingly bloody French Revolution. Adams and fellow Federalists tried to stifle their foreign policy critics with the Alien and Sedition Acts. This legislation placed harsh restrictions on immigrants and free speech, among other effects. Adams influenced the courts with his judicial appointments, including that of Chief Justice

> **"I am but an ordinary man. The times alone have destined me to fame."**
>
> John Adams, diary entry, April 26, 1779

John Marshall, but his so-called midnight judges were named too late in his term to be confirmed.

In 1801 Adams retired to his home in Massachusetts with his wife, Abigail. The pair shared a deep relationship of mutual admiration and friendship in one of the longest marriages in presidential history—54 years.

After their presidencies were over, John Adams and Thomas Jefferson restored the friendship of their Revolutionary War days through lively letter writing. The two men were the only signers of the Declaration of Independence to become presidents. Curiously, they both died on the same day—the 50th anniversary of the approval of the Declaration of Independence. That day, Adams observed: "It is the glorious Fourth of July. God bless it." His final words were: "Thomas Jefferson still survives." He did not know his friend had died only a short while earlier. Adams, who had been ill, stopped breathing later that day.

THE WHITE HOUSE
THE BUILDING AND ITS HISTORY

Since 1800 every U.S. president has lived in the national landmark known today as the White House. George Washington was the only president who never slept there, but he left his mark on the structure by choosing its location and approving its design. The place has been endlessly modified, expanded, and rebuilt ever since John Adams moved into the incomplete house near the end of his term of office.

Thomas Jefferson, the home's second resident, directed many early improvements to the structure and its grounds. Subsequent presidents have added basic conveniences such as running water, toilets, and electricity; others have modernized it with telephones, elevators, and a movie theater. Theodore Roosevelt developed what became known as the West Wing in 1909. This addition to the White House features essential working areas for the administration, including the Oval Office used by the president. Harry S. Truman had the original White House structure shored up and rebuilt after one inspector proclaimed that the

BUILDING THE FIRST WHITE HOUSE

WASHINGTON D.C. 1798

building "was standing up purely from habit." More recently, workers painstakingly removed all of the building's exterior paint, some 30 layers thick, then repainted it its trademark white. Today the president's home includes more than 100 rooms on four floors (plus two basement levels).

Over the years the occupants of the White House have sat for portraits, collected priceless furnishings, and obtained notable works of art. Many of these items remain in use today, making the White House a living museum. Citizens may take a self-guided tour of public areas in the White House by obtaining free tickets in advance through their members of Congress. An off-site visitors center provides general information for anyone.

The President's House (left, George Washington with architect James Hoban) was renamed the White House in 1901 by Theodore Roosevelt. More than 200 enslaved persons helped to build it. Another 100 or more worked there in bondage during a majority of pre–Civil War presidencies.

The modern White House (left, and cutaway and key, opposite) serves as office and residence for the president and family. Its surrounding 18 acres are enjoyed by modern first families for croquet, tennis, horseshoes, golf, swimming, basketball, and jogging. Interests expressed by White House residents can influence the nation as a whole, from Jacqueline Kennedy's enthusiasm for historic preservation to the Obama family's devotion to organic gardening.

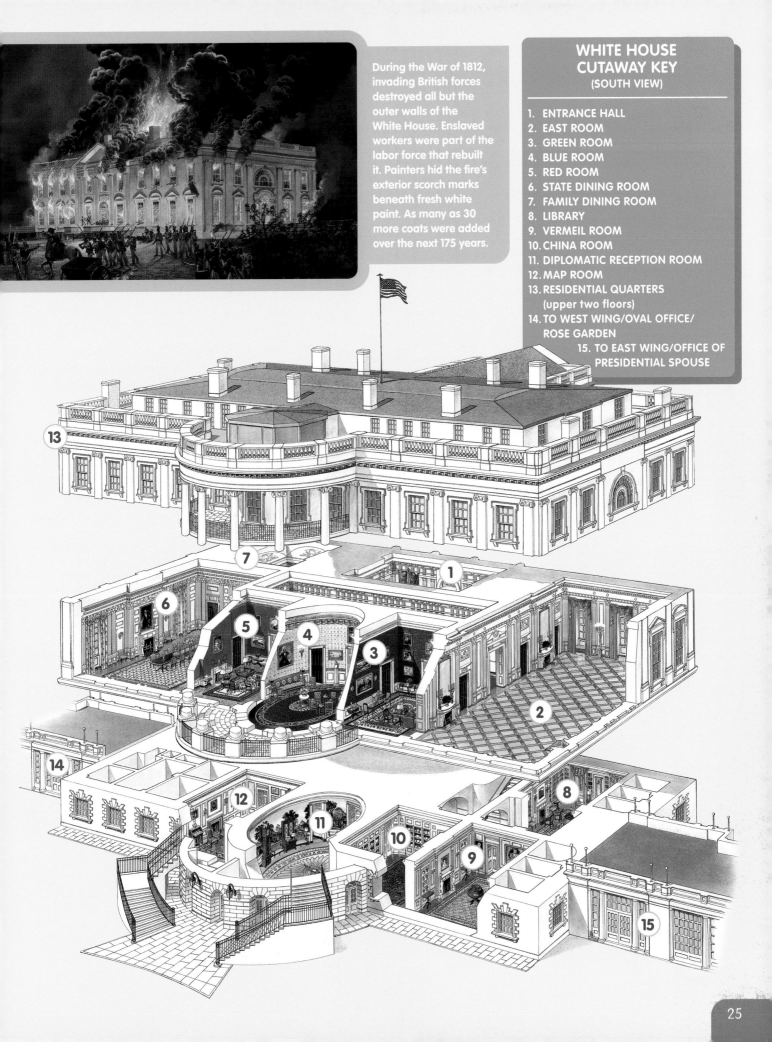

During the War of 1812, invading British forces destroyed all but the outer walls of the White House. Enslaved workers were part of the labor force that rebuilt it. Painters hid the fire's exterior scorch marks beneath fresh white paint. As many as 30 more coats were added over the next 175 years.

WHITE HOUSE CUTAWAY KEY
(SOUTH VIEW)

1. ENTRANCE HALL
2. EAST ROOM
3. GREEN ROOM
4. BLUE ROOM
5. RED ROOM
6. STATE DINING ROOM
7. FAMILY DINING ROOM
8. LIBRARY
9. VERMEIL ROOM
10. CHINA ROOM
11. DIPLOMATIC RECEPTION ROOM
12. MAP ROOM
13. RESIDENTIAL QUARTERS (upper two floors)
14. TO WEST WING/OVAL OFFICE/ ROSE GARDEN
15. TO EAST WING/OFFICE OF PRESIDENTIAL SPOUSE

THOMAS JEFFERSON
3RD PRESIDENT OF THE UNITED STATES 1801–1809

Before his death, Thomas Jefferson listed the accomplishments he wanted carved on his gravestone. Serving as the nation's third president did not make his list. Jefferson's achievements in the White House and beyond have earned him enduring notice, but his fame as a champion of liberty stands in troubling contrast to his lifelong dependence upon enslaved labor.

Jefferson had the skills for many careers. However, because he came of age during the American Revolution, he devoted himself most notably to service as a statesman. Jefferson was born in 1743 in colonial Virginia. His father, who died when Jefferson was 14, was a landowner with enslaved laborers. His son would likewise hold others in bondage. Beginning at age nine, Jefferson studied away from home, living with his tutor. Later he enrolled at the College of William and Mary in Williamsburg, Virginia. His education was broad and comprehensive, including science, mathematics, philosophy, law, English language and literature, Latin, Greek, French, and even how to dance at social events.

After college Jefferson became an attorney. By age 26 he was a member of Virginia's House of Burgesses. Jefferson spoke out there against British policies during the final years of colonial government. On June 7, 1776, Jefferson and other delegates at the Second Continental Congress in

NICKNAME
Father of the Declaration of Independence

BORN
April 13, 1743, at Shadwell, Goochland (now Albemarle) County, VA

POLITICAL PARTY
Democratic-Republican

CHIEF OPPONENTS
1st term: President John Adams, Federalist (1735–1826), and Aaron Burr, Democratic-Republican (1756–1836); 2nd term: Charles Cotesworth Pinckney, Federalist (1746–1825)

TERM OF OFFICE
March 4, 1801–March 3, 1809

AGE AT INAUGURATION
57 years old

NUMBER OF TERMS
two

VICE PRESIDENTS
1st term: Aaron Burr (1756–1836); 2nd term: George Clinton (1739–1812)

FIRST LADIES
Dolley Dandridge Payne Todd Madison (1768–1849), friend; Martha (Patsy) Jefferson Randolph (1772–1836), daughter

WIFE
Martha Wayles Skelton Jefferson (1748–1782), married Jan. 1, 1772

CHILDREN
Born to Martha Jefferson (wife): Martha, Mary, plus three daughters and a son who died young; born to Sally Hemings (1773–1835, enslaved woman): Beverly, Harriet, Madison, Eston, plus two daughters who died young

GEOGRAPHIC SCENE
16 states

NEW STATES ADDED
Ohio (1803)

DIED
July 4, 1826, at Monticello, Charlottesville, VA

AGE AT DEATH
83 years old

SELECTED LANDMARKS
Monticello, Charlottesville, VA (homestead and grave); Jefferson Memorial, Washington, DC; Mount Rushmore National Memorial, Keystone, SD

Thomas Jefferson (standing) drafted the Declaration of Independence in consultation with, among others, Benjamin Franklin (seated at left) and John Adams. Adams suggested that Jefferson compose the document. "You can write ten times better than I can," said Adams, plus "I am obnoxious, suspected, and unpopular."

During the Tripolitan War of 1801–1805, the U.S. fought against the Barbary pirates and their allies in North Africa to stop lawlessness on the seas.

French troops turned over New Orleans and the territory of Louisiana to U.S. forces on December 20, 1803. During the ceremony (left), the Stars and Stripes of the U.S. replaced the tricolor French flag at the Mississippi River port. Eventually all or parts of 15 states would be carved from Thomas Jefferson's Louisiana Purchase.

Philadelphia were asked to consider whether "these United Colonies are, and of right ought to be, free and independent States."

Soon after, Jefferson, Benjamin Franklin, John Adams, and two others were appointed to draft a declaration, or statement, in favor of independence. Jefferson spent about two weeks putting their ideas on paper. On July 2 the delegates agreed to declare their independence. Two days later, after a few revisions, members approved Jefferson's official declaration. This document is treasured for its persuasive calls for freedom and equality. It is the first achievement Jefferson listed on his gravestone.

During the Revolutionary War, Jefferson tried to put his democratic dreams into action. He wrote the "Statute for Religious Freedom" while serving in the Virginia Legislature. This document called for the separation of church and state, a concept that says it is improper for religious groups and the government to interact. Later this idea was adopted as one of the basic principles of the national government. Jefferson listed this achievement on his gravestone, too.

Over the next 20 years, Jefferson served as governor of Virginia, a representative to the Continental Congress, U.S. minister to France, secretary of state for George Washington, and vice president for John Adams. These last two posts left Jefferson frustrated. Some government leaders, known as Federalists, favored a strong federal, or national, government ruled by the country's most prosperous and well-educated citizens. Jefferson and his supporters, many of whom farmed using enslaved laborers, opposed these ideas. They favored greater freedom for the individual states and called themselves Anti-Federalists or Democratic-Republicans and, eventually, Democrats. Jefferson expressed his dislike of Federalism by resigning from Washington's administration. He also chose not to powder his hair, and he encouraged states to disobey federal laws that they disliked.

When the Electoral College voted in 1800, Jefferson and Aaron Burr tied for the presidency. It took the House of Representatives 36 ballots and two months to decide that Jefferson should be the winner. The Constitution was amended by the time of the next presidential election, so that separate votes were held for president and vice president. Jefferson was then easily reelected.

As president, Jefferson reversed what he saw as the

> **"We hold these truths to be self-evident, that all men are created equal, that they are endowed by their Creator with certain unalienable Rights, that among these are Life, Liberty and the pursuit of Happiness."**
>
> Thomas Jefferson,
> Declaration of Independence, July 4, 1776

most offensive Federalist programs. He restored full freedom of speech to the press, reduced restrictions on immigration, increased land sales in the West, ended federal taxation, decreased the national debt, closed the national bank, and canceled the last-minute "midnight judges" appointments that Adams had made as he left office. During his second term, with his approval, Congress ended the practice of importing enslaved people, but nothing was done to stop the trade for those already here.

Jefferson invented new codes of presidential behavior, too. He dressed casually around guests, even answered the White House door himself sometimes,

Jefferson is called a Renaissance man because of his broad range of talents. He excelled as a farmer, an architect, an inventor, a lawyer, a writer, a musician, and an educator, as well as a statesman. Among his inventions were swivel chairs and the polygraph (right), a machine that duplicated an original document as it was being composed.

Jefferson designed and founded the University of Virginia in Charlottesville (below) during his retirement years. His personal library of 6,500 books became the foundation for a new Library of Congress after its original collections were destroyed during the War of 1812.

Jefferson's life was fundamentally intertwined with the institution of slavery. Enslaved workers helped build his beloved Monticello. They likewise labored there, both indoors and out (left, with Jefferson and his newly invented plow). Enslaved people served him at the White House, too. Jefferson's namesake memorial (below) opened in 1943. He is the only person to serve two full terms as president after being vice president.

"I shall not die without a hope that light and liberty are on a steady advance."

Thomas Jefferson, letter to John Adams, September 12, 1821

and added an Independence Day open house for ordinary citizens to the White House calendar. His administration, and the two like-minded ones that followed it, led to the end of the Federalist Party.

Jefferson's most noted presidential triumph was the Louisiana Purchase of 1803. When Jefferson tried to buy the port of New Orleans, the French offered to sell all of their western lands, not just the port. They were too busy preparing to fight the British to defend this distant territory. The price was 60 million francs, or about $15 million. The United States nearly doubled in size by gaining more than 800,000 square miles of territory west of the Mississippi River. Many Federalists failed to see the value of buying "a howling wilderness." Jefferson, however, was thrilled.

Even before the Louisiana Purchase, Jefferson had been planning an exploration of the West. He asked Meriwether Lewis, his personal secretary, to lead the trip. News of the Louisiana Purchase reached the U.S. on Independence Day in 1803, just as Lewis was about to set off from the East. Lewis joined forces with William Clark and a small corps of explorers in St. Louis, Missouri. The next spring they set off up the Missouri River in search of a water passageway to the Pacific. Instead they found the Rocky Mountains. They finally reached the Pacific Ocean by way of the Columbia River in December 1805. The Lewis and Clark expedition returned by a similar route to St. Louis the following fall. Their 8,000-mile trip helped open the Louisiana Purchase for settlement.

Jefferson spent five decades perfecting his beloved mountaintop home, Monticello. In Italian, "Monticello" (pronounced mont-ti-CHELL-o) means "little mountain." Jefferson added clever details to his house (above) such as hidable beds, dumbwaiters, octagonal rooms, skylights, revolving storage space, a clock that kept track of the days of the week, and pairs of doors that opened when only one of them was pushed.

Jefferson married a young widow when he was 28 years old. She died 10 years later; no pictures of her survive. Their daughter Martha (left) served sometimes as her father's first lady.

Before the era of the Oval Office, presidents worked in the White House itself (right, Jefferson in what is now the State Dining Room).

Jefferson retired to Monticello at the end of his second term. For the remaining 17 years of his life he made improvements to his beloved home, surrounded himself with grandchildren, entertained distinguished guests, and juggled the mounting debts that came with his lavish lifestyle. He accomplished the third and final credit for his gravestone during these years: Jefferson is called the Father of the University of Virginia for designing and organizing this institution. Jefferson, like his old Revolutionary War friend John Adams, died 50 years to the day after the approval of the Declaration of Independence.

Jefferson left a complicated legacy. His estate was so in debt that Monticello and some 200 enslaved workers had to be sold. Historical and scientific evidence, including genetic testing, supports the case that Jefferson had a long-term relationship with Sally Hemings, his enslaved servant, and fathered six children with her. Four of them survived to adulthood; all were eventually freed by Jefferson or released without fear of capture. After his death, Hemings was likewise released, apparently by his daughter Martha.

Today it is hard to reconcile Jefferson's passionate calls for freedom during the nation's founding with his lifelong reliance on the labor of enslaved people. Jefferson maintained an unjustified racial prejudice even though he witnessed countless examples of Black intelligence, skill, and humanity. He recognized that slavery was morally wrong but chose not to end his own dependence on the shameful institution—or the nation's.

JAMES MADISON
4TH PRESIDENT OF THE UNITED STATES 1809–1817

James Madison is remembered most for the hand he had in creating the basic rules for governing the United States—the Constitution and its Bill of Rights. Madison made sure that his new country had a strong and democratic government. Later, as president, he struggled to lead the United States safely through its first war since the American Revolution: the War of 1812.

Madison devoted his adult life to the creation of the United States. Born to a life of privilege on a slavery-based Virginia plantation, he completed his education in New Jersey at what is now called Princeton University. Madison was the smallest president in U.S. history at five feet four inches and 100 pounds.

After serving in the Virginia Legislature and with the Continental Congress, Madison was sent to the Constitutional Convention of 1787. He and other delegates spent 86 days inventing the structure of the U.S. government, including its Congress, presidency, and federal court system. His detailed notes remain a valuable record of the entire event. As one of the authors of *The Federalist Papers*, Madison helped influence states to ratify, or accept, the new Constitution. These 85 essays supported the idea of a strong federal, or national, government.

First Lady Dolley Madison

NICKNAME
Father of the Constitution

BORN
March 16, 1751, at Belle Grove, Port Conway, VA

POLITICAL PARTY
Democratic-Republican

CHIEF OPPONENTS
1st term: Charles Cotesworth Pinckney, Federalist (1746–1825); 2nd term: DeWitt Clinton, Federalist (1769–1828)

TERM OF OFFICE
March 4, 1809–March 3, 1817

AGE AT INAUGURATION
57 years old

NUMBER OF TERMS
two

VICE PRESIDENTS
1st term: George Clinton (1739–1812); 2nd term: Elbridge Gerry (1744–1814)

FIRST LADY
Dolley Dandridge Payne Todd Madison (1768–1849), wife (married Sept. 15, 1794)

CHILDREN
none; 1 stepson from his wife's first marriage

GEOGRAPHIC SCENE
17 states

NEW STATES ADDED
Louisiana (1812), Indiana (1816)

DIED
June 28, 1836, at Montpelier, Orange County, VA

AGE AT DEATH
85 years old

SELECTED LANDMARKS
Montpelier, Orange County, VA (homestead and grave); The Octagon, Washington, DC (temporary executive home after destruction of the White House)

James Madison had studied hundreds of books on history and government by the time delegates gathered at the Constitutional Convention of 1787 to organize a new government (above). Madison joked that he earned the scar on his nose in "defense of his country." Actually, it resulted from the frostbite he suffered during a long ride home after a 1788 debate with James Monroe during a U.S. congressional campaign.

Wars raged on many fronts during Madison's presidency. U.S. soldiers led by future president William Henry Harrison (far left, in 1811) fought with Native Americans who resisted the expansion of white settlements onto Native lands in Indiana Territory.

Forced recruitment of American sailors by the British Navy helped draw the U.S. into the War of 1812 with Great Britain.

As a representative in the first U.S. Congress, Madison helped secure passage of the Bill of Rights. This companion document to the Constitution sets down the basic civil liberties of the nation's citizens and states. Because Madison played such a central role in these events, he became known as the Father of the Constitution. Madison preferred to share the credit. The Constitution was not "the off-spring of a single brain," he insisted, but "the work of many heads and many hands." Madison and George Washington are the only signers of the Constitution who later became presidents.

Madison served four terms in Congress and then worked in Virginia's state government before his friend Thomas Jefferson asked him to join his new presidential administration as secretary of state. At the end of his two terms, Jefferson favored Madison as his successor. Madison easily defeated his opponent, Charles Pinckney, and became president. Pinckney, noting the popularity of Madison's wife, Dolley, observed that he "might have had a better chance had I faced Mr. Madison alone."

When Madison became president, the United States was being drawn into conflict with the British over their war with France. Americans were frustrated because the British were halting U.S. cargo ships bound for France and seizing U.S. sailors and goods. If modern forms of communication had existed in Madison's time, war might have been avoided. Not knowing that the British were ending these seizures, the U.S. declared war against Great Britain.

During the War of 1812 (which lasted until 1815), American forces were beaten regularly on land and at sea. The greatest humiliation occurred late in the war when the British entered Washington and set fire to the White House and the U.S. Capitol Building. The final contest, the Battle of New Orleans,

The War of 1812 featured many battles at sea.

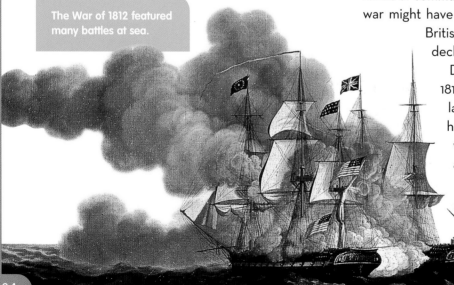

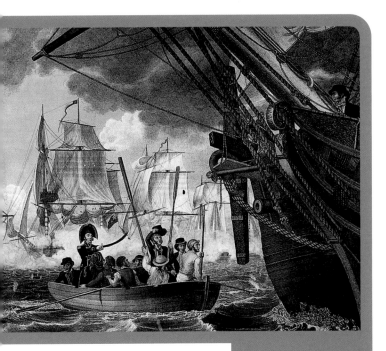

Dolley Madison supervised the packing of White House valuables as the British marched on the nation's capital in 1814.

The U.S. gained control of the Great Lakes during the second year of the War of 1812 (Commodore Oliver Hazard Perry, above with sword, on Lake Erie).

"If men were angels, no government would be necessary."

James Madison, *The Federalist Papers*, #51, 1788

was fought after a peace treaty had been signed in Europe but before that news could reach North America. Madison was praised after the war for having allowed others to criticize his wartime policies without fear of trial or imprisonment. He insisted it was important for the United States to be able to fight a war without limiting the constitutional rights of its citizens, including the right of free speech.

First Lady Dolley Madison gained lasting fame during the war. She organized the rescue of government documents and a famous portrait in the White House of George Washington just hours before the British raided the capital. She was famous, too, for her role as a hostess. She gave lively parties, made pleasant conversation, and dressed lavishly, often topping her head with a turban, jewels, or feathers.

In 1817 the couple retired to their Virginia homestead, Montpelier. James Madison helped Jefferson create the University of Virginia, argued against secession (the right of states to withdraw from the Union), and organized his notes from the Constitutional Convention. He outlived all other Founding Fathers and died in 1836. By the end of their lives, the Madisons had become so dependent upon the monetary value of their enslaved workers that few of them gained their freedom, even after the couple died. Most were sold to clear family debts.

Francis Scott Key (above, standing hatless) captured the drama of a British naval attack on Fort McHenry in Baltimore in 1814 by writing the poem that became the U.S. national anthem.

THE POWERS OF THE PRESIDENT
THE EXECUTIVE BRANCH IN GOVERNMENT

The structure of the United States government was established by the Constitution in 1787. That document and its 27 amendments are the foundation for the nation's three branches, or divisions, of government power. These branches are the legislative, judicial, and executive. The U.S. Congress, as the legislative branch, is tasked with passing new laws through its House of Representatives and Senate. The judicial branch settles disputes about legal matters using the federal court system, including the U.S. Supreme Court.

The executive branch is headed by the president, who directs the actions of the U.S. government. The work of a presidential administration is distributed among various departments, each of which is led by a director known as a secretary. These secretaries are nominated to their posts by the president and must be approved by Congress in order to formally join the Cabinet that advises the Chief Executive.

Originally there were only three departments of the federal government—State, War, and Treasury. Today there are 15, including ones added over time to address such national interests as education, labor, energy, and homeland security. Each has its own duties and responsibilities. For example, the Department of Justice is expected to enforce the laws of the land with consistency and to defend them when they are challenged in the courts.

The Constitution outlines a brief list of presidential powers: Serve as commander in chief of the armed forces; make treaties with other nations; grant pardons; inform Congress on the state of the Union; and appoint ambassadors, officials, and judges. In addition, the president is responsible for reviewing the legislation passed by Congress and deciding whether or not to sign its bills so that they become law.

By creating three branches of government, the framers of the Constitution established a mechanism for each branch to use its power to counter the influence of the others. This system of checks and balances can keep one branch from

The president's Cabinet helps the Chief Executive address the complex challenges of governing a world superpower (below, meeting with Donald Trump).

Informal meetings shape the policies of the United States government, too (above, advisers gather in the Oval Office with Barack Obama, seated far left).

The Government of the United States

THE CONSTITUTION

LEGISLATIVE BRANCH
U.S. Senate
U.S. House of Representatives

EXECUTIVE BRANCH
President
Vice President
Cabinet

JUDICIAL BRANCH
U.S. Supreme Court
U.S. Circuit Courts
U.S. District Courts

The U.S. Constitution divides the nation's government into three branches of responsibility. The president directs the executive branch.

dominating the others. For example, although the president takes the lead on negotiating treaties, Congress must ratify, or approve, them before they can take effect. If Congress passes legislation that the president rejects, members of the House and Senate can try to override that veto. If two-thirds of all legislators still support the bill, then it becomes law without needing the president's approval.

At various times in the nation's history, presidents have sought to expand their power and influence. For example, in recent decades presidents have sidestepped the war-making powers assigned to Congress by the Constitution. No president since World War II has asked Congress to declare war during a time of conflict. Instead, presidents have sought general authorizations to use military force. These open-ended requests have granted the president the flexibility to deploy troops to various locations over many years. They also have spared members of Congress from having to take potentially unpopular votes on specific military engagements.

Another way presidents have increased their power is through the issuing of executive orders. Such orders play an essential role in guiding the departments of the administration, but they can also be used to put policies into place that might not otherwise gain the approval of Congress.

In 1917 Woodrow Wilson asked members of Congress to declare war on Germany during what became known as World War I.

These directives do not have the permanence of laws. Subsequent presidents may overturn them by issuing new executive orders. Members of Congress can likewise pass legislation that ends a president's order, although it would take two-thirds of them to do so if the president vetoed their initial attempt. Federal courts may also be asked to review a president's directives. Sometimes orders remain in effect, but at other times the courts may rule them to be unconstitutional.

JAMES MONROE
5TH PRESIDENT OF THE UNITED STATES **1817–1825**

James Monroe was the last U.S. president who had been an adult during the Revolutionary War. He presided over a country in the midst of widespread change. New thinking was developing about the role of political parties, the issue of slavery, and the fate of European colonies in the Americas.

As with prior Virginia-born presidents, Monroe's family depended upon the labors of enslaved people in their homes and beyond. That same dependency continued throughout his own life. Tensions increased between American colonists and Great Britain during his youth, and his education at the College of William and Mary was interrupted by early revolutionary activities. At age 17 he and other students raided the local armory; the next year he left college to join the Continental Army. Monroe served under the command of General George Washington, rising in rank to major. He crossed the Delaware River with Washington's troops, was severely wounded during a heroic capture of British cannons in the Battle of Trenton, and wintered at Valley Forge.

Near the end of the war, Monroe studied law in Thomas Jefferson's law practice and later opened his own. He also began his lifelong career of public service. Before being elected president, Monroe served in the Virginia Assembly, the Continental Congress, the U.S. Senate, and as governor of Virginia. He held foreign affairs posts under three of the first four presidents. He was Washington's minister to France, Jefferson's minister to Great Britain, and secretary of state and secretary of war for James Madison.

James Monroe

NICKNAME
Era of Good Feelings President

BORN
April 28, 1758, in Westmoreland County, VA

POLITICAL PARTY
Democratic-Republican

CHIEF OPPONENT
1st term: Rufus King, Federalist (1755–1827);
2nd term: none

TERM OF OFFICE
March 4, 1817–March 3, 1825

AGE AT INAUGURATION
58 years old

NUMBER OF TERMS
two

VICE PRESIDENT
Daniel D. Tompkins (1774–1825)

FIRST LADY
Elizabeth Kortright Monroe (1768–1830), wife (married Feb. 16, 1786)

CHILDREN
Eliza, Maria, plus a son who died young

GEOGRAPHIC SCENE
19 states

NEW STATES ADDED
Mississippi (1817), Illinois (1818), Alabama (1819), Maine (1820), Missouri (1821)

DIED
July 4, 1831, in New York, NY

AGE AT DEATH
73 years old

SELECTED LANDMARKS
Highland (Ash Lawn), Charlottesville, VA (homestead); James Monroe Museum and Memorial Library, Fredericksburg, VA; Hollywood Cemetery, Richmond, VA

James Monroe was a tall president, just over six feet in height. He chose to be inaugurated outdoors in 1817.

In 1803 President Jefferson sent him to France to help negotiate the Louisiana Purchase.

Both Jefferson and his successor, President Madison, favored Monroe's election as president in 1816. Some Democratic-Republicans spoke of their desire to pass over Monroe, a Virginian, and end the "Virginia Dynasty" of presidents. (Three of the first four presidents had come from Virginia. Eventually seven of the first 12 would be Virginians.) Monroe's abilities were more important than concerns about his birthplace, though, and he was elected by a wide margin.

Monroe added to his popularity as president by taking two extensive "goodwill tours" during his administration. In 1817 he traveled north and west as far as Maine and Michigan. Two years later he headed south to

Georgia, went as far west as the Missouri Territory, and traveled back to Washington through Kentucky. He ran for reelection without opposition and earned all but one electoral vote. Legend says he lost this single vote because an elector wanted to preserve George Washington's record of unanimous election. Facts suggest, however, that the elector simply did not support Monroe and put forth another candidate (John Quincy Adams) instead. During his presidency a newspaper credited Monroe with bringing the nation an "era of good feelings." The phrase stuck and came to be associated with him like a nickname.

The United States underwent significant geographic changes during Monroe's leadership. Five new states

> **"The American continents ... are henceforth not to be considered as subjects for future colonization by any European powers."**
>
> James Monroe,
> Monroe Doctrine, December 2, 1823

The building of canals and locks expanded the opportunities for travel and commerce during Monroe's presidency.

The White House (above, center) and adjacent federal office buildings as they appeared in 1820

As president, Monroe (standing by globe) framed a new vision for the role of the U.S. government in the Western Hemisphere.

joined the nation. Only one administration would add more. (Six states joined the nation during Benjamin Harrison's single term in office.) In addition, Monroe purchased Florida from Spain and resolved key border concerns with Canada. Most important, he stated a vital U.S. position about the Western Hemisphere: The American continents were off-limits for further colonizing by European nations. This policy came to be known as the Monroe Doctrine. It set the stage for the expansion of the United States westward to the Pacific Ocean during the next two decades.

The greatest controversy of Monroe's administration was whether Missouri should enter the Union as a state that permitted slavery. Politicians organized along regional lines—North against South—over this issue. In the end, the Missouri

During Monroe's diplomatic service, his wife, Elizabeth, influenced French radicals to free the condemned wife of Revolutionary War ally the Marquis de Lafayette.

Compromise admitted Missouri as a "slave state" with Maine entering as a "free state." Since each side in the debate gained one state, the balance between opposing viewpoints was maintained. Legislators agreed to prohibit further expansion of slavery north and west of Missouri's southern border. This position would be reconsidered by future administrations during an increasingly tense debate over slavery.

Monroe was among those who supported returning formerly enslaved people to Africa. The colonization site of Monrovia, in Liberia, was named in his honor. But like other early presidents from Virginia, Monroe depended on the labor of enslaved people throughout his life. He is known to have granted liberty to only one man, which happened after his death in 1831. Monroe is the third and last U.S. president to die on the Fourth of July.

JOHN QUINCY ADAMS
6TH PRESIDENT OF THE UNITED STATES **1825–1829**

John Quincy Adams, like his father, earned more lasting fame for his accomplishments beyond the White House than for his presidency. His single term of office took place following important overseas service and preceded a celebrated career in Congress. Adams was the only son of a Chief Executive to seek and gain the presidency until George W. Bush did so in the 2000 election.

Adams grew up in Massachusetts during the American Revolution. He witnessed the Battle of Bunker (Breed's) Hill at age eight. He traveled abroad while his father was a diplomat and later earned a degree from Harvard University. After studying law, he served his country with each of the nation's first presidents. He was a U.S. ambassador for both George Washington and his father, a senator under Thomas Jefferson, an ambassador for James Madison, and secretary of state for James Monroe.

The 1824 electoral votes failed to give majority support to one candidate. After an ugly debate, the House of Representatives named Adams the victor. As Chief Executive, Adams ignored political strategy, stuck to his principles, and found himself generally miserable. It seemed that no one supported him. Jealous political rivals accused him of corruption. Congress refused to fund his plan for a national transportation system of roads and canals. Newspapers slandered him. In 1828 Adams felt it was undignified to personally campaign for reelection and lost the first presidential election influenced by popular vote.

John Quincy Adams enlivened his

John Quincy Adams won his congressional seat in 1830 at age 63. He served until his death (above, taking ill in the House chamber).

gloomy White House years by playing billiards, writing in his diaries, and exercising. Often he swam nude in the Potomac River. Once someone stole his clothes, and he had to ask a passing boy to fetch new ones for him from the White House. Even though Adams never held people in bondage, historians know that members of his wife's family did. They believe some of these enslaved people lived and worked at the White House for the extended first family during his presidency.

Later Adams spoke against slavery as the only former president to become a member of the House of Representatives. He earned the nickname Old Man Eloquent for his passionate speeches against the 1836 "gag rule" that prohibited discussion of slavery there. After the order was lifted, he condemned slavery itself.

After Adams had a stroke in the House, the gravely ill former president asked to rest nearby so he could die in his beloved Capitol Building. He did so two days later.

John Quincy Adams

NICKNAME
Old Man Eloquent

BORN
July 11, 1767, in Braintree, MA (location later designated Quincy, MA)

POLITICAL PARTY
Democratic-Republican

CHIEF OPPONENT
Andrew Jackson, Democratic-Republican (1767–1845)

TERM OF OFFICE
March 4, 1825–March 3, 1829

AGE AT INAUGURATION
57 years old

NUMBER OF TERMS
one

VICE PRESIDENT
John Caldwell Calhoun (1782–1850)

FIRST LADY
Louisa Catherine Johnson Adams (1775–1852), wife (married July 26, 1797)

CHILDREN
George, John, Charles, plus a daughter who died young

GEOGRAPHIC SCENE
24 states

NEW STATES ADDED
none

DIED
Feb. 23, 1848, at the U.S. Capitol, Washington, DC

AGE AT DEATH
80 years old

SELECTED LANDMARKS
Adams National Historical Park, Quincy, MA (birthplace and family home); United First Parish Church, Quincy, MA (grave)

WHITE HOUSE TRADITIONS
FROM EASTER EGGS TO PRESIDENTIAL PORTRAITS

John and Abigail Adams established one of the oldest and longest-lasting White House traditions soon after their arrival at the incomplete mansion in the fall of 1800. The following New Year's Day they invited members of the public to visit their home at an open house. All were welcomed. Those first guests would have exchanged bows with the presidential couple, but handshakes came into fashion with the presidency of Thomas Jefferson.

As the popularity of the New Year's Day open house grew, so did the length of the lines of waiting visitors. Abraham Lincoln found himself shaking hands for three hours on New Year's Day in 1863. Herbert Hoover ended the practice; he held the last such reception in 1932.

A newer tradition that continues to this day is the annual Easter Egg Roll on the South Lawn of the White House. This activity migrated to the president's yard in 1878 after it was banned from the lawn of the U.S. Capitol as too damaging to the turf. The custom has continued with some interruptions (such as during wartime) ever since and has gained in popularity in recent decades. The tradition of decorating a Christmas tree at the White House dates back almost as far as the Easter Egg Roll; it began in 1889 during Benjamin Harrison's administration.

The Easter Egg Roll gets under way as children race to the finish line on the South Lawn of the White House. In 1933 Eleanor Roosevelt greeted visitors and listeners to the Egg Roll for the first time over the radio. She introduced games at the event, but the most famous activity during the modern Easter Egg Roll, the egg-rolling race, began in 1974. More than 20,000 children participate annually.

At state dinners, world leaders exchange toasts of praise and thanks (above, George W. Bush during a visit by Queen Elizabeth II in 2007).

Candles lit the first White House Christmas tree in 1889. Frances Cleveland switched to electric lights in 1895. In 1923 the first family began decorating an outdoor tree with electric lights, too. The 2015 tree (above) commemorated the centennial of the National Park Service in 2016.

Sometimes the president hosts a state dinner for a visiting leader from another country. These ceremonial events honor important international allies of the United States. Tradition calls for the presidential couple to escort the visiting dignitaries to dinner by way of what is known as the grand staircase of the White House. The U.S. Marine Band performs, and the presidential party pauses for news photographers when they reach the adjoining entrance hall. If dancing is planned, custom dictates that the presidential hosts exchange dances with their guests of honor. They usually offer gifts to one another, too, and deliver ceremonial toasts to the health of the leaders and their nations.

Guests lucky enough to be invited to stay at the White House often sleep in what is known as the Lincoln Bedroom. Lincoln never actually slept there, but furnishings from his administration help decorate the room.

First Lady Caroline Harrison helped establish the tradition of preserving and displaying china and other dishes used at official events. Periodically a presidential couple will order new dishes for the White House. Considerable thought is given to the design and manufacturing of the china. In early administrations, such tableware had to be imported from Europe; now preference is given to goods made in the United States.

Over the years, it has become a tradition for multiple artists to paint separate portraits of the outgoing president and spouse. Paintings of each person are then hung at the White House with those from prior administrations. Additional compositions are displayed in the National Portrait Gallery.

Presidents and first ladies are among the people represented at the National Portrait Gallery (above, Michelle Obama).

ANDREW JACKSON
7TH PRESIDENT OF THE UNITED STATES 1829–1837

The election of Andrew Jackson put in the White House for the first time a man who seemed to represent the background and ambitions of "ordinary" Americans. His leadership style differed from that of his predecessors, too. Jackson set new patterns for presidential power that continue to be used today.

Jackson grew up earning his "man of the people" reputation. He was the son of Scotch-Irish immigrants, born to a family on the move following the sudden death of his father just a few days earlier. His exact birthplace remains uncertain. He is considered the first of the log cabin presidents. In 1776 he was able, at age nine, to read aloud the text of the new Declaration of Independence to nonreading neighbors. Although he never

The Inauguration of Andrew Jackson, 1829

learned proper written grammar and spelling, he was well-spoken.

Jackson's education was interrupted by the American Revolution. At age 13 he served as a messenger for American troops and was captured by the British. Jackson is the only president who was a prisoner of war, and the last one who served in the Revolutionary War.

NICKNAME
Old Hickory

BORN
March 15, 1767, in the Waxhaw border region of North and South Carolina

POLITICAL PARTY
Democratic (formerly Democratic-Republican)

CHIEF OPPONENTS
1st term: President John Quincy Adams, National Republican (1767-1848);
2nd term: Henry Clay, National Republican (1777-1852)

TERM OF OFFICE
March 4, 1829–March 3, 1837

AGE AT INAUGURATION
61 years old

NUMBER OF TERMS
two

VICE PRESIDENTS
1st term: John Caldwell Calhoun (1782-1850);
2nd term: Martin Van Buren (1782-1862)

FIRST LADY
Emily Donelson (1807-1836), niece

WIFE
Rachel Donelson Robards Jackson (1767-1828), married Aug. 1791 and Jan. 17, 1794

CHILDREN
Andrew (adopted)

GEOGRAPHIC SCENE
24 states

NEW STATES ADDED
Arkansas (1836), Michigan (1837)

DIED
June 8, 1845, in Nashville, TN

AGE AT DEATH
78 years old

SELECTED LANDMARKS
The Hermitage, Nashville, TN (homestead and grave)

A British officer attacked Jackson (above) after he refused to polish his captor's boots during the Revolutionary War. His face bore a lifelong scar from the wound.

Jackson gained fame during the War of 1812. The general's reputation as a war hero (right, with military officers in 1818) made him a popular candidate for president.

Jackson tried several professions after the war before he took up the study of law and became an attorney. He settled in Tennessee. Jackson practiced law there and established a cotton plantation named the Hermitage where his enslaved laborers worked. Later he served briefly in both the House and Senate of the U.S. Congress.

More than a decade later—during the War of 1812—Jackson earned the national reputation that carried him to the White House. He served as an officer for volunteers from Tennessee and became a U.S. general. General Jackson became famous for his leadership during the Battle of New Orleans, the last conflict in the War of 1812. Jackson's soldiers thought their leader was as tough as an old hickory tree. The nickname Old Hickory stuck with Jackson for life.

During the 1828 presidential election, the opposition party sought to discredit Jackson. It issued a thick booklet about his "youthful indiscretions," or mistakes, including accounts of his numerous fights and duels. (Jackson lived the last four decades of his life with a bullet lodged near his heart from one of his duels.) Jackson's supporters dished out their own round of slander, and Jackson defeated his rival, President John Quincy Adams. Jackson's wife, Rachel, became ill when she learned that their marital history was a campaign issue. The couple had been married twice; the second ceremony occurred after they learned that their first wedding had taken place before she was properly divorced from an earlier husband. Rachel died of a heart attack before her husband became president.

Citizens stormed the White House during Jackson's Inaugural reception. They were eager to see the "People's President." Guests with muddy boots climbed on silk chairs, fists flew, china crashed, and ladies fainted in the crush of visitors. Jackson escaped out a back door to the safety of a hotel. Finally, staff members placed tubs of punch on the White House lawn to lure the crowd outside, and then they locked the doors.

Jackson marked his two terms of office by assuming greater powers of leadership than any prior president.

General Jackson went on to become the first president to have his life threatened by an assassin. The assailant (who was later ruled insane) fired two guns at the president from close range in the U.S. Capitol Rotunda, but neither one fired properly. Jackson was so angry that he beat the gunman with his cane.

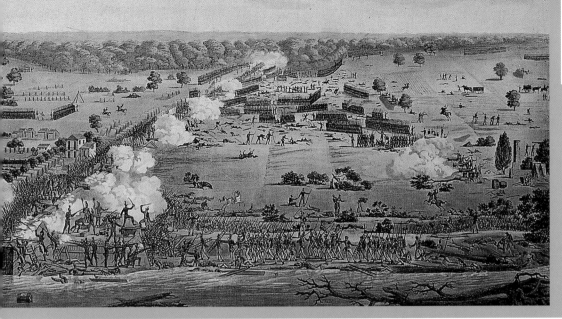

General Jackson became the "hero of New Orleans" after his forces killed or wounded 2,000 British soldiers who were attacking the city at the end of the War of 1812. U.S. casualties were only 71. Jackson's fame helped earn him the presidency 14 years later.

Jackson, who grew up in a simple log cabin, was called "a barbarian who ... hardly could spell his own name" by political rival John Quincy Adams.

Although slavery had not been part of his early life, Jackson held people in bondage throughout adulthood. Some of these enslaved people helped care for him at the White House, but most were forced to labor at his cotton plantation, the Hermitage (above). At the time of Jackson's death some 150 enslaved people worked there. Although his land and home were valuable, these enslaved individuals accounted for much of his wealth.

Critics nicknamed him King Andrew the First. But his bold style appealed to many of his successors, and some of his policies did, too. Jackson insisted that presidents could hire and fire their Cabinet members, and he replaced one who refused to follow his orders. He upheld the authority of the U.S. government over state governments by insisting it was treasonous for South Carolina to ignore federal import tax law. He encouraged the practice of awarding federal jobs to political supporters. He defied the Supreme Court by ignoring its support of the Cherokee people. Jackson forced Native Americans living east of the Mississippi to move against their will to new land farther west.

His bold actions often shocked politicians but were popular with the era's white male voters. Jackson was the last two-term president until Abraham Lincoln. After his second term he retired to the Hermitage, where he continued to influence politics. He took particular pleasure in the election to the presidency of two of his protégés—his former vice president Martin Van Buren and, later on, James K. Polk, a fellow Tennessean. Old Hickory died shortly after Polk became president.

> "The great can protect themselves, but the poor and humble require the arm and shield of the law."
>
> Andrew Jackson, 1821

FROM SEA TO SHINING SEA

1837–1861

Presidents faced a delicate balancing act before the Civil War. Efforts to expand U.S. landholdings always seemed to spark renewed debate over whether to expand slavery as well. Presidents had greater success at adding land than at resolving what to do about slavery. Native Americans suffered when they were pushed from their homelands by new waves of settlers. None of the presidents from this era served more than one term in office. Rather, they left by choice, lost reelection bids, or died in office.

1838–1839
When the U.S. Army forced 15,000 Cherokee to move from Georgia to present-day Oklahoma, nearly a third of them died. The harsh 1,000-mile journey is called the Trail of Tears.

1845
Frederick Douglass increased public concern over the treatment of enslaved people when he published his autobiography. He worked with abolitionists to end slavery.

1846–1848
The Mexican War began with battles at disputed Texas border spots such as Palo Alto. By the end of the war, U.S. boundaries stretched to include the future state of California.

1849
The 1848 discovery of gold in California triggered a massive gold rush the next year. Prospectors flocked to the region in search of the valuable metal.

Travelers head west on the Oregon Trail with livestock and belongings (an artist's rendering of the scene circa 1869).

1850s
The number of miles of railroad track in use throughout the United States tripled during the 1850s. A spreading web of routes moved people and freight across vast distances.

1854
Commodore Matthew C. Perry, backed up by a strong show of military might, established trading rights between the United States and Japan during his visit there.

1860
By 1860 more than one-third of all Southerners—nearly four million people—were enslaved Blacks. Disagreement over the expansion of slavery erupted into the Civil War a year later.

1860–1861
Pony Express riders could deliver mail between Missouri and California in 10 days or less. Rides ceased after telegraph wires spanned the continent in October 1861.

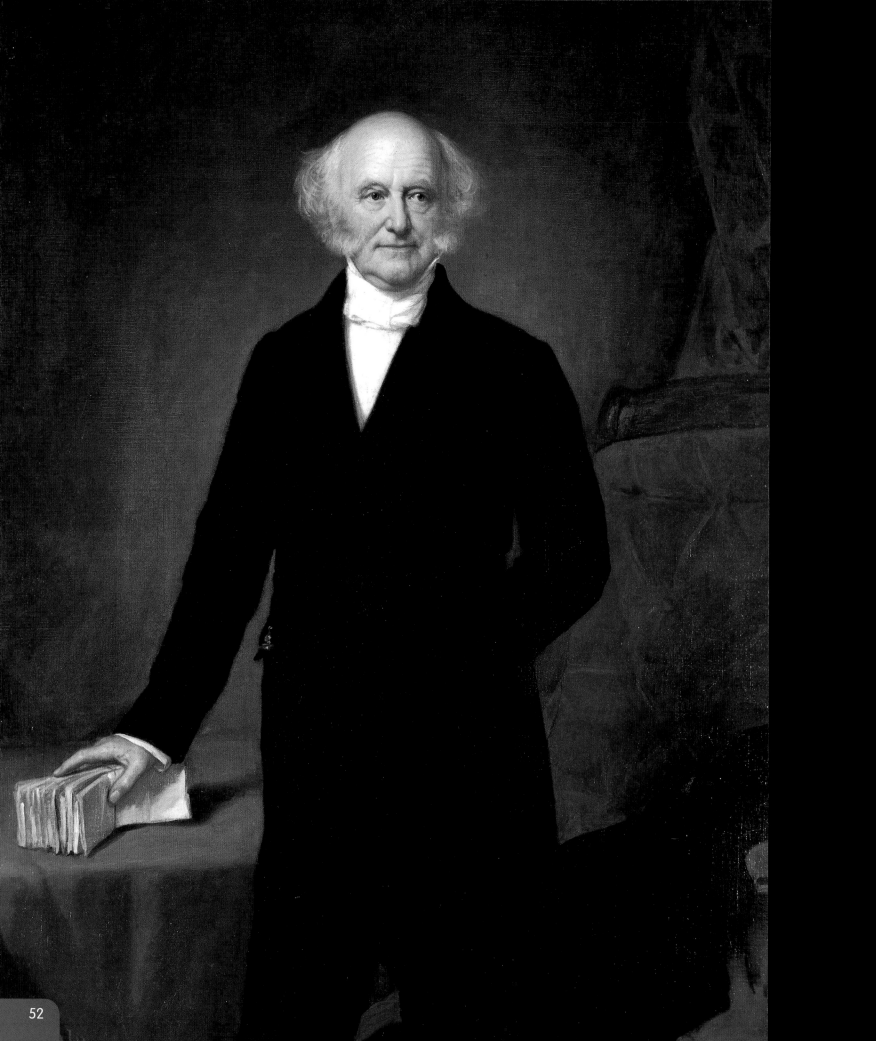

MARTIN VAN BUREN
8TH PRESIDENT OF THE UNITED STATES **1837–1841**

Martin Van Buren rose to prominence in the Democratic Party by developing new systems for rewarding political supporters. After serving as Andrew Jackson's vice president, he succeeded him as president. Nationwide financial hardships undercut his popularity, though, and he was limited to a single term of office.

Van Buren, who descended from Dutch immigrants, was the first Chief Executive to be born as a citizen of the United States. Earlier presidents had all been born in colonial America, making them British subjects at birth. Van Buren completed his formal education when he was 13, then turned to the study of law. By age 21 he was a practicing attorney.

After Van Buren entered New York State politics, he became so skilled at helping to defeat influential wealthy opponents that he was nicknamed the Little Magician. He and his supporters identified themselves by affixing deer tails to their hats. These Bucktail Democrats rewarded their supporters with thousands of state jobs, a practice that came to be known as the spoils system. This

Martin Van Buren's ties to Kinderhook, New York (above, his birthplace), led him to be nicknamed Old Kinderhook, or O.K., which came to mean "all right."

base of support boosted Van Buren into the U.S. Senate and led him to serve briefly as governor of New York.

President Jackson brought this clever politician into his administration, first as secretary of state and then as vice president. With Jackson's encouragement, Van Buren sought—and won—the presidency. His administration struggled to deal with the financial Panic of 1837 but had better luck quieting tensions between Mexico and the Republic of Texas. He also avoided war with Great Britain over disputes involving Canada and continued Jackson's forced relocation of Native Americans westward. An improving economy came too late to save his reelection bid. Although the staff at his vice presidential home and White House had included enslaved laborers, Van Buren grew increasingly opposed to slavery. This stance contributed to two subsequent failures to regain the presidency. Van Buren died while the Civil War raged.

NICKNAMES
Little Magician; Old Kinderhook (O.K.)

BORN
Dec. 5, 1782, in Kinderhook, NY

POLITICAL PARTY
Democratic

CHIEF OPPONENT
William Henry Harrison, Whig (1773–1841)

TERM OF OFFICE
March 4, 1837–March 3, 1841

AGE AT INAUGURATION
54 years old

NUMBER OF TERMS
one

VICE PRESIDENT
Richard M. Johnson (1780–1850)

FIRST LADY
Angelica Singleton Van Buren (1816–1878), daughter-in-law

WIFE
Hannah Hoes Van Buren (1783–1819), married Feb. 21, 1807

CHILDREN
Abraham, John, Martin, Smith

GEOGRAPHIC SCENE
26 states

NEW STATES ADDED
none

DIED
July 24, 1862, in Kinderhook, NY

AGE AT DEATH
79 years old

SELECTED LANDMARKS
Lindenwald, Kinderhook, NY (homestead); Kinderhook Cemetery, Kinderhook, NY

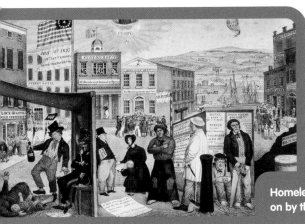

Homelessness, unemployment, and despair (shown in this illustration) brought on by the Panic of 1837 marked most of Van Buren's presidency.

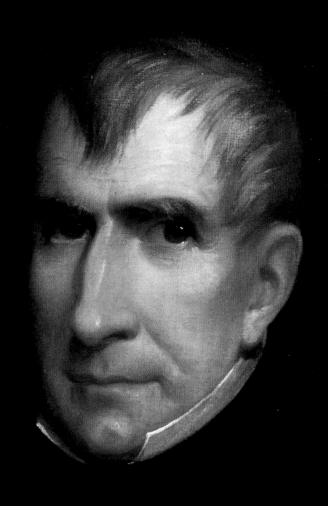

54

WILLIAM HENRY HARRISON
9TH PRESIDENT OF THE UNITED STATES 1841

William Henry Harrison had a presidency of extremes. At age 68 he was the oldest person at that point in time to become president. He gave the longest Inaugural Address ever—one hour and 40 minutes—and he was the first president to die in office. But Harrison is remembered most for having the shortest term of office: one month.

Harrison was also the last president born before the American Revolution. He and his father, who had signed the Declaration of Independence, both held enslaved people in bondage. Harrison attended Hampden-Sydney College in Virginia before studying medicine and becoming a soldier. He battled Shawnee people at the Tippecanoe River (hence his nickname) and fought in the War of 1812. He was the governor of Indiana Territory, an Ohio state senator, the ambassador to Colombia, and a U.S. representative and senator before seeking the presidency. Harrison represented the Whigs, a new party that evolved from the Federalists. He and his 1840 presidential running mate were billed as the ticket of "Tippecanoe and Tyler Too." They won.

Harrison delivered his lengthy Inaugural

William Henry Harrison's efforts to seize Native American lands made Tecumseh, leader of the Shawnee, furious during their 1810 meeting.

Address outdoors in brisk weather, yet he refused to wear a hat or coat. He became ill soon after, a fact that many attributed to his disregard of the weather. Renewed study of the historical record, however, suggests a different cause: contaminated drinking water due to an open sewer located near the White House. Harrison died exactly one month after taking office. His death triggered the first promotion of a vice president to the presidency without benefit of an election. Years later, Harrison's grandson Benjamin Harrison became the nation's 23rd president.

The Whig Party urged voters to "keep the ball rolling on to Washington" by supporting its candidate.

JOHN TYLER
10TH PRESIDENT OF THE UNITED STATES 1841–1845

John Tyler was the first vice president to complete a different Chief Executive's term. He took firm command of the office immediately after the death of William Henry Harrison. This confident action set the standard for future midterm presidential successions.

A Virginian like his predecessor, Tyler was a graduate of the College of William and Mary in Williamsburg. Before being named to the 1840 presidential ticket, he had served Virginia in the state legislature, as governor, and in the U.S. House of Representatives and the U.S. Senate.

Tyler was dubbed His Accidency after Harrison's unexpected death. The Constitution was vague about how a vice president should take over as president. Tyler insisted that he was a true president, not an acting one. He took the oath of office, moved into the White House, and prepared to serve out Harrison's term. He even delivered a brief Inaugural Address (and did not catch cold).

As president, Tyler favored greater power for state governments and less for the federal government. His policies added to North-South tensions and helped lead the country to civil war later

During John Tyler's administration the Morse telegraph machine revolutionized long-distance communication by sending coded messages with electric current.

on. Tyler supported settlement of the West, helped resolve a dispute with Great Britain over Canada's boundaries with Maine, and led efforts to bring the Republic of Texas (then an independent country) into the Union.

Tyler was kicked out of the Whig Party after he vetoed its pro-banking legislation. Without the backing of a party, he had no easy way to seek reelection. Tyler, who was married twice, had 15 children—more than any other president. He and his family retired to Virginia. When civil war seemed likely, the pro-slavery Tyler encouraged his state to leave the Union.

He was elected to serve in the Confederate Congress, but he died before he could take office.

Tyler and his future wife, Julia, escaped harm in 1844 when a cannon misfired during their visit to the U.S.S. Princeton. After Julia hosted a popular White House ball at the end of her husband's presidency, Tyler, who had been kicked out of his political party, joked: "They cannot say now that I am a president without a party."

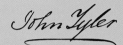
John Tyler

NICKNAME
His Accidency

BORN
March 29, 1790, in Charles City County, VA

POLITICAL PARTY
Whig

CHIEF OPPONENT
none; succeeded William Henry Harrison

TERM OF OFFICE
April 6, 1841–March 3, 1845

AGE AT INAUGURATION
51 years old

NUMBER OF TERMS
one (partial)

VICE PRESIDENT
none

FIRST LADIES
Letitia Christian Tyler (1790–1842), first wife (married March 29, 1813); Priscilla Cooper Tyler (1816–1889), daughter-in-law; Letitia Tyler Semple (1821–1907), daughter; Julia Gardiner Tyler (1820–1889), second wife (married June 26, 1844)

CHILDREN
Born to Letitia Tyler (first wife): Mary, Robert, John, Letitia, Elizabeth, Alice, Tazwell, plus a daughter who died young; born to Julia Tyler (second wife): David, John, Julia, Lachlan, Lyon, Robert, Pearl

GEOGRAPHIC SCENE
26 states

NEW STATES ADDED
Florida (1845)

DIED
Jan. 18, 1862, in Richmond, VA

AGE AT DEATH
71 years old

SELECTED LANDMARKS
Sherwood Forest Plantation, Charles City County, VA (homestead); Hollywood Cemetery, Richmond, VA

THE VICE PRESIDENTS
LEADERS JUST A HEARTBEAT AWAY

Forty-nine individuals have served as vice president of the United States since 1789. Fifteen have eventually become president, starting with John Adams, the first vice president. The others, although important political figures in their day, have tended to fade from popular memory.

The vice presidency was created at the same time as the presidency with the writing of the U.S. Constitution in 1787. The office received only brief definition. It took two constitutional amendments to clarify how vice presidents should be chosen and what role they should play when a president becomes ill or dies in office.

The earliest vice presidents earned their posts by being the runners-up in the voting for president by the Electoral College. By the late 1820s political parties began identifying their own candidates for the two offices. Today this selection is directed by each presidential nominee. Vice presidential nominees often balance and broaden the appeal of an election ticket by representing a different age, political perspective, or geographic region—and, more recently, a different race or gender.

Early vice presidents were not seen as presidents-in-waiting the way they are today. In fact, lawmakers disagreed over whether the vice president even had that responsibility. It was not until the death of President William Henry Harrison in 1841 that this uncertainty was resolved. John Tyler, Harrison's vice president, insisted that he deserved all the rights and responsibilities of a president. His decisive example set the pattern for future presidential successions.

The Constitution spells out one main responsibility for the vice president: to preside over the U.S. Senate. In that role, the vice president is expected to cast the deciding vote whenever senators are deadlocked in a tie. Vice President John Adams was called upon to fulfill this duty on 29 occasions, more than any other vice president.

With such a limited job description, early vice presidents often spent little time in the nation's capital, especially

> The vice president's official residence lies a short drive from the White House.

Aaron Burr was among the most notorious vice presidents, particularly after he shot Alexander Hamilton in an 1804 duel (above). Hamilton later died, leaving Burr open to murder charges as Thomas Jefferson's vice president.

when the Senate was out of session. Many returned to their home states and took up other responsibilities. It was not until the 1970s that the vice president even earned an official residence. The home is a 33-room house on the grounds of the U.S. Naval Observatory, which continues to operate. Walter Mondale, second in command to President Jimmy Carter, became the first vice president to inhabit this space.

Over the years vice presidents have shared similar

Former vice president Joe Biden tapped Kamala D. Harris to be his running mate on the Democratic ticket in 2020 (right, Harris during the announcement). The pair's victory made her the first female vice president in U.S. history and the first Black person and the first person of South Asian descent to hold the post.

Vice presidents represent the administration at events (Hubert Humphrey, right, greeting Martin Luther King, Jr., at a dinner in New York, 1965).

Only two vice presidents, John C. Calhoun and Spiro T. Agnew, have resigned from office. Calhoun left Andrew Jackson's administration to become a U.S. senator. Agnew (right), Richard Nixon's vice president, resigned after admitting he had cheated on his income taxes. Ten months later, scandal forced Nixon to resign, too.

The complexity of national affairs makes vice presidents valuable advisers and consultants for their bosses (Al Gore, left, at work with President Bill Clinton).

backgrounds with presidents, starting with a common average age of about 55 years. New York State, a popular home for presidents, has given more vice presidents to the country than any other state. Eight have been born there, and four others settled there before taking office. Like presidents, many vice presidents served first as governors (16) or members of Congress (36) before assuming national office. Many had presidential ambitions of their own but settled for the post of vice president, perhaps with the hope that the job would serve as a stepping-stone to the presidency later on.

More than half of the vice presidents have served at least one four-year term in office; only nine have completed two terms as vice president. Others either became president because the sitting president died (on eight occasions) or resigned (once), died in office themselves (in seven instances), resigned from their duties (twice), or filled unexpired terms of other vice presidents (once). Former vice presidents have either retired from political life; won seats in Congress; or, in the case of six men, gone on to be elected president. Charles Dawes (Coolidge's vice president) and Al Gore (Bill Clinton's) even earned Nobel Peace Prizes.

Until the U.S. Constitution was amended in 1967, vacancies in the office of vice president remained unfilled until the next presidential election. Now the 25th Amendment directs the president to nominate someone to serve as vice president, subject to approval by a majority of both houses of Congress. Richard Nixon was the first president to use this provision. Before then there had been 19 occasions totaling nearly 38 years when the nation had no one serving as vice president.

The role a vice president plays in an administration is set by each individual president. During the 20th century, vice presidents gained greater influence and were given increasingly important duties. Today's vice presidents juggle a growing range of responsibilities. At the same time, they live each day knowing they are but a heartbeat away from becoming president of the United States.

JAMES K. POLK
11TH PRESIDENT OF THE UNITED STATES 1845–1849

Using a combination of war and rough diplomacy, James Knox Polk significantly increased the nation's size. By the end of his single term, he had taken control of the land that would form almost all of the 48 contiguous United States. However, disagreements over the expansion of slavery into the new territories left the nation more divided than ever.

Polk came to Washington with the nickname Young Hickory because of his ties to Andrew Jackson, the famed "Old Hickory" president. Like Jackson, Polk was born in the Carolinas. His family later moved to Tennessee, where they established a prosperous plantation with the help of enslaved laborers. Polk's formal education began at age 17. He earned a degree with honors from the University of North Carolina, studied law, became an attorney, and sought a career in politics.

Salutes of "Hail to the Chief" began with James K. Polk (above, with his wife, Sarah).

After a few years in the Tennessee Legislature, Polk gained election to the U.S. House of Representatives. He served there for 14 years and was eventually elected speaker, or leader, of the House. He earned Andrew Jackson's friendship

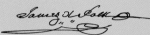

NICKNAME
Young Hickory

BORN
Nov. 2, 1795, near Pineville, Mecklenburg County, NC

POLITICAL PARTY
Democratic

CHIEF OPPONENT
Henry Clay, Whig (1777–1852)

TERM OF OFFICE
March 4, 1845–March 3, 1849

AGE AT INAUGURATION
49 years old

NUMBER OF TERMS
one

VICE PRESIDENT
George Mifflin Dallas (1792–1864)

FIRST LADY
Sarah Childress Polk (1803–1891), wife (married Jan. 1, 1824)

CHILDREN
none

GEOGRAPHIC SCENE
27 states

NEW STATES ADDED
Texas (1845), Iowa (1846), Wisconsin (1848)

DIED
June 15, 1849, in Nashville, TN

AGE AT DEATH
53 years old

SELECTED LANDMARKS
Pineville, NC (reconstructed birthplace); State Capitol Grounds, Nashville, TN (grave)

Polk (left, camping with his father on a surveying trip) pushed U.S. boundaries to the Pacific Ocean as president. The first U.S. postage stamps, the U.S. Naval Academy, and the Smithsonian Institution began during his administration.

Polk was a "dark horse," or unexpected choice, for the Democratic Party in the election of 1844. When word of his nomination reached Washington, D.C., by the new Morse telegraph, some doubted that the machine was working correctly.

> "The people of this continent alone have the right to decide their own destiny."
>
> James K. Polk,
> Message to Congress, December 2, 1845

in those years by supporting the president's policies. Later Polk served as governor of Tennessee.

Despite this record of public service, the nomination of Polk for president in 1844 came as a surprise. Most Democrats had expected the party to renominate former president Martin Van Buren, with Polk as a possible vice presidential candidate. Van Buren, however, had lost favor because of his antislavery stand against Texas statehood. Polk, who depended upon enslaved laborers himself, supported bringing Texas into the Union as a slave state and became the compromise nominee. He narrowly defeated the noted statesman Henry Clay at the polls.

Polk came into office determined, as were many citizens then, to expand his country's borders to the Pacific Ocean. This belief—that the U.S. had the right to take over lands in the West—was called Manifest Destiny. This unquestionable confidence was used to justify the nation's expansion regardless of how it forced Native Americans from their homelands.

Polk started with the Oregon Territory. Previously, this northwestern region, which included parts of present-day Oregon, Idaho, Washington State, and Canada's British Columbia, had been settled by British and Americans alike. U.S. pioneers traveled to it by way of

An artist illustrated Polk's policy of Manifest Destiny by showing the symbolic figure of Columbia leading settlers westward.

the Oregon Trail. Polk bluffed that he expected the British to give up all land south of latitude 54° 40' N, the southern border of Russia's Alaskan Territory. Otherwise he would fight to take it, leading to the popular slogan "fifty-four forty, or fight." In the end, Polk was delighted to settle on the 49th parallel, which still forms most of the U.S.–Canada border.

Next Polk concentrated on the southern U.S. border. Texans had won their independence from Mexico in 1836. Polk angered Mexico by granting Texas statehood soon after he became president. Then a boundary dispute erupted over how to define the new state's southern border. Mexico said the previous boundary of the Nueces River should be maintained. The U.S. claimed the border extended to the Rio Grande River.

On Polk's instructions, U.S. soldiers provoked the Mexicans to attack by crossing into the disputed region in early 1846. From then on, U.S. forces never lost a battle in a war that ultimately took them all the way to Mexico City. When the Mexican War ended in the fall of 1847, the United States had gained not only the border it wanted for Texas but considerable other new land as well. Eventually, some or all of the states of Arizona, California,

This political cartoon questions whether trouble caused by President Polk's policies will collapse on him like a house of cards.

Colorado, Nevada, New Mexico, Utah, and Wyoming would be included in a transfer that reduced the original size of Mexico almost by half. The U.S. government paid Mexico $15 million for its loss of land. Ulysses S. Grant, the future Civil War general and U.S. president, was among those who fought in the war. He described the conflict as "one of the most unjust ever waged by a stronger against a weaker nation."

In all, Polk added 1.2 million square miles of territory to the country, but it came with a heavy price. Northerners opposed to the expansion of slavery and Southerners who supported it debated furiously over whether slavery had a place in the vast new lands. The two sides seemed ready to come to blows over the issue, and they finally did when the Civil War erupted some dozen years later.

Polk left the White House after one term, fulfilling an election promise not to run again. He enjoyed the shortest retirement of any president—three months—in part because he had literally exhausted himself on the job. Polk became ill, possibly with cholera, and died. His wife, Sarah, lived in their Tennessee home 42 years longer, remaining neutral during the Civil War.

Sarah Polk outlived her husband by 42 years, longer than any other first lady. She wore black throughout (above, visiting the Hermitage in 1890 with her great-niece).

President Polk and his wife are buried on the state capitol grounds in Nashville, Tennessee.

WE WANT TO VOTE

BATTLES FOR THE BALLOT

During the country's earliest years, the only Americans with voting rights were almost exclusively white men who owned property. The range of people denied the right to vote in the past—and even still today in some cases—has included women, enslaved persons, African Americans, Native Americans, Asian Americans, immigrants, the impoverished, people imprisoned for a felony or who have served time for one, and adults unable to read and write.

The expansion of U.S. suffrage, or voting, is an ongoing process that has unfolded through the centuries in incremental steps. The granting of rights at one time hasn't necessarily guaranteed their continuation, and laws adopted to expand the franchise haven't always been enforced. Although the federal government has the last word on voting rights, states administer the casting and counting of votes, and state laws vary on voter registration, who can vote, and how they vote.

In an effort to restrict the ability of others to vote, local authorities have at times imposed taxes on the voting process (known as poll taxes), redrawn the boundaries of voting districts to suit a political advantage (a process called gerrymandering), required long periods of residency, constructed illogical tests and other obstacles to registration, refused to comply with laws, and harassed and even murdered people attempting to register, or prove their qualifications, for voting.

A series of three amendments to the U.S. Constitution has widened the franchise, beginning with the 15th Amendment.

It took almost two centuries for a nation born out of a desire for equality to achieve something close to universal suffrage—that is, the right of all citizens to have a voice in their governance. Early efforts to extend voting rights to African-American males occurred after the Civil War (left), but it took another 100 years for people of color to achieve equal suffrage.

The dramatic 1965 voting rights march in Alabama (led by Martin Luther King, Jr., center, and other activists) influenced Congress to pass the year's landmark Voting Rights Act. Five decades later, states began challenging the ongoing federal review of their voting laws.

In 1971 18-year-olds became eligible to vote. Until then, voters had to be 21 years of age.

In 1920 the 19th Amendment granted voting rights to women (shown marching for the cause in 1912), but southern states continued to deny the ballot to people of color until passage of the Voting Rights Act of 1965. Only then did Blacks and other minorities more nearly achieve their long-promised right to vote.

In 1993 passage of the so-called Motor Voter Act made it easier for everyone to register—even at state motor vehicle offices. Political parties may work to expand voting rights because they hope to attract the votes of the newly enfranchised. Or they may back laws that make it easier for their traditional supporters (or harder for their opponents' supporters) to vote. Sometimes leaders even set politics aside and embrace the arguments of those who want to vote.

It was ratified in 1870 and granted African-American males the right to vote. Although the amendment initially enabled thousands of formerly enslaved people to vote, its effectiveness faded after whites used intimidation and legal maneuvers to prevent Blacks from voting. Not until the federal government passed the Voting Rights Act of 1965 were local authorities forced to uphold the 15th Amendment.

This 1965 legislation protected voters from discrimination for decades, but its power was weakened in 2013 by the Supreme Court *Shelby County* v. *Holder* ruling. This decision made it easier for states to change their voting laws, and since then a number of them have done so in ways that have made it harder to vote. These changes are most likely to affect poor people, minorities, and younger voters.

The 19th Amendment—the next one to address voting rights—was ratified in 1920. It granted suffrage to women after a 72-year-long fight for voting rights. Because of ongoing discrimination, particularly in the South, women of color waited another 45 years to have their voting rights enforced under the Voting Rights Act of 1965.

In 1971 Americans expanded the ranks of voters again when the 26th Amendment lowered the voting age from 21 to 18. A period of war contributed to this constitutional change. At the height of the Vietnam War, young people objected to forced military service for 18-year-olds who could not yet vote on government policies. Such objections led Congress and the states to reduce the voting age to match the age for military service.

Wars had influenced passage of the previous suffrage amendments as well. The Union victory in the Civil War directly contributed to the granting of voting rights to formerly enslaved men, and the national commitment to supporting democracy abroad during World War I led to the granting of voting rights to women at home.

Debates continue over who should vote and how. Should voters have to obtain photo IDs to prove their identities? Should there be a paper record of every vote cast? Should convicted felons have the right to vote? Should immigrants be allowed to vote, even if they are not yet citizens? Should the voting age be lowered to 16? Answers may come through the work of politicians, the courts—and voters!

ZACHARY TAYLOR
12TH PRESIDENT OF THE UNITED STATES 1849–1850

Zachary Taylor was a soldier by training, not a politician, but he discovered unexpected similarities between those two professions after becoming president. Politicians in the nation's capital could become as combative as soldiers, he learned, particularly when the matter of slavery was discussed. He threatened to use military force to keep all states in the Union; then he died in office before he could carry out his threat.

Taylor was the first president who had never held another elected office. In fact, he had never even voted in a presidential election because he felt his loyalty as a soldier for the U.S. government required him to stay neutral politically. Born in Virginia, Taylor was raised in Kentucky on a plantation with enslaved laborers. He held people in bondage for much of his life. Taylor bypassed college to pursue a 40-year career in the U.S. Army. His relaxed style of military dress, bravery, and battle success earned him the nickname Old Rough-and-Ready.

Being a military hero helped Taylor win the election, but his Army career was

After Zachary Taylor died in office, his 1848 running mate became president.

poor training for the national debate on slavery. He is thought to be the last president who brought enslaved laborers to the White House. An uproar developed after he suggested that new states should decide for themselves whether to be slave or free. Northerners wanted Taylor to restrict slavery, not expand it. Southerners feared new antislavery states would diminish their own pro-slavery influence in Congress. When Southerners threatened to secede from, or leave, the Union, Taylor offered to lead the U.S. Army against them. We must "preserve the Union at all hazards," he said.

Then Taylor died. Evidence now suggests that he, as with William Henry Harrison, may have become ill because of contaminated drinking water at the White House. He died within days of contracting an intestinal infection.

General Taylor often wore old farm clothes into battle. He made a straw hat part of his standard battle dress. Taylor's legs were so short that he needed help mounting a horse. He liked to ride sidesaddle.

NICKNAME
Old Rough-and-Ready

BORN
Nov. 24, 1784, in Orange County, VA

POLITICAL PARTY
Whig

CHIEF OPPONENT
Lewis Cass, Democrat (1782–1866)

TERM OF OFFICE
March 4, 1849–July 9, 1850

AGE AT INAUGURATION
64 years old

NUMBER OF TERMS
one (cut short by death)

VICE PRESIDENT
Millard Fillmore (1800–1874)

FIRST LADIES
Margaret Mackall Smith Taylor (1788–1852), wife (married June 21, 1810); Mary Elizabeth Taylor Bliss (1824–1909), daughter

CHILDREN
Ann, Sarah, Mary, Richard, plus two daughters who died young

GEOGRAPHIC SCENE
30 states

NEW STATES ADDED
none

DIED
July 9, 1850, in the White House, Washington, DC

AGE AT DEATH
65 years old

SELECTED LANDMARKS
Zachary Taylor National Cemetery, Louisville, KY

MILLARD FILLMORE
13TH PRESIDENT OF THE UNITED STATES 1850–1853

Millard Fillmore offered compromise, in contrast to the threatening style of his predecessor, as a way to end the tense, ongoing debate over slavery. Despite being born a Northerner, Fillmore seemed to sympathize with Southern concerns. In the end, the compromises he signed only delayed civil war between North and South.

Born in a log cabin in upstate New York, Fillmore fulfilled the American dream of rising from simple beginnings to national importance. He was poorly educated. He is said to have seen his first map of the United States upon entering school at age 19. (Later he married his schoolteacher.) He never attended college, but he trained himself to be a lawyer. He won election to government posts in New York State and the U.S. House of Representatives before agreeing to run for vice president on Zachary Taylor's ticket in 1848.

When Fillmore became president after Taylor died in office, he chose to compromise with lawmakers over quarrelsome debates about slavery. Their five agreements became known as the Compromise of 1850. These deals admitted California as a free state, gave

In 1856 Millard Fillmore finished third in his attempt to regain the presidency.

territory status to New Mexico, settled border disputes between it and Texas, closed the markets in the nation's capital where people were sold into slavery, and allowed federal agents to return freedom-seeking enslaved persons to captivity. Each side gained something, and war seemed less likely.

Fillmore showed little interest in the next election, so the Whigs selected a different candidate and lost in 1852, making him the "Last of the Whigs" when the party disintegrated. Some former Whigs supported the new Know-Nothing Party and nominated Fillmore for president in 1856. Fillmore disapproved of the group's anti-immigrant views but ran and finished third. He died in Buffalo, New York, in 1874.

NICKNAME
Last of the Whigs

BORN
Jan. 7, 1800, in Cayuga County, NY

POLITICAL PARTY
Whig

CHIEF OPPONENT
none; succeeded Zachary Taylor

TERM OF OFFICE
July 10, 1850–March 3, 1853

AGE AT INAUGURATION
50 years old

NUMBER OF TERMS
one (partial)

VICE PRESIDENT
none

FIRST LADIES
Abigail Powers Fillmore (1798–1853), wife (married Feb. 5, 1826; Mary Abigail Fillmore (1832–1854), daughter

OTHER MARRIAGES
Caroline Carmichael McIntosh Fillmore (1813–1881), married Feb. 10, 1858

CHILDREN
Born to Abigail Fillmore (first wife): Millard, Mary

GEOGRAPHIC SCENE
30 states

NEW STATES ADDED
California (1850)

DIED
March 8, 1874, in Buffalo, NY

AGE AT DEATH
74 years old

SELECTED LANDMARKS
Fillmore Glen State Park, Moravia, NY (reconstructed birthplace); The Millard Fillmore House, East Aurora, NY; Forest Lawn Cemetery, Buffalo, NY

Fillmore was tall, handsome, and well mannered, in striking contrast with the rough-and-ready image of his predecessor. He and his wife Abigail established the first permanent library at the White House. Abigail traveled in an elegant carriage (right). Sadly she caught cold and died after attending the inauguration of Franklin Pierce, her husband's successor.

U.S. POLITICAL PARTIES
THE TWO-PARTY SYSTEM

The Founding Fathers hoped that representatives of the new United States government would work together in harmony without dividing into opposing groups called parties. Yet, soon after George Washington became president, political parties began to form. Leaders partnered with others who shared their geographic background, foreign policy beliefs, or other ideas for governing the country.

Today, as then, the party with the largest number of elected members in the U.S. House of Representatives and the U.S. Senate holds a majority of influence over those chambers. Its members outnumber those of the minority, or opposing, parties. Occasionally the same party will control both chambers of Congress and the presidency. The concentration of that much political power in one party can give it significant influence. Usually each party will control only one or two of these three areas. In that case, political parties will have to compromise and cooperate with one another to enact new laws and policies.

During George Washington's presidency, lawmakers divided into two groups, depending on whether or not they believed that a strong federal government should oversee weaker state governments. Ever since, although names and opinions may change, two political parties have dominated the U.S. government. Today's leaders are primarily members of the Democratic and Republican Parties. Each group can trace its origins well back into the 19th century.

A 19th-century political cartoonist popularized the use of animals to symbolize the Republican and Democratic Parties. He drew an elephant to represent the colossal size of Republican Party support in 1874. He chose a donkey for the Democrats, knowing that Andrew Jackson had adopted that symbol after being called a jackass during the feisty campaign of 1828.

A campaign banner promotes the 1920 ticket of the Democratic Party. (It lost.)

The Democratic Party evolved from the early groups who opposed a strong federal government. Leaders such as Thomas Jefferson shaped these lawmakers into a collection of politicians who referred to themselves by such terms as Anti-Federalists and Democratic-Republicans. By 1828 they were known simply as Democrats.

The modern Republican Party was formed during the 1850s to combat the spread of slavery. Its first successful presidential candidate was Abraham Lincoln. Sometimes it is referred to as the Grand Old Party (GOP).

The Democratic and Republican Parties have shared fairly equally in the control of the White House. There have been several occasions, however, when one party has had a long period of domination. From Lincoln's election in 1860 through the election of 1908, for example, all but two presidents were Republicans. The Democratic Party earned its longest streak of control—20 years—from 1933 to 1953. Its predecessor, the Democratic-Republican Party, had an even longer streak—28 years, from 1801 to 1829.

Two other political parties had members become Chief Executives, too. Washington and his successor, John Adams, were associated with the Federalist Party. The Whig Party evolved from these early Federalists. Four of its members became president. Two Whigs won outright election: William Henry Harrison and Zachary Taylor. Both of them died in office. Their Whig vice presidents, John Tyler and Millard Fillmore, replaced them.

70

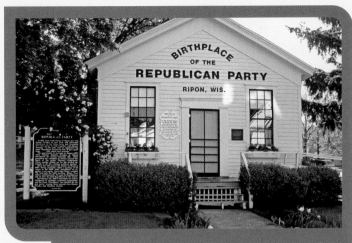

The Republican Party was founded in 1854. Party beliefs have evolved with the changing interests of politicians and voters.

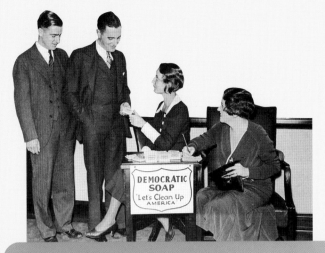

The Democratic Party became fully formed with the presidency of Andrew Jackson. Franklin D. Roosevelt led the Democrats for 12 years following the election of 1932 (above, party supporters). There have been many attempts to start new parties over the years. These range from the Free Soil and Know-Nothing Parties of the 19th century to the Libertarian and Green Parties of modern times. These third parties may try to offer an alternative to the established parties on all fronts or may form around a single issue.

Often the presidential ballot will include candidates from third parties, those groups that exist beyond the two major parties. Since the turn of the last century notable third-party candidates have run as Populists, Socialists, and Progressives. Occasionally a candidate will run for office as an "independent"—that is, without the support of a political party. No independent or third-party candidate has ever made it to the White House. Even so, these candidates may influence an election by dividing the support of voters or by directing attention to a particular issue or cause. In recent decades third-party and independent candidates have frequently siphoned support away from Republican and Democratic candidates in ways that helped secure a victory for the opposing major party.

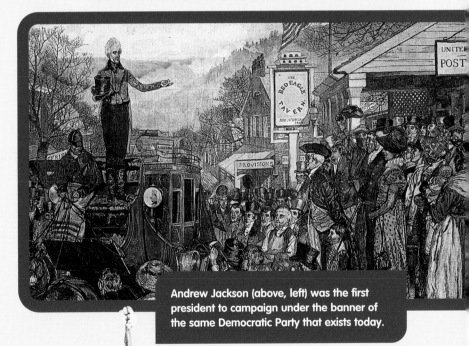

Andrew Jackson (above, left) was the first president to campaign under the banner of the same Democratic Party that exists today.

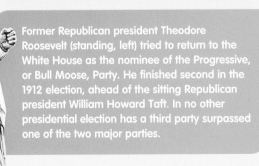

Former Republican president Theodore Roosevelt (standing, left) tried to return to the White House as the nominee of the Progressive, or Bull Moose, Party. He finished second in the 1912 election, ahead of the sitting Republican president William Howard Taft. In no other presidential election has a third party surpassed one of the two major parties.

FRANKLIN PIERCE
14TH PRESIDENT OF THE UNITED STATES 1853–1857

When Franklin Pierce became president, the national debate about slavery had quieted. Pierce, a man with an undistinguished record in public office, renewed the controversy by supporting the option of slavery in Kansas Territory. This stand reopened the slavery issue and helped push the country closer to civil war.

In large part, Pierce was nominated for president because he had not made many political enemies or taken a firm stand on slavery. His party decided it would be easier to elect "Handsome Frank" than other, more controversial Democrats. Pierce had been born in a log cabin in New Hampshire. A graduate of Maine's Bowdoin College, he took up law and served in the New Hampshire Legislature. Later he spent 10 years in Washington, D.C., as a representative and a senator. While there Pierce earned more notice for his heavy drinking than for his lawmaking. Democrats campaigned for his presidency with the slogan "We Polked you in 1844; we shall Pierce you in 1852."

Benjamin Pierce (above, with his mother) died in a train crash shortly before his father's Inauguration.

As president, Pierce infuriated Northerners by supporting the Kansas-Nebraska Act of 1854. This measure ended the Missouri Compromise of 1820 by permitting slavery to spread north of Missouri's southern border. Using a policy called popular sovereignty, the act suggested that residents of new territories should determine for themselves whether to permit slavery within their borders. Casualties climbed to about 200 in "Bleeding Kansas" after both pro-slavery and antislavery settlers rushed in and began fighting there.

The Democratic Party was so embarrassed by the scene that it did not renominate Pierce for a second term. Pierce retired to New Hampshire in disgrace. His death in 1869 went largely unrecognized.

Although Franklin Pierce scored small victories overseas by negotiating favorable trade agreements with Great Britain and Japan, he invariably encountered trouble wherever he tried to influence domestic policy during the stormy pre–Civil War years of his presidency. Debates over slavery turned particularly ugly in "Bleeding Kansas" (left). Life did improve at the White House during his tenure with the addition of hot and cold running water and a hot-water-based heating system.

JAMES BUCHANAN
15TH PRESIDENT OF THE UNITED STATES 1857–1861

James Buchanan, in an effort to hold the Union together, offered concession after concession to the South, regardless of the anger his actions provoked in the North. When Southern states began to secede anyway, he protested but claimed to have no constitutional authority to force them to stay in the Union.

Buchanan's dissatisfying single term in the White House followed a distinguished, 40-year career of public service in the United States and abroad. Buchanan was born in a log cabin in Pennsylvania. He had one good eye for each type of vision—close-up and distant. In order to see well, he cocked his head to one side or the other, depending on which eye he needed to use.

The son of an Irish immigrant, Buchanan graduated from Dickinson College, studied law, and ran for public office. He served briefly in the state legislature and then spent a decade each in the U.S. House and Senate. In addition, he was minister to Russia under Andrew Jackson, James K. Polk's secretary of state, and minister to Great Britain for Franklin Pierce. This final post helped earn him the presidential nomination. By being abroad he had avoided the latest slavery debates.

Dred Scott lost his bid for freedom from enslavement in 1857.

Shortly after Buchanan's Inauguration, the Supreme Court issued its *Dred Scott* ruling. Dred Scott, an enslaved African American, had argued he should be free because he had been relocated to a free state by the man who held him in bondage. The Court disagreed, saying the enslaved should be viewed as property, not citizens, and they remained enslaved anywhere. Although Buchanan disliked slavery (he even bought enslaved people in order to free them), he hated breaking laws even more. (His nickname recalled his insistence on precise bookkeeping, for example.) Buchanan stood by the ruling, infuriating Northerners. He could not stop southern states from seceding or resolve the financial Panic of 1857. Having stated he would serve only one term, Buchanan was delighted to leave office. The only president who never married, he retired to Pennsylvania to write his memoirs. He died in 1868.

NICKNAME
Ten-Cent Jimmy

BORN
April 23, 1791, in Cove Gap, PA

POLITICAL PARTY
Democratic

CHIEF OPPONENT
John C. Frémont, Republican (1813–1890)

TERM OF OFFICE
March 4, 1857–March 3, 1861

AGE AT INAUGURATION
65 years old

NUMBER OF TERMS
one

VICE PRESIDENT
John Cabell Breckinridge (1821–1875)

FIRST LADY
Harriet Lane (1830–1903), niece

WIFE
never married

CHILDREN
none

GEOGRAPHIC SCENE
31 states

NEW STATES ADDED
Minnesota (1858), Oregon (1859), Kansas (1861)

DIED
June 1, 1868, in Lancaster, PA

AGE AT DEATH
77 years old

SELECTED LANDMARKS
Mercersburg Academy, Mercersburg, PA (relocated boyhood home); Wheatland, Lancaster, PA (homestead); Woodward Hill Cemetery, Lancaster, PA

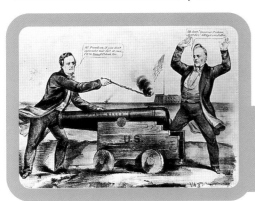

James Buchanan (hands raised, urging South Carolina to resist fighting until "I get out of office"), told his successor, Abraham Lincoln: "If you are as happy, my dear sir, on entering this house as I am on leaving it and returning home, you are the happiest man on earth."

A NEW BIRTH OF FREEDOM

1861–1897

Years of disagreement between Northerners and Southerners over slavery and related issues finally led to civil war between the two regions. After the four-year war ended in 1865, a series of presidents struggled with Reconstruction, the process of reuniting and rebuilding the splintered nation. Post–Civil War presidents more often found themselves watching history unfold than shaping it. The growth of industry in the East and the expansion of western settlement drove the United States toward its modern form.

1863
U.S. treaty violations pushed the starving Dakota to attack whites (above left, Chief Taoyateduta, or Little Crow). Later, the government hanged 38 warriors in its largest mass execution.

1869
A continuous railway line spanned the country coast to coast for the first time on May 10 when a ceremonial gold spike was pounded into place at Promontory, Utah.

1879
Thomas Edison invented the electric lightbulb. Other inventions by Edison included the phonograph, microphone, and motion pictures. He developed the scientific research laboratory, too.

1882
The Chinese Exclusion Act banned most immigrants from China—America's first such restriction to entry. Chinese had lost the right to become U.S. citizens 12 years earlier. Both laws stood until 1943.

Union admiral David G. Farragut's three-masted ship fights its way up river to New Orleans in April 1862. The city fell from Confederate control soon after, but Civil War battles continued elsewhere for three more years.

1886
The Statue of Liberty became a beacon of welcome to immigrants after its dedication. Within a decade, more than 350,000 newcomers were arriving annually. That figure had more than doubled by 1906.

1889
The U.S. government reversed policy and permitted settlement in Oklahoma on land previously set aside for relocated Native nations. Some 50,000 white "sodbusters" rushed to stake claims the first day.

1890
Susan B. Anthony worked most of her life on the fight to earn women the right to vote. In 1890 she became president of the National American Woman Suffrage Association. The cause succeeded 30 years later.

1896
With only one dissenting vote, the Supreme Court affirmed the legality of separation by race in *Plessy v. Ferguson*. Racial segregation remained legal into the 1960s (above, Jackson, Mississippi, 1961).

ABRAHAM LINCOLN
16TH PRESIDENT OF THE UNITED STATES 1861–1865

When Abraham Lincoln was inaugurated in 1861, he became president of states that were not united. In fact, after arguing for years about slavery and states' rights, Northerners and Southerners were on the brink of civil, or internal, war. Lincoln, expressing his commitment to the highest ideals of democracy, succeeded in reuniting the country and ending slavery. He was assassinated just after the end of the Civil War in 1865.

Lincoln's humble beginnings are a schoolbook legend. He was born in a log cabin in Kentucky to parents who could neither read nor write. The sum of his schoolhouse education was about one year's time, so he taught himself by reading books he borrowed from others. When Lincoln was nine years old, his mother died. His father, a carpenter and farmer, remarried and moved his family farther west, eventually settling in Illinois. Lincoln was taller (at six feet four inches) than any other president. His high-pitched

First Lady Mary Todd Lincoln

voice and thick frontier accent (saying "git" for "get" or "thar" for "there") made an odd contrast with his dignified figure and inspiring words.

Lincoln worked as a flatboat navigator, storekeeper, soldier, surveyor, and postmaster before being elected at age 25 to the Illinois Legislature in Springfield. Once there, he taught himself law, opened a law practice, and earned the nickname Honest Abe. He served one term in the U.S. House of Representatives during 1847–1849 but lost two U.S. Senate races in the 1850s. He spoke in opposition to the expansion of slavery during his famed 1858 debates with Stephen Douglas. This stance helped earn him the Republican presidential nomination two years later.

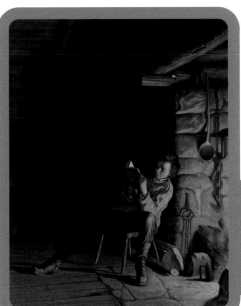

Abraham Lincoln's lifelong love of reading whenever and wherever he could began in his youth, when books often took the place of school. Favorite reading included U.S. history, *Aesop's Fables*, *Robinson Crusoe*, the Bible, and works by Shakespeare.

Abraham Lincoln

NICKNAME
Honest Abe

BORN
Feb. 12, 1809,
near Hodgenville, KY

POLITICAL PARTY
Republican (formerly Whig)

CHIEF OPPONENTS
1st term: Stephen Arnold Douglas, Northern Democrat (1813–1861); John Cabell Breckinridge, Southern Democrat (1821–1875); John Bell, Constitutional Unionist (1797–1869); 2nd term: George Brinton McClellan, Democrat (1826–1885)

TERM OF OFFICE
March 4, 1861–April 15, 1865

AGE AT INAUGURATION
52 years old

NUMBER OF TERMS
two (cut short by assassination)

VICE PRESIDENTS
1st term: Hannibal Hamlin (1809–1891); 2nd term: Andrew Johnson (1808–1875)

FIRST LADY
Mary Todd Lincoln (1818–1882), wife (married Nov. 4, 1842)

CHILDREN
Robert, Edward (died young), William, Thomas (Tad)

GEOGRAPHIC SCENE
23 United States;
11 Confederate States

NEW STATES ADDED
West Virginia (1863),
Nevada (1864)

DIED
April 15, 1865,
in Washington, DC

AGE AT DEATH
56 years old

SELECTED LANDMARKS
Hodgenville, KY (birthplace); Springfield, IL (home, grave, and library); Lincoln Memorial, President's Cottage, Washington, DC; Mount Rushmore National Memorial, Keystone, SD

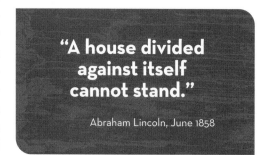

Native Americans fought on both sides during the Civil War (right, Lincoln asks tribal leaders to side with the North).

Lincoln grew strong by splitting logs into thousands of rails for fences. At age 21 he "paid" 400 rails per yard for pants fabric.

Lincoln triumphed in the four-way race.

Lincoln gained the presidency on a platform that considered it treason for Southern states to secede, or withdraw, from the nation. It agreed to continue slavery in the South but outlawed its spread elsewhere. Southern leaders threatened to secede rather than accept this Republican plan. After Lincoln's victory, but before his Inauguration, these states began to act on their threat to leave the Union. The Civil War officially began on April 12, 1861, at Fort Sumter, South Carolina, when forces from the new Confederate States of America attacked this U.S. fort.

Lincoln had promised in his Inaugural oath to "preserve, protect, and defend" the Union. Now he began to act, competing with Confederate leaders for the allegiance of states not yet committed to either side. With Congress out of session until July, Lincoln broke laws when they stood in his way of protecting the Constitution. "Often a limb must be amputated to save a life," he reasoned. Lincoln expanded the size of the Army and Navy, jailed people who might encourage states to secede from the Union, stopped trade with the Confederacy, and spent government funds without the approval of lawmakers. His efforts strengthened the North's cause; later they were approved by Congress and the courts. In the end, 11 states joined

> ## "A house divided against itself cannot stand."
>
> Abraham Lincoln, June 1858

the Confederacy and 23 remained in the Union, including several that practiced slavery—Delaware, Kentucky, Maryland, Missouri, and what became West Virginia.

The outcome of the Civil War remained unclear during the early years of fighting. While the North held the upper hand on the seas, the South generally beat Union forces on land. It was not until the Battle of Gettysburg, in July 1863, that Southern dominance of the battlefield ended. Through speeches such as his Gettysburg Address, Lincoln encouraged Northerners to keep fighting, whatever the costs. In this famous dedication of the battlefield cemetery, he urged citizens to ensure "that these dead shall not have died in vain—that this nation, under God, shall have a new birth of freedom—and that government of the people, by the people, for the people, shall not perish from the earth." Earlier that year Lincoln issued his Emancipation Proclamation, calling for the end of slavery.

Consistent military victories, including the capture of Atlanta, Georgia, in September 1864, helped Lincoln's reelection bid. He selected as his running mate Andrew Johnson, who was Southern-born but Union-loyal, in an effort to represent the complexity of the divided nation. Only Union states participated in the voting, and Lincoln won. By the following March, Northern victory in the war was certain; the only question was when. Lincoln's second Inaugural Address made it clear that the Union states would keep fighting "until every drop of blood drawn with the lash, shall be paid by another drawn with the sword." Yet Lincoln urged citizens to end the war free from bitterness, "with malice toward none; with charity for all." Victory came on April 9, 1865, at Appomattox Court House, Virginia, when Confederate general Robert E. Lee surrendered to Union general Ulysses S. Grant. Some 750,000 soldiers had died during the four-year conflict.

Seeing the Union successfully through the Civil War was Lincoln's greatest presidential responsibility, but it was not his only accomplishment. Together with Congress, he inaugurated a national banking system; established the Department of Agriculture; standardized paper currency; supported the development of a transcontinental railroad; enacted the Homestead Act, which opened up vast holdings of federal land to settlers; and crafted the 13th Amendment, which ended slavery.

Lincoln's personal life in the White House revolved around his wife, Mary, and two young sons, William and Thomas, better known as Willie and Tad. (Their oldest son, Robert, was studying at Harvard.) Lincoln often romped with his sons and their friends. A teenage guest recalled how she once entered a room to find the President flattened on the floor with four boys holding down his limbs. "Come quick and sit on his stomach," invited Tad. Lincoln forgave the boys their wildness. "It's a diversion," he told a visitor, "and we need diversion at the White House." Lincoln told jokes, tall tales,

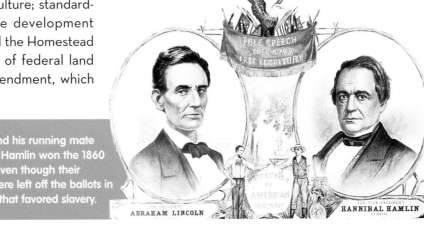

The Fugitive Slave Act of 1850 remained in effect in northern states until its repeal in 1864. Thus, for most of the Civil War, freedom seekers were at risk of being returned to enslavement (below, 19th-century artist Theodor Kaufmann depicted a group of women and children on a perilous quest for liberty).

Lincoln and his running mate Hannibal Hamlin won the 1860 election even though their names were left off the ballots in 10 states that favored slavery.

ABRAHAM LINCOLN

HANNIBAL HAMLIN

The invention of photography made it possible to capture and widely share the grim horrors of the Civil War (left, Confederate casualties from the Battle of Gettysburg, 1863).

Photographic portraits of Abraham Lincoln document the toll the four-year-long Civil War took on the president (photo taken November 15, 1863).

anecdotes, and stories to relieve wartime tensions.

In 1862 humor lost its place for a while when Willie became the only child to die in the White House. He was a victim of typhoid fever. Mary, already saddened by criticism of her actions as first lady, grieved deeply and long. First falsely accused of being sympathetic to the Confederacy (because some of her relatives fought against the Union), then scolded for her lavish spending, she was now chided by the public for neglecting her official duties. The subsequent deaths of her husband and Tad left her so grief-stricken that some people considered her insane.

Left to right: Mary, Willie, Robert, Tad, and President Lincoln. By 1871 only Mary and Robert remained alive.

Lincoln spent much of the final weeks of his life away from the White House. He met with military commanders, such as Ulysses S. Grant (who would become the 18th president), and discussed surrender terms. Lincoln's plans for Reconstruction, or the reunification of the United States, were flexible and generous. However, he would barely live to enjoy the end of the war, much less shape its peace. He became the first president to be assassinated when he was shot on April 14, 1865.

Lincoln had received thousands of death threats since 1860. The day he was shot, he confided to his daytime bodyguard that he had recently dreamed of being assassinated. His nightmare became a reality that evening when he went out to see a play. Lincoln and his wife watched the performance from box seats that could be accessed by a private door. This entrance was poorly guarded, allowing the actor John Wilkes Booth to enter the seating area uninvited. Booth hoped to revive the Confederate cause by killing the president.

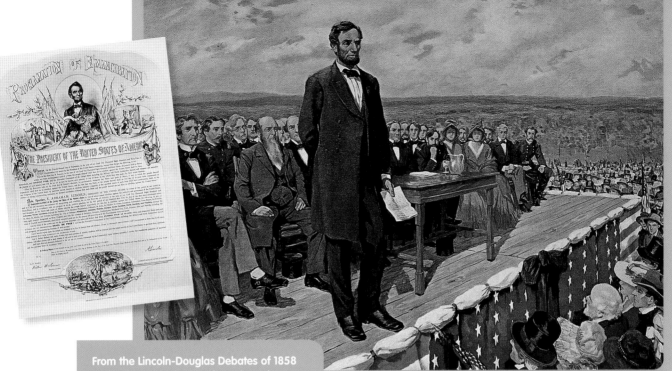

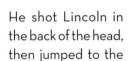

From the Lincoln-Douglas Debates of 1858 to the Emancipation Proclamation (above, left) and Gettysburg Address of 1863 (above, right), Lincoln promoted freedom and unity.

Lincoln was assassinated at Ford's Theatre on April 14, 1865.

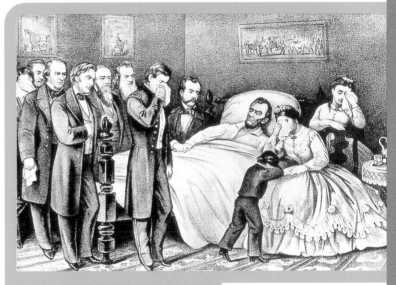

The president's death at the end of the Civil War unsettled the fragile nation.

He shot Lincoln in the back of the head, then jumped to the stage floor, breaking his leg in the process. He escaped the theater nonetheless and remained on the loose for nearly two weeks. He was shot during his eventual capture and died from his wounds.

The wounded and unconscious president was carried to a boardinghouse across the street. His long body had to be placed diagonally across the standard-size bed in order to recline properly. He died the following morning, said to be wearing an expression of happiness and repose on his face. His body lay in state at the U.S. Capitol and at other sites in the North before traveling home for burial in Illinois.

"All persons held as slaves within any State ... in rebellion against the United States, shall be then, thenceforward, and forever free."

Abraham Lincoln, Emancipation Proclamation, January 1, 1863

ANDREW JOHNSON
17TH PRESIDENT OF THE UNITED STATES 1865–1869

The crisis of war between the states was followed by a crisis within the U.S. presidency. It began with the assassination of Abraham Lincoln and continued through the presidency of his successor, Andrew Johnson. The climax came with Johnson's impeachment and near removal from office by Congress.

Johnson grew up with more poverty and hardship than any other president. His parents were illiterate laborers; his father died when Andrew was three. He never attended a day of school. Nonetheless, by age 20 Johnson had been elected to be an alderman, or city council member, in Tennessee. Later he became a mayor, then a state senator, U.S. representative, the state's governor, and, ultimately, a U.S. senator. During this period he held enslaved people in bondage in his household. Johnson was the only southern legislator who stayed on to work in the U.S. Senate during the Civil War. Southerners branded him a traitor, but Lincoln rewarded him a year later by making him the military governor of Tennessee.

As a gesture of national reconciliation, Lincoln chose the southern Democrat as his running mate on the Republican ticket in 1864. Thus, the party of the presidency changed from Republican to Democrat with Lincoln's death. Johnson's southern perspective put him at odds with the Republican-led Congress on how to "reconstruct" the United States after the Civil War. He routinely vetoed, or rejected, Congress's ideas and became known as the Veto President.

Legislators reached a breaking

Andrew Johnson opened a tailor's shop when he was 17. He continued to make his own clothes even after becoming a legislator.

point in 1868 when Johnson fired his secretary of war, Edward Stanton, in defiance of the newly enacted Tenure of Office Act. Enraged members of the House of Representatives impeached him, declaring he should be removed from office for this and other offenses. Senators considered the 11 House charges and voted on three tied to the war secretary post. Each result fell one vote short of conviction, so the president completed his term of office.

During his presidency the U.S. purchased the territory Alaska from Russia. In 1875 the retired president returned to the U.S. Senate. No other president has gone on to become a senator. At his request he was buried wrapped in a U.S. flag with his head resting on his copy of the Constitution.

NICKNAME
Veto President

BORN
Dec. 29, 1808, in Raleigh, NC

POLITICAL PARTY
Democratic

CHIEF OPPONENT
none; succeeded Abraham Lincoln

TERM OF OFFICE
April 15, 1865–March 3, 1869

AGE AT INAUGURATION
56 years old

NUMBER OF TERMS
one (partial)

VICE PRESIDENT
none

FIRST LADIES
Eliza McCardle Johnson (1810–1876), wife (married May 17, 1827); Martha Johnson Patterson (1828–1891), daughter

CHILDREN
Martha, Charles, Mary, Robert, Andrew Jr.

GEOGRAPHIC SCENE
36 states

NEW STATES ADDED
Nebraska (1867)

DIED
July 31, 1875, in Carter's Station, TN

AGE AT DEATH
66 years old

SELECTED LANDMARKS
Mordecai Historic Park, Raleigh, NC (relocated birthplace); Andrew Johnson National Historic Site, Greeneville, TN (includes two residences and grave)

Johnson—the first president ever impeached—receives a summons for his Senate trial.

IMPEACHMENT
THE PROCESS FOR ENDING A PRESIDENCY

n 1787, when representatives of the new American states drafted a national Constitution, they sought to assure that no individual ever presided over the country the way Britain's King George had ruled the Colonies. As a safeguard they outlined a two-part mechanism for removing a president from office. The same process applies to federal judges and other key government officials. They instructed that such action should be taken for only the gravest of offenses: "treason, bribery, or other high crimes and misdemeanors."

The framers could have granted this responsibility to the judicial branch as a legal matter, but instead they entrusted it to Congress. This choice assures that removal from office is both a legal and a political process. Part one—the power to impeach, or bring charges—resides with the House of Representatives. A majority of its members must support the accusations before further action can be taken against an office holder.

Successful articles of impeachment then pass to the Senate for part two of the process—a trial with senators serving as jurors. In cases of presidential impeachment the Chief Justice of the United States presides. The framers set a high bar for conviction—two-thirds of all participating senators must support one or more articles for someone to be removed from office. In the course of U.S. history, only 20 individuals, including three presidents, have been impeached by the House and tried in the Senate. Just eight people—all of them federal judges—have lost their posts. No president has ever been removed from office by Congress.

Andrew Johnson, a Democrat with southern roots, was the first Chief Executive to be impeached by the House. He had become president in 1865 after the assassination of Abraham Lincoln, a Republican. Johnson clashed repeatedly with the views of members of the Republican-dominated Congress. Finally, in 1868, House members judged him unfit to lead. His trial in the Senate lasted almost three months and ended with votes on a trio of charges. Although most Republicans found Johnson guilty, some did not. Their decisions, when added to those of all the Democrats, secured the continuation of his presidency by a margin of one vote.

One hundred years passed before the actions of another president—Richard Nixon, a Republican—drew sufficient scrutiny to threaten an administration's survival. His offenses sprang from the cover-up of actions he and others had taken to secure his reelection in 1972. Once again the president and congressional leaders represented opposing political parties, but this time it appeared that enough of Nixon's fellow Republicans might join Democrats to assure his Senate conviction. Rather than face that disgrace, the president resigned. Nixon's brush with impeachment came so close that many people mistakenly believe it actually happened.

Nearly a quarter-century later, in 1998, members of the House impeached a president for the second time in history. Once again the accused—Bill Clinton, a Democrat—faced a Congress where both chambers were controlled by the opposing

Richard Nixon resigned from office during the sixth year of his presidency to avoid being impeached and removed by Congress (left, parting salute from the White House, August 9, 1974).

Banner headlines appeared (above, August 18, 1998) after Bill Clinton admitted he had lied to hide his romantic affair with White House intern Monica Lewinsky. His deception led to impeachment, but his presidency survived when the Senate failed to convict him.

In the 19th century, members of Congress tried unsuccessfully to remove Andrew Johnson from office. Special tickets to his impeachment trial (below) allowed visitors to watch the proceedings at the U.S. Capitol.

party. After a five-week-long trial, members of the Senate agreed to vote on two of the four charges leveled by the House. This time results were far below the two-thirds majority required for removal. As with Johnson, no members of the president's party found him guilty. Instead of being forced from the White House, the president completed the remaining months of his two-term administration.

Donald Trump, a first-term Republican, was the most recent president to be impeached. Unlike during the Johnson and Clinton proceedings, this time control of Congress was split between the two parties. Democrats initiated the process in the House in late 2019, and the Republican-led Senate considered a pair of charges for three weeks in early 2020. Unlike in previous trials, one member of the president's party voted for his conviction. This vote is the only one ever made against a fellow party member out of 223 votes cast during the three presidential trials. Even so, total votes fell far short of the required two-thirds majority, and Trump remained in office.

These examples demonstrate that the drafters of the Constitution devised a challenging mechanism for removing a president. The logistics of the process are complex and time-consuming, and the proceedings themselves

"Maybe we'll frame it," Donald Trump said of a *Washington Post* report of the news that he had been acquitted during his 2020 impeachment trial in the U.S. Senate.

become politically contentious. Legal scholars continue to debate what the framers meant by the phrase "high crimes and misdemeanors." So far no behavior has met that threshold in a way that rallies the broad bipartisan support required to prematurely end a presidency.

ULYSSES S. GRANT
18TH PRESIDENT OF THE UNITED STATES 1869–1877

By the end of the Civil War, Ulysses Simpson Grant was the highest ranking U.S. general since George Washington. He was a national hero, too. Grant's popular appeal helped him become president in the first post–Civil War national election. Mastery of military tactics did not prepare him for the world of politics, however. His administration is remembered more for its scandals than for its accomplishments.

As a child Grant seemed an unlikely person to triumph on the battlefield. He disliked hunting, got sick in his father's leather tanning shop, and later resisted attending the U.S. Military Academy at West Point. Once there, however, Grant distinguished himself as a horseman and excelled at math. Within a few

Birthplace of Ulysses S. Grant in Point Pleasant, Ohio. As a child Grant imagined becoming a farmer or a river trader.

years Grant was on active duty in the Mexican War. Later he farmed. Although his own family opposed slavery, his wife's family did not. Grant benefited from the labor of people enslaved by his relatives, and he himself held one man in bondage. Grant was the last president directly tied to slavery.

When the Civil War began, Grant led Illinois troops as a brigadier general. His aggressive assault on Fort Donelson, Tennessee, during February 1862, gave the Union its first notable victory in the Civil War. Citizens boasted that his initials stood for "Unconditional Surrender," the

The name of the nation's 18th president was accidentally changed from Hiram Ulysses Grant to Ulysses Simpson Grant when he was enrolled at the U.S. Military Academy. (His local congressman incorporated the maiden name of Grant's mother into his appointment recommendation by mistake.) Classmates nicknamed him Uncle Sam, after the already popular patriotic character. His initials gained new meaning after he demanded the "unconditional and immediate surrender" of Confederates at Fort Donelson in 1862.

NICKNAME
Unconditional Surrender Grant

BORN
April 27, 1822, in Point Pleasant, OH

POLITICAL PARTY
Republican

CHIEF OPPONENTS
1st term: Horatio Seymour, Democrat (1810–1886); 2nd term: Horace Greeley, Democrat (1811–1872)

TERM OF OFFICE
March 4, 1869–March 3, 1877

AGE AT INAUGURATION
46 years old

NUMBER OF TERMS
two

VICE PRESIDENTS
1st term: Schuyler Colfax (1823–1885);
2nd term: Henry Wilson (1812–1875)

FIRST LADY
Julia Boggs Dent Grant (1826–1902), wife (married Aug. 22, 1848)

CHILDREN
Frederick, Ulysses, Ellen, Jesse

GEOGRAPHIC SCENE
37 states

NEW STATES ADDED
Colorado (1876)

DIED
July 23, 1885, in Mount McGregor, NY

AGE AT DEATH
63 years old

SELECTED LANDMARKS
Point Pleasant, OH (birthplace); Georgetown, OH (boyhood home); White Haven, St. Louis, MO (home); General Grant National Memorial, New York, NY (grave)

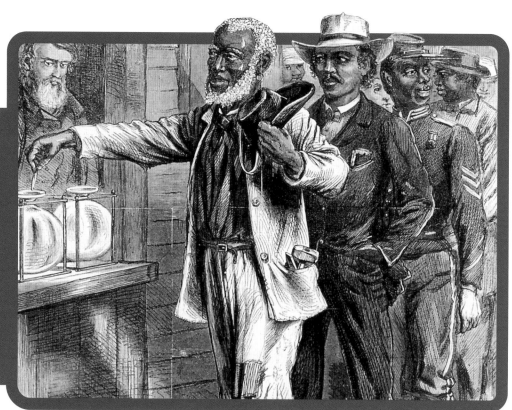

Passage of the 15th Amendment in 1870 permitted large numbers of African Americans to begin voting. In 1872 Victoria Claflin Woodhull became the first female presidential candidate. She suggested that the formerly enslaved Frederick Douglass run as her vice president. He declined, and her third-party campaign fizzled.

> ## "War and politics are so different."
>
> Ulysses S. Grant, 1871

terms he had set for the Southern rebels at the fort. When Northerners learned he had smoked a cigar during the assault, they sent him as many as 10,000 boxes of them to help guarantee future victories. (Thus developed Grant's custom of smoking some 20 cigars a day, a habit that probably helped cause his death.) Some called him Butcher Grant for the casualties that came with his victories, but Abraham Lincoln was impressed. "I cannot spare this man—he fights," he said. Lincoln named him commander of all Federal troops in March 1864. Grant, who was superstitious about retracing his steps, did not like to retreat. He persisted on the battlefield, and, supported by Union commanders fighting aggressively elsewhere, he wore down the Confederate side until it was forced to surrender.

After the political infighting that filled Andrew Johnson's administration, voters were enthusiastic about electing Grant—the respected war hero—as their president. He was the only man to complete two presidential terms during the 76-year span between Andrew

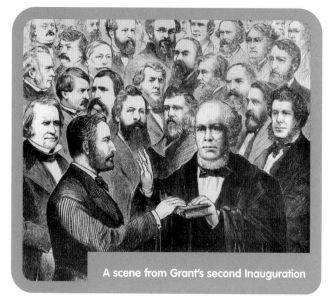

A scene from Grant's second Inauguration

Jackson and Woodrow Wilson. Under Grant's leadership the government established the world's first national park (Yellowstone, founded in 1872), avoided war with Great Britain about Civil War damage claims, established the Department of Justice, and championed the new 15th Amendment. This legislation granted voting rights regardless of "race, color, or previous condition of servitude" to all men. (Women only began to gain voting rights nationwide in 1920.)

These accomplishments were overshadowed, however, by controversies. The federal government failed

Grant's appeal as a presidential nominee in 1880 was undercut by the scandal-plagued reputation of his prior administration. *Puck* magazine (cartoon, above) warned readers that his administration would be weighed down by corruption if he returned for a third term.

Grant found he had much in common with the viceroy of China when they met during a world tour after his presidency (above). Both men liked to eat—the viceroy hosted an eight-hour, 70-course dinner for his guest. Both leaders had defended their countries as generals during civil wars, too.

Enslaved laborers were part of the upbringing of Missouri-born Julia Dent. She married a Northern-born soldier even though neither of their families approved. Julia Grant was the first first lady to write a memoir about her life.

to prevent white Southerners from using violence and political tricks to limit the rights of formerly enslaved people. The financial Panic of 1873 put millions of laborers out of work. Worst of all were the scandals of Grant's administration—from corrupt banking and currency deals to the stealing of federal liquor taxes by manufacturers and public officials. Although none of these crimes involved Grant directly, his reputation as a leader suffered.

Grant failed to win nomination for a third presidential term. (A constitutional amendment in 1951 limited a president to two elected terms of office, but no such barrier existed before then.) After leaving the White House, Grant, his wife, and their teenage son embarked on a 30-month tour of the world. Along the way he met Queen Victoria in England and became the first person ever allowed to shake hands with a Japanese emperor. In 1880 he failed yet again to win the Republican

nomination for president. Grant invested in a family business venture during his retirement in New York City, but a dishonest business partner brought financial ruin to the project. Congress provided Grant with much needed income by putting him back on the Army payroll as a general, even though he was not on active duty.

At the suggestion of author and publisher Mark Twain, Grant tried to make more money by writing his autobiography. Grant raced to complete the book before his life could be claimed by throat cancer. He finished only days before his death. The book became a best seller and earned his family a small fortune. Grant and his wife, Julia, who died 17 years after him, are buried in the New York City landmark popularly known as Grant's Tomb.

RUTHERFORD B. HAYES
19TH PRESIDENT OF THE UNITED STATES 1877-1881

Rutherford Birchard Hayes started his administration amid controversy. Politicians argued about how to count the national election returns. In the end, Hayes won office by one electoral vote, the narrowest presidential victory in history. He went on to bring dignity, honesty, and reform to the federal government.

Hayes came to the White House with a solid background of service to his country. He was born in Delaware, Ohio, graduated from Kenyon College in Ohio, and earned a law degree from Harvard University. In 1861 Hayes interrupted law practice in his home state to join the Union Army. He rose to the rank of major general by the end of the Civil War and survived having four horses shot out from under him. Hayes declined to leave the battlefield after he was nominated for a seat in Congress. He wrote home that soldiers who campaigned for office "ought to be scalped" for deserting their posts. (These patriotic words ensured his election.) Later he served three terms as Ohio's governor.

Widespread ballot fraud, or illegal vote-casting, clouded the results of the popular and electoral voting in the 1876 presidential election. Victory belonged to the candidate with the greatest number of electoral votes, but politicians disagreed on how to allocate them. Eventually a 15-person commission of legislators and Supreme Court justices was created to break the stalemate. When it voted along party lines and chose Hayes, a Republican, southern Democrats were

Lucy Hayes, with Fanny (above, right) and Scott and a friend, was the first first lady to finish college. She was nicknamed Lemonade Lucy for supporting temperance by serving soft drinks instead of alcohol at the White House.

outraged. To placate them Hayes promised to end federal Reconstruction of the South. The dealmaking earned Hayes the offensive nicknames of His Fraudulency and Rather*fraud* B. Hayes. As president, Hayes left scandal behind. He actually worked to increase the standards of behavior for civil servants, or employees who make a career out of government service.

Alexander Graham Bell personally installed the first White House telephone while Hayes was president. Another inventor, Thomas Edison, visited the first family to demonstrate his new phonograph. The Hayes family held the first public Easter Egg Roll on the White House lawn.

Having always planned to serve only one term, Hayes retired to Ohio where he took an active role in local and state causes. He died in 1893.

NICKNAME
His Fraudulency

BORN
Oct. 4, 1822, in Delaware, OH

POLITICAL PARTY
Republican

CHIEF OPPONENT
Samuel Jones Tilden, Democrat (1814–1886)

TERM OF OFFICE
March 4, 1877–March 3, 1881

AGE AT INAUGURATION
54 years old

NUMBER OF TERMS
one

VICE PRESIDENT
William Almon Wheeler (1819–1887)

FIRST LADY
Lucy Ware Webb Hayes (1831–1889), wife (married Dec. 30, 1852)

CHILDREN
Birchard Austin, Webb Cook, Rutherford Platt, Frances (Fanny), Scott, plus three sons who died young

GEOGRAPHIC SCENE
38 states

NEW STATES ADDED
none

DIED
Jan. 17, 1893, in Fremont, OH

AGE AT DEATH
70 years old

SELECTED LANDMARKS
Spiegel Grove National Historic Landmark, Fremont, OH (adult home, memorial library, museum, grave)

RACE TO THE FINISH
HOW CANDIDATES, CONVENTIONS, AND CASH SET THE PACE FOR PRESIDENTIAL ELECTIONS

The presidential campaigns of modern times are vastly different from those waged by earlier candidates for president. In fact, the concept of campaigning for the presidency did not even gain favor until well into the 19th century. Prior to that time, supporters spoke on behalf of candidates. Sitting presidents, in particular, preferred not to mix the politics of campaigning with their work as Chief Executive. Today's candidates usually launch their presidential campaigns more than a year before Election Day and spend months traveling the country to gain public support for themselves and their varying visions for the country.

Multiple rounds of voting take place before the outcome is decided. The first ballots are cast during the opening months of an election year. States, the District of Columbia, and U.S. territories hold primaries or caucuses where voters identify their preferred candidates. These votes help determine the number of delegates, or candidate representatives, who are sent to summer nominating conventions for the next step in the process.

Each political party holds its own convention, but the largest and most consequential ones are those of the Democrats and Republicans, the country's leading parties. Delegates at these events are grouped geographically and announce their various tallies of support with great ceremony. If no candidate receives a majority of votes, a so-called brokered convention begins. Delegates are then allowed to change their preferences until a candidate wins the nomination. Delegates also approve the nominee's choice for a vice presidential running mate. This pair represents the party in the upcoming nationwide general election.

Nominees spend the remaining months of the election season traveling the country to meet with potential voters. Others campaign for them, too, including grassroots supporters who spread out to recruit additional allies. Campaigns employ every innovation in communications technology in an effort to attract voters—including use of the telephone, radio, television, text messaging, the internet, and carefully targeted postings on social media. Campaigns are expensive. They require multimillion-dollar budgets to pay for staff, offices, travel, advertising, and so on. Candidates typically raise money directly from supporters, but they may also rely on their own wealth for some or all of the expense.

Americans who watched the first televised presidential debate in 1960 liked John F. Kennedy's youthful appearance and preferred him to Richard Nixon. Radio listeners, who could only hear the candidates, were more impressed by Nixon than Kennedy.

When rail travel served as the best link between cities, politicians often embarked on so-called whistle-stop campaigns (above, Warren G. Harding in 1920).

Opportunities to vote increased during the 1960s when reforms ended an era that sought to exclude African Americans from participating in southern elections (above, marking ballots in Alabama, 1966).

A 2010 Supreme Court ruling known as *Citizens United* made it much easier for corporations, unions, and other special interests as well as wealthy individuals to have a financial impact on elections. Previously there had been limits on individual campaign contributions, and donations from businesses were more restricted. After the ruling, unlimited funds began to flow from these sources to outside groups known as PACs (short for "political action committees"). PACs are permitted to support a specific candidate or group of candidates. All this outside money has raised concerns about how it may influence victorious candidates to favor the policies of their financial supporters.

Many more people vote today than in earlier centuries. (See pages 64-65 for a brief history of voting rights.) Laws have changed through the years so that U.S. citizens age 18 or older may register to vote, regardless of race, gender, or beliefs. Some people still face barriers, though, due to such factors as voter ID requirements, long lines at polling places, and work commitments that conflict with voting schedules.

Each state sets its own rules for voter registration and for how ballots are cast. Voter turnout, the number of people who actually vote, can be a critical factor in a candidate's success or defeat. Although a surprising number of people choose not to participate, many others view voting as a fundamental democratic responsibility.

Election Day occurs in November on the first Tuesday after the first Monday in the month. It marks the third phase in the process of choosing a president. Many states allow

In 2008 a record-breaking crowd of more than 80,000 people gathered in Denver at its Mile High Stadium to celebrate the nomination of Barack Obama as the Democratic Party's nominee for president. The occasion featured political speeches, performances by pop stars, and celebration.

votes to be cast ahead of time or by mailed-in absentee ballots. Election results may be known within hours of the closing of polling places, but sometimes they can take much longer. The delayed arrival of mailed ballots, faulty equipment, and concerns about the accuracy of vote tallies can impede the process and create uncertainty about results. Tallies of the popular vote are then used to predict the outcome of the Electoral College—the final stage of voting for president. (See pages 174-175 for more information about how this process works.)

Winning candidates celebrate with victory speeches. Losers are expected to concede, or admit defeat, as a sign of respect for the rule of law and the will of the people. When elections are won by narrow margins, there can be bitterness and anger over the outcome, and these divisions may endure—and even expand—long after an election ends. Sometimes candidates win with a landslide of overwhelming support. These presidents are said to have a mandate, or level of approval, from voters that gives them considerable political influence.

JAMES A. GARFIELD
20TH PRESIDENT OF THE UNITED STATES **1881**

James Abram Garfield, like William Henry Harrison, barely had a chance to establish himself as president before death removed him from office. He was shot by an assassin early in his term and died 79 days later.

Garfield was the last president born in a log cabin. His election followed notable service as an educator, soldier, and statesman. A graduate of Williams College in Massachusetts, Garfield returned to his home state of Ohio to be a college professor. He had considered a career as a sailor until he fell overboard while working on a canal boat and caught a bad cold. A nonswimmer, he decided to teach instead. Later he became a lawyer, Ohio state senator, Civil War colonel, and U.S. congressman from his home state.

Garfield served 18 years in the House of Representatives before receiving his unexpected nomination for president in 1880. He became known as the Preacher President for his talents as a public speaker. Garfield was the nation's first left-handed president. He was actually ambidextrous, or able to write with either hand. Friends said he could write Latin with one hand and Greek with the other hand—at the same time!

As president, Garfield surprised legislators by how diligently he sought to end political corruption, or improper influence, especially within his own Republican Party. He refused to be bullied by powerful party leaders in the Senate when making political appointments; in the end, two senators resigned, and he got his way. Garfield fought similar battles on a smaller scale at the White House. The place swarmed with job hunters. People expected to be rewarded with posts in Garfield's administration because they had supported the Republican Party.

One disappointed and mentally ill job hunter shadowed Garfield and his staff for weeks. He shot the president at a Washington, D.C., train station on July 2, 1881. Although Garfield survived the initial wound, the bullet could not be found and removed. He died from complications two and a half months later. His assassin was tried and hanged. Reacting to Garfield's murder, lawmakers wrote new rules for how to fill many government posts. These jobs were to be given as a reward for talent and experience, not as political favors.

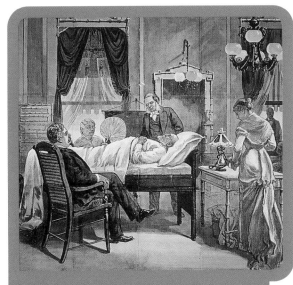

James A. Garfield became the second president to die by assassination, and the fourth to die in office. X-rays, surgery, and antibiotics might have saved him, had they been available.

NICKNAME
Preacher President

BORN
Nov. 19, 1831, near Orange, OH

POLITICAL PARTY
Republican

CHIEF OPPONENT
Winfield Scott Hancock, Democrat (1824–1886)

TERM OF OFFICE
March 4, 1881–Sept. 19, 1881

AGE AT INAUGURATION
49 years old

NUMBER OF TERMS
one (cut short by assassination)

VICE PRESIDENT
Chester A. Arthur (1829–1886)

FIRST LADY
Lucretia Rudolph Garfield (1832–1918), wife (married Nov. 11, 1858)

CHILDREN
Harry, James, Mary, Irvin, Abram, plus a son and a daughter who died young

GEOGRAPHIC SCENE
38 states

NEW STATES ADDED
none

DIED
Sept. 19, 1881, in Elberon, NJ

AGE AT DEATH
49 years old

SELECTED LANDMARKS
Lawnfield, Garfield National Historic Site, Mentor, OH (birthplace and replica homestead); Lake View Cemetery, Cleveland, OH

CHESTER A. ARTHUR
21ST PRESIDENT OF THE UNITED STATES **1881–1885**

Many citizens were as shocked at the thought of Chester Alan Arthur becoming president as they were by the shooting of his predecessor, James A. Garfield. Once again—as with John Tyler, Millard Fillmore, and Andrew Johnson—a vice president chosen for political reasons instead of leadership skills became president.

Arthur had never been elected to public office until he became Garfield's vice president. Born in Vermont, Arthur was a graduate of Union College in New York and an attorney. In 1871 he was made collector of the port of New York City and was responsible for collecting import fees for goods arriving at the nation's busiest harbor. Arthur built his personal and political fortune there by using the "spoils system" and "machine politics." He awarded jobs, raises, and favorable regulations (the spoils) to employees and businesses who supported his political candidates with their votes and donations (the vote-buying "machine" that influenced elections). This favoritism led the *New York Times* to call his pre-White House career a "mess of filth."

Arthur was deeply shocked that Garfield had been shot by someone caught up in the greed of machine politics. As president, he angered old friends and surprised the nation by supporting passage of the Pendleton Act. This legislation created a Civil Service Commission to oversee the government's

Chester A. Arthur (above, with daughter Nell) entered the White House a widower, his wife having died the previous year. His sister served as first lady and helped him care for 13-year-old Nell. "Elegant Arthur" changed his clothes for each occasion of the day; he was said to own 80 pairs of pants.

civilian (nonmilitary) workers. It established procedures to ensure that a core of basic federal jobs were filled by competitive exam, not presidential appointment. It also protected these employees from being fired because of their political views.

After Arthur learned that he suffered from a fatal kidney disease, he did not care if he was renominated for a second term (he was not). Arthur retired to New York City. He died 20 months later.

NICKNAME
Elegant Arthur

BORN
Oct. 5, 1829, in Fairfield, VT

POLITICAL PARTY
Republican

CHIEF OPPONENT
none; succeeded James A. Garfield

TERM OF OFFICE
Sept. 20, 1881–March 3, 1885

AGE AT INAUGURATION
51 years old

NUMBER OF TERMS
one (partial)

VICE PRESIDENT
none

FIRST LADY
Mary Arthur McElroy (1842–1917), sister

WIFE
Ellen Lewis Herndon Arthur (1837–1880), married Oct. 25, 1859

CHILDREN
Chester, Ellen (Nell), plus a son who died young

GEOGRAPHIC SCENE
38 states

NEW STATES ADDED
none

DIED
Nov. 18, 1886, in New York, NY

AGE AT DEATH
57 years old

SELECTED LANDMARKS
Fairfield, VT (reconstructed birthplace); Albany Rural Cemetery, Menands, NY

President Arthur (seated, center) visited Yellowstone National Park in 1883. He modernized the U.S. Navy by ordering the construction of four steel warships.

GROVER CLEVELAND
22ND AND 24TH PRESIDENT OF THE UNITED STATES 1885–1889, 1893–1897

Grover Cleveland was the first Democrat to be elected president after the Civil War. Although he lost his reelection bid in 1888 to Benjamin Harrison, he returned to the White House four years later after winning a rematch in the 1892 election. Thus, Cleveland is the only president to serve two nonconsecutive terms of office. His disregard of popular and political opinion cost him reelection after each term.

Cleveland's political career developed rapidly; he went from county sheriff to U.S. president in only 11 years. Although born in New Jersey, he grew up in New York State, the son of a Presbyterian minister. His school years ended at age 16 with the death of his father. Eventually Cleveland studied law and entered into private practice in Buffalo, New York. His firm hand as the local sheriff led citizens to elect him mayor. Cleveland succeeded so well at ending corruption, waste, and scandal that he was nominated for governor of New York. He won by a landslide. His popularity in New York State made him a natural candidate for president in 1884.

Gossip and scandal fueled the presidential campaign. Republicans were delighted to discover that the bachelor Cleveland might have fathered a child. They chanted: "Ma, Ma, where's my Pa? Gone to the White House, ha, ha, ha!" However, the public seemed less concerned about Cleveland's private life than about the professional actions of his opponent. Democrats joked about "James Blaine, James Blaine, the continental liar from the state of Maine."

Grover Cleveland and First Lady Frances Cleveland aboard the presidential train

Cleveland claimed "Public Office Is a Public Trust." Republican "Mugwumps" (an Algonquian word meaning "big chief") deserted their own party's candidate and favored him instead. Cleveland narrowly won the race.

Cleveland, who weighed 250 pounds, was nicknamed Uncle Jumbo. He was the first president since the Civil War who had not fought in that conflict. Cleveland avoided military service then by paying a Polish immigrant $150 to take his place. Although this practice was legal, it was not considered admirable. As a presidential candidate, Cleveland had been criticized for avoiding combat.

During his first administration, Cleveland vetoed more than twice as many pieces of legislation (413 total) as had all previous presidents combined. As with Andrew Johnson two decades

NICKNAME
Uncle Jumbo

BORN
March 18, 1837, in Caldwell, NJ

POLITICAL PARTY
Democratic

CHIEF OPPONENTS
1st administration: James Gillespie Blaine, Republican (1830–1893); 2nd administration: President Benjamin Harrison, Republican (1833–1901)

TERM OF OFFICE
1st administration: March 4, 1885–March 3, 1889; 2nd administration: March 4, 1893–March 3, 1897

AGE AT INAUGURATION
1st administration: 47 years old; 2nd administration: 55 years old

NUMBER OF TERMS
two (nonconsecutive)

VICE PRESIDENTS
1st administration: Thomas Andrews Hendricks (1819–1885); 2nd administration: Adlai Ewing Stevenson (1835–1914)

FIRST LADIES
Rose Elizabeth Cleveland (1846–1918), sister; Frances Folsom Cleveland (1864–1947), wife (married June 2, 1886)

CHILDREN
Ruth, Esther, Marion, Richard, Francis

GEOGRAPHIC SCENE
1st administration: 38 states; 2nd administration: 44 states

NEW STATES ADDED
Utah (1896)

DIED
June 24, 1908, in Princeton, NJ

AGE AT DEATH
71 years old

SELECTED LANDMARKS
Caldwell, NJ (birthplace); Westland (home) and Princeton Cemetery, Princeton, NJ

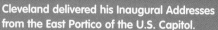
Cleveland delivered his Inaugural Addresses from the East Portico of the U.S. Capitol.

Cleveland became the only president to marry at the White House when he wed Frances Folsom during his first administration. The couple changed their wedding vows so Frances could pledge to "love, honor, and keep" her husband instead of agreeing to "love, honor, and obey" him. Their first child, nicknamed Baby Ruth, had a candy bar named after her. Their second child, Esther, was the only child of a president born in the White House.

earlier, critics called him the Veto President. Children sang: "A fat man once sat in the president's chair, singing 'Ve-to,' 'Ve-to.'" Although Cleveland worked hard to hire loyal Democrats to fill government posts, other party members were often angered by his choices. He was more popular for his unexpected marriage, at age 49, to 21-year-old Frances Folsom, who was the daughter of a deceased friend.

During the election of 1888, Cleveland again won a greater share of the popular vote than his opponent. However, the presidency went to Benjamin Harrison because he earned the most votes in the Electoral College. The story goes that the departing first lady assured the White House staff that she and her husband would return after the next election. They did. Cleveland won by a sizable margin in both popular and electoral voting when he faced Harrison in 1892.

Cleveland campaigned on his party's ties to revered early presidents, including Democrats Thomas Jefferson and Andrew Jackson as well as the nonpartisan George Washington. His two administrations were interrupted by Benjamin Harrison's single term.

Cleveland hunted with a rifle he nicknamed "Death and Destruction." The president was forced to take a break from outdoor recreation in 1893 after developing mouth cancer. To avoid media attention, Frances Cleveland arranged for doctors to operate on the president aboard a private yacht. Doctors removed the tumor and part of Cleveland's jaw, then inserted a rubber shape to take the place of the missing bone. It left no visible scars. Some two dozen years passed before news of the operation leaked out.

> "What is the use of being elected or reelected unless you stand for something?"
>
> Grover Cleveland, 1887

Public support of Cleveland began to fall soon after his reelection, however, with the start of a new round of economic hard times. The Panic of 1893 lasted for the rest of Cleveland's presidency and brought widespread suffering. Cleveland argued with Congress over what, if anything, to do. Should the government issue more money, or less money, or should it do nothing? Should paper money continue to be worth a standard amount of gold? Should extra money be created in the form of silver coins? Was it better for the government to hoard precious metals or to share them? No one was quite sure how all the elements of national finance influenced one another, so it was hard to know what might help end

the panic. Meanwhile, politicians gave little thought to the suffering of the nation's citizens. Some people joked that if a hungry man started eating grass on the White House lawn, Cleveland, instead of offering him food, would suggest he move to the backyard, where the grass was taller.

By the next election, Democrats were ready for a new candidate, and the public was ready for an entirely different party. Republicans, who had dominated the presidency since the Civil War, became the favored party again. Except for Cleveland and Woodrow Wilson, Republicans controlled the White House from 1861 until 1933.

Cleveland retired to New Jersey and became a lecturer and trustee for Princeton University. His dying words, 11 years after leaving the White House, were: "I have tried so hard to do right."

The Clevelands (from left to right: Esther, Francis, Mrs. Cleveland, Ruth, Richard, and the former president) posed for a family snapshot on the porch of the president's retirement home in New Jersey. Frances outlived her husband by 39 years. She became the first widow of a president to remarry when she wed a professor in 1913.

PRESIDENTIAL FACTS AND COMPARISONS
A LOOK AT THE STATS

Forty-five individuals have served their nation as president in 46 administrations. (Grover Cleveland is counted twice—once for each of his two separate presidencies.) The oldest president on taking office was Joe Biden, age 78; the youngest was Theodore Roosevelt, age 42. The president who served the shortest term in office—32 days—was William Henry Harrison. Franklin D. Roosevelt served the longest term; he was elected four times and was president for 12 years before dying in office at age 63.

Eight presidents have been born in Virginia, earning that state the nickname "Mother of Presidents." Many presidents have come from Massachusetts, New York, and Ohio, too. In all, 24 presidents have been born in one of these four states. Some half a dozen presidents were born in log cabins; Jimmy Carter was the first president born in a hospital. Carter, like many earlier presidents, was the son of a farmer.

Nine presidents have failed to complete their terms of office. Eight have died on the job. One, Richard Nixon, resigned from office because of political scandal.

Throughout the course of the nation's history the presidential salary has grown from $25,000 a year (for George Washington) to $400,000 a year today. Each president receives a significant expense allowance, too.

In 1897 William McKinley became the first sitting president to play golf. Most Chief Executives have played since then, too.

Harry S. Truman (standing far left) owned a clothing store before he entered politics.

William Howard Taft began a presidential tradition when he tossed out a ceremonial first pitch for the baseball season in 1910.

During the final month of his presidency, George W. Bush (center) hosted a luncheon for the incoming Chief Executive. The guests at this rare gathering of presidential power were (from left, posing in the Oval Office) Bush's father, former president George H. W. Bush; President-elect Barack Obama; and former presidents Bill Clinton and Jimmy Carter.

All but eight of the presidents have attended college; 33 have been college graduates. More than half of all presidents have been members of the armed services, although not all witnessed combat. Eleven presidents were former generals. Fifteen presidents have been vice presidents of the country first. More than two dozen had served in the U.S. Congress. Seventeen were governors before becoming president. Twenty-seven had studied law and become attorneys. Other pre-presidential occupations include farmer, teacher, journalist, college professor, actor, engineer, business owner, and tailor.

Presidents have enjoyed hobbies including fishing, golf, and stamp collecting. Two played the piano (Harry S. Truman and Richard Nixon); two played the violin (Thomas Jefferson and John Tyler). Calvin Coolidge's instrument was the harmonica. Bill Clinton played the saxophone.

Most presidents have been affiliated with Protestant churches, including 12 Episcopalians and seven Presbyterians. Two have been Catholics. No one from the Jewish or Muslim faiths has yet served as president. Four presidents, including Thomas Jefferson and Abraham Lincoln, listed no preferred religious affiliation.

James K. Polk enjoyed the shortest presidential retirement (103 days). In 2012 Jimmy Carter broke Herbert Hoover's record-long retirement (31 years). No president has lived longer than Carter, either. John F. Kennedy died at the youngest age: 46. Three presidents died on the Fourth of July: John Adams, Thomas Jefferson, and James Monroe.

PRESIDENTIAL CAREER PATHS

No.	President	College Education	Graduate School	Military Service	Lawyer	Educator	State & Local Politics	House of Representatives	U.S. Senate	Governor	Diplomat	Cabinet Secretary	Vice President	Agriculture	Business
1.	George Washington			●			●						●		
2.	John Adams	●			●		●				●		●		
3.	Thomas Jefferson	●			●		●			●	●	●	●		
4.	James Madison	●	●	●			●	●				●			
5.	James Monroe	●		●	●		●		●	●	●	●			
6.	John Quincy Adams	●			●		●		●		●	●			
7.	Andrew Jackson			●	●		●	●	●	●					
8.	Martin Van Buren				●		●		●	●	●		●		
9.	William Henry Harrison	●	●	●			●	●	●	●	●				
10.	John Tyler	●			●		●	●	●	●			●		
11.	James K. Polk	●			●		●	●		●					
12.	Zachary Taylor			●											
13.	Millard Fillmore				●		●	●					●		
14.	Franklin Pierce	●		●	●		●	●	●						
15.	James Buchanan	●			●		●	●	●		●	●			
16.	Abraham Lincoln			●	●		●	●							●
17.	Andrew Johnson			●			●	●	●	●			●		●
18.	Ulysses S. Grant	●		●							●	●			
19.	Rutherford B. Hayes	●	●	●	●			●		●					
20.	James A. Garfield	●		●	●	●	●	●	●						
21.	Chester A. Arthur	●			●	●	●						●		
22. & 24.	Grover Cleveland				●		●			●					
23.	Benjamin Harrison	●		●	●				●						
25.	William McKinley	●		●	●			●		●					
26.	Theodore Roosevelt	●	●				●			●			●	●	
27.	William Howard Taft	●	●		●	●					●	●			
28.	Woodrow Wilson	●	●		●	●				●					
29.	Warren G. Harding	●					●		●		●				●
30.	Calvin Coolidge	●			●		●			●			●		
31.	Herbert Hoover	●										●			●
32.	Franklin D. Roosevelt	●	●	●			●			●					
33.	Harry S. Truman			●			●		●				●	●	
34.	Dwight D. Eisenhower	●	●	●		●									
35.	John F. Kennedy	●		●				●	●						
36.	Lyndon B. Johnson	●		●		●		●	●				●		
37.	Richard Nixon	●		●	●			●	●				●		
38.	Gerald R. Ford	●		●	●			●					●		
39.	Jimmy Carter	●		●			●			●			●	●	
40.	Ronald Reagan	●		●						●					
41.	George H. W. Bush	●		●				●			●		●		●
42.	Bill Clinton	●	●		●	●				●					
43.	George W. Bush	●	●							●					●
44.	Barack Obama	●	●		●	●			●						
45.	Donald Trump	●													●
46.	Joe Biden	●	●		●		●		●				●		

Presidents have taken many pathways to the presidency. This chart makes it easy to see the career paths of individuals or to study specific vocations and the evolving popularity of common routes to the White House.

BENJAMIN HARRISON
23RD PRESIDENT OF THE UNITED STATES 1889–1893

Benjamin Harrison's single term of office was sandwiched between the two presidential terms of Grover Cleveland. Harrison and Cleveland competed for the presidency in the consecutive elections of 1888 and 1892. In both cases Cleveland won the popular vote. However, Harrison was awarded the presidency in 1888 after receiving a majority of Electoral College votes.

Harrison grew up in the shadow of another resident of the White House—his grandfather. "Little Ben" was a seven-year-old boy living in Ohio when William Henry Harrison became president. The younger Harrison went on to graduate from Ohio's Miami University and become an attorney in Indiana. He served one term in the U.S. Senate before being nominated for president.

Harrison, as was customary at the time, chose to run a low-key campaign. He spoke only to the crowds who were encouraged to gather at his home in Indianapolis. For one campaign stunt,

President Benjamin Harrison facing the latest round of office seekers

40,000 drummers from 11 states were organized to visit him. Harrison's well-financed campaign earned him victories in enough key states so that he topped his opponent in the Electoral College. Cleveland's slim lead in popular votes—about 90,000—became irrelevant.

As president, Harrison authorized the first peacetime federal budget to reach the $1 billion mark. This money improved harbors, established naval fleets on both U.S. coasts, and helped pay the costs of building steamship lines. More states (six) were added to the nation during Harrison's single administration than during any other presidency.

Harrison's support of import tariffs cost him reelection when Cleveland mounted a bid to retake the White House. He returned to Indianapolis a widower, his wife having died of tuberculosis the previous year. He resumed his law practice and married his late wife's niece. He died of pneumonia five years later.

NICKNAME
Little Ben

BORN
Aug. 20, 1833, in North Bend, OH

POLITICAL PARTY
Republican

CHIEF OPPONENT
President Grover Cleveland, Democrat (1837–1908)

TERM OF OFFICE
March 4, 1889–March 3, 1893

AGE AT INAUGURATION
55 years old

NUMBER OF TERMS
one

VICE PRESIDENT
Levi Parsons Morton (1824–1920)

FIRST LADIES
Caroline Lavinia Scott Harrison (1832–1892), wife (married Oct. 20, 1853); Mary Scott Harrison McKee (1858–1930), daughter

OTHER MARRIAGES
Mary Scott Lord Dimmick Harrison (1858–1948), married April 6, 1896

CHILDREN
Born to Caroline Harrison (first wife): Russell, Mary; born to Mary Harrison (second wife): Elizabeth

GEOGRAPHIC SCENE
38 states

NEW STATES ADDED
Montana, North Dakota, South Dakota, and Washington (1889); Idaho and Wyoming (1890)

DIED
March 13, 1901, in Indianapolis, IN

AGE AT DEATH
67 years old

SELECTED LANDMARKS
Indianapolis, IN (home); Crown Hill Cemetery, Indianapolis, IN

As a Union officer in the Civil War, Harrison fought in more battles in one month than his famous grandfather had in a lifetime. They are the only grandfather-grandson pair of presidents.

AMERICA TAKES CENTER STAGE

1897–1945

Presidents took firm control of the federal government at the start of the 20th century. They helped develop the United States into a global power, both economically and politically. The era featured fantastic advances in science, technology, transportation, and exploration. Leaders were challenged to expand the rights of citizens and curb the power of businesses. They struggled to cope with worldwide war and widespread economic suffering, too. Public opinion of federal policies played a central role in national elections.

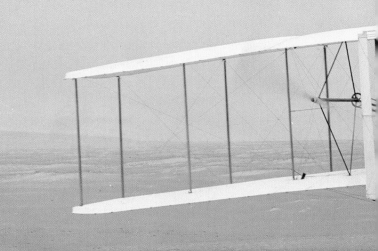

CIRCA 1890s
By the late 19th century, laborsaving inventions such as the mechanical washing machine were changing the way families handled routine household chores.

1912
The "unsinkable" *Titanic* went down on its first voyage after it struck an iceberg in the North Atlantic Ocean on April 14. More than 1,500 people died.

1913–1920
Women intensified their efforts to gain suffrage, or voting rights. In 1920 the 19th Amendment to the Constitution finally granted all female U.S. citizens the right to vote.

1914–1919
World War I raged for nearly three years before U.S. forces arrived in 1917. Their presence helped win the war even as soldiers and civilians faced a related global flu pandemic that killed 40 million.

Wilbur (below, right) and Orville Wright made the first successful airplane flight—12 seconds long—on December 17, 1903, near Kitty Hawk, North Carolina (colorized image).

1924
The Immigration Act of 1924 used quotas to limit entry based on country of origin. Eastern and southern European countries were targeted in particular. The act banned Japanese from seeking citizenship.

1930s
A decade of economic suffering followed the stock market collapse of October 1929. Citizens who had lost their jobs and even their homes sought free food in breadlines.

1933
German physicist Albert Einstein settled in the U.S. to avoid Nazi persecution of Jews. His scientific breakthroughs led to the development a decade later of the atomic bomb.

1941
The U.S. was compelled to enter World War II after Japan attacked a U.S. naval base on December 7 (above, ships burn at Pearl Harbor, Hawaii).

WILLIAM McKINLEY
25TH PRESIDENT OF THE UNITED STATES 1897–1901

William McKinley was the last Chief Executive who fought in the Civil War. However, McKinley's witness of an earlier era did not stop him from pushing the nation and his office into modern times. He did everything from using telephones on a regular basis to expanding the political influence of the United States around the globe. Early in his second term, McKinley became the fifth president to die in office, and the third one to be assassinated.

The state of Ohio sent five of her sons, including McKinley, to the White House in 28 years. (Two more followed him over the next 24 years.) As a youth, McKinley played army games with friends or went fishing, ice-skating, and horseback riding. He attended public schools where he excelled at speechmaking, and he studied briefly at Allegheny College in Pennsylvania. He served in the Civil War under future president Rutherford B. Hayes. Despite four years of duty, he escaped all injury and illness. Twice he won promotions for acts of bravery. After the war McKinley took up the study of law and became an attorney. His final wartime rank of major remained his nickname among close friends for years.

"The Major" spent a dozen years in the U.S. House of Representatives and gained national notice for his McKinley Tariff legislation. Once implemented, however, this tax on imported goods brought unexpectedly high prices to consumer goods at home. Many Republicans, including McKinley and President Benjamin Harrison, lost their elected posts as a result. Nonetheless, McKinley persuaded Ohioans to elect him as their governor two years later. He served two terms before being nominated for president in 1896. McKinley defeated his opponent, William Jennings Bryan, in part because he spent five times as much money during the campaign as his rival. Bryan, a noted

When William McKinley was Ohio's governor, each day at 3 p.m. he waved to his wife from his office window, and Ida McKinley (above) waved back from their home across the street.

NICKNAMES
Idol of Ohio, The Major

BORN
Jan. 29, 1843, in Niles, OH

POLITICAL PARTY
Republican

CHIEF OPPONENT
1st and 2nd terms: William Jennings Bryan, Democrat (1860–1925)

TERM OF OFFICE
March 4, 1897–Sept. 14, 1901

AGE AT INAUGURATION
54 years old

NUMBER OF TERMS
two (cut short by assassination)

VICE PRESIDENTS
1st term: Garret Augustus Hobart (1844–1899); 2nd term: Theodore Roosevelt (1858–1919)

FIRST LADY
Ida Saxton McKinley (1847–1907), wife (married Jan. 25, 1871)

CHILDREN
two daughters who died young

GEOGRAPHIC SCENE
45 states

NEW STATES ADDED
none

DIED
Sept. 14, 1901, in Buffalo, NY

AGE AT DEATH
58 years old

SELECTED LANDMARKS
National McKinley Birthplace Memorial, Niles, OH; McKinley Museum and McKinley National Memorial (grave), Canton, OH

McKinley (right, reelection banner) was the only president between Andrew Johnson and Woodrow Wilson not to have facial hair. He liked to wear a red carnation in the buttonhole of his jacket. Ohio went so far as to make this bloom its official flower in honor of the "Idol of Ohio." McKinley liked cigars, too. Sometimes he broke one in two and chewed the halves instead of smoking the whole cigar.

FOR PRESIDENT
WILLIAM McKINLEY

WE STAND FOR
The Gold Standard,
Protection and Prosperity,
Just Pension Laws,
And To Redeem All
REPUBLICAN PLEDGES
To The People.

FOR VICE PRESIDENT
THEODORE ROOSEVELT

President McKinley (seated, center), celebrated his second Inauguration in 1901 but did not live to complete his term.

orator, traveled 18,000 miles around the country during a three-month-long speaking tour. McKinley, as Benjamin Harrison had done in 1888, ran a "front porch" campaign from his home in Ohio and relied on others to campaign for him nationally.

As president, McKinley focused on U.S. relations with foreign countries. He started with Spain. This European nation still ruled Cuba and other Caribbean islands near the United States, as well as the Philippine Islands in the Pacific. Diplomatic talks gave way to war in 1898 after the suspicious destruction of the U.S. battleship *Maine* while it was anchored near Cuba. Future president Theodore Roosevelt rode to national fame as the head of the Rough Riders once the fighting began. Meanwhile, the U.S. Navy destroyed Spain's Atlantic and Pacific fleets during the four-month-long Spanish-American War.

Americans pledged to "Remember the *Maine!*" by going to war with Spain soon after the ship's destruction. McKinley helped lead the United States to victory in the Spanish-American War of 1898.

LOCATION OF THE MAINE-HAVANA HARBOR.

RECOVERING THE DEAD BODIES.

McKinley proposed linking the Atlantic and Pacific Oceans by building a canal through Central America. He made full use of new technologies while in office. The president communicated with the war front by telegraph, kept in touch with newspaper editors by telephone, and established the first White House press room. He even had telegraph lines installed there so reporters could easily dispatch stories to their newspaper offices. He controlled the slant reporters gave to news by putting his own twist on details released to them. Sometimes he completely censored, or kept secret, certain facts.

Combat ended when Spain withdrew its claim to Cuba. Spain put Puerto Rico, Guam, and the Philippine Islands under U.S. control in exchange for a $20 million settlement. Guam and the Philippines gave the United States a Pacific base from which to influence Asian affairs, particularly in China. McKinley further increased the U.S. presence in the Pacific by annexing, or taking over, the Hawaiian Islands. In addition, he initiated plans to build what would become the Panama Canal, linking the Atlantic and Pacific Oceans through Central America.

McKinley's first vice president died in office. Theodore Roosevelt was nominated to fill the job during the election of 1900. Roosevelt talked himself hoarse while campaigning for "Four More Years of the Full Dinner Pail." Buoyed by a strong economy and satisfaction with the war's outcome, McKinley triumphed over Bryan again. This time he won by an even greater margin.

In the fall of 1901, barely six months into his second administration, McKinley attended the Pan-American Exposition in Buffalo, New York. During the events a lone assassin joined a crowd of spectators waiting to shake the president's hand. When McKinley reached out to greet him, the man fired two shots at the president from a hidden gun. McKinley died eight days later after developing gangrene from his wounds. The assailant, an unemployed laborer, said he was an anarchist, someone who believes all forms of government are tyrannical. He was convicted of murder and executed.

"War should never be entered upon until every agency of peace has failed."

William McKinley,
Inaugural Address, March 4, 1897

McKinley often charmed strangers by presenting them with the carnation he wore on his jacket. Once, when two brothers were introduced to him, he carefully replaced the flower in his buttonhole with a fresh one so each boy could receive a bloom from the president. McKinley had just presented his lapel flower to a young girl when he was shot (above, right). The president died eight days later.

THEODORE ROOSEVELT
26TH PRESIDENT OF THE UNITED STATES 1901–1909

Theodore Roosevelt took charge of the White House after the assassination of William McKinley. He filled it with his own personality and vision. He was the first "accidental" president to later win outright election to the office. During his tenure he expanded the reach of the U.S. government into such areas as industry, labor, the environment, consumer rights, and foreign affairs.

Few presidents, if any, could compete with the unique background that Roosevelt brought to the White House. He was the son of a wealthy New York family. Sickly and asthmatic as a youth, he was schooled at home. Finally, "Teedie's" father encouraged him to improve his health through vigorous physical exercise. By the time he attended Harvard University, he was physically fit enough to compete in the campus boxing program. Roosevelt graduated with honors, married, and became a member of New York's state assembly.

Theodore Roosevelt wrote more than 30 books.

Then tragedy struck. Roosevelt's mother and wife both died from illnesses on Valentine's Day in 1884. Roosevelt took his grief to the western United States and worked as a cowboy and a rancher. Locals came to respect the eyeglasses-wearing "Four Eyes" as the East Coast "dude" whose strongest curse was "By Godfrey!" Roosevelt did not hesitate to punch out an offensive cowboy, fire a dishonest ranch hand, or capture thieves.

In the fall of 1886 Roosevelt returned to East Coast life. He remarried, took up

Not since Thomas Jefferson had a president enjoyed as many talents and diverse interests as Roosevelt. He loved being active outdoors. Roosevelt would swim through shark-infested waters to explore a shipwreck or lead cross-country hikes on an unwavering straight course, taking each obstacle as a fresh challenge. After being wounded by a would-be assassin during his 1912 presidential campaign, Roosevelt insisted on speaking for nearly an hour, dripping blood, before seeking medical care. The folded copy of his speech and his metal eyeglass case had slowed the path of the bullet and prevented the wound from being too severe.

Theodore Roosevelt

NICKNAME
T. R.

BORN
Oct. 27, 1858, in New York, NY

POLITICAL PARTY
Republican

CHIEF OPPONENT
1st term: none, succeeded William McKinley; 2nd term: Alton Brooks Parker, Democrat (1852–1926)

TERM OF OFFICE
Sept. 14, 1901–March 3, 1909

AGE AT INAUGURATION
42 years old

NUMBER OF TERMS
one, plus balance of William McKinley's term

VICE PRESIDENT
1st term: none; 2nd term: Charles Warren Fairbanks (1852–1918)

FIRST LADY
Edith Kermit Carow Roosevelt (1861–1948), second wife (married Dec. 2, 1886)

OTHER MARRIAGE
Alice Hathaway Lee Roosevelt (1861–1884), married Oct. 27, 1880

CHILDREN
Born to Alice Roosevelt (first wife): Alice; born to Edith Roosevelt (second wife): Theodore, Kermit, Ethel, Archibald, Quentin

GEOGRAPHIC SCENE
45 states

NEW STATES ADDED
Oklahoma (1907)

DIED
Jan. 6, 1919, in Oyster Bay, NY

AGE AT DEATH
60 years old

SELECTED LANDMARKS
New York, NY (birthplace); Sagamore Hill National Historic Site (homestead) and Young's Memorial Cemetery, Oyster Bay, NY; Theodore Roosevelt Island, Washington, DC; Mount Rushmore National Memorial, Keystone, SD

writing, and reentered public service. He worked on the U.S. Civil Service Commission for Benjamin Harrison, headed the New York City Police Board, and served as William McKinley's assistant secretary of the Navy. When the Spanish-American War broke out, Roosevelt recruited a volunteer company of cowboys, college football players, New York City police officers, and Native Americans. Roosevelt's "Rough Riders" became famous for their charge near San Juan Hill, in Cuba. Roosevelt was elected governor of New York after the

> "Speak softly and carry a big stick; you will go far."
>
> Theodore Roosevelt's version of an African saying

war. In 1901 Roosevelt became vice president and then president. He won outright election to the post in 1904.

Roosevelt's political background as an administrator prepared him to take aggressive charge of the office. He expanded the role of the national government in protecting the lives of its citizens. He went head-to-head with large corporations that had formed monopolies—called trusts—in railroad, beef, oil, tobacco, and other industries. Trusts had become so powerful from lack of competition that citizens and workers were suffering from high prices, low wages, and poor working conditions. Roosevelt became known as a trustbuster for breaking up these monopolies.

In other domestic affairs Roosevelt forced coal mine owners to settle labor disputes with 150,000 striking miners by threatening to have the government take control of the mines. He set aside vast areas of the country for conservation and resource development. He increased safety standards for the preparation of meat, other food products, and medicine.

In foreign policy Roosevelt outlined what became known as big stick diplomacy. He declared that the United States would serve as "an

Roosevelt gained fame during the Spanish-American War as the commander of his fearless troop of Rough Riders.

Roosevelt's second wife, Edith (seated with their family), served as her husband's secretary during his administration. Her research aided his Nobel Peace Prize–winning treaty negotiations.

Roosevelt continued the work begun by his predecessor for the construction of a waterway connecting the Atlantic and Pacific Oceans across Central America. Roosevelt (in white suit) visited the Panama Canal construction site in 1906.

Roosevelt hoped his continuing popularity (below, in 1911, two years after leaving office), would lead to his reelection in 1912. It did not.

During his retirement, Roosevelt (above, right) spent seven months exploring the River of Doubt in the jungles of Brazil. He suffered periodically from malaria and other ailments during the trip and for the rest of his life.

international police power" throughout the Western Hemisphere of the globe if it felt threatened by other nations. He proved an effective mediator in disputes among other nations, too. He won the Nobel Peace Prize in 1905 for his role in negotiating an end to the war between Russia and Japan.

Roosevelt, the youngest man ever to become president, was very much a family man when he entered the White House. His eldest daughter, Alice, was married there. His younger children grew up in its corridors and on its grounds. Once a son and his friends disrupted work at a nearby government building by using mirrors to bounce sunlight through the windows. When informed about the problem, Roosevelt, always playful, arranged for someone at the office building to send the boys a message with signal flags: "Attack on this building must immediately cease ..." A friend observed: "You must always remember that the President is about six."

Roosevelt left the White House in 1909. On an extended safari in Africa he collected hundreds of animals for the Smithsonian Institution. He made an unsuccessful attempt to regain the White House in 1912 by running as a third-party candidate for the Progressive, or Bull Moose, Party. Roosevelt's offer to raise a fighting force during World War I was refused, but all four of his sons joined the service. The combat death in 1918 of his youngest son, Quentin, left Roosevelt shaken. With his health deteriorating, he died the following year.

Roosevelt (center, with envoys of Japan and Russia) is known for being first at many things, both great and trivial. He was the first president to travel by car and submarine while in office. During his retirement years, he became the first president to ride in an airplane. He was the first president to have his initials become his nickname. He made the first overseas trip by a sitting president (to Panama). He was the first president and first American to be awarded a Nobel Peace Prize. The teddy bear was named after Roosevelt by a toymaker who heard how he had spared the life of a bear cub during a hunting trip.

KIDS IN THE WHITE HOUSE
AT HOME IN THE SPOTLIGHT

The first residents of the White House—John and Abigail Adams—were also the first occupants to bring children to the president's home. Their four-year-old granddaughter, Susanna, traveled with her grandmother to stay at the residence in 1800. A parade of children has continued to live there off and on ever since.

In 1806 Thomas Jefferson's grandson James became the first presidential relative born in the Executive Mansion. His was not the first birth there, though. Five years earlier an enslaved teenager had given birth at the residence to a daughter who was likewise considered to be in bondage. In 1893 Grover Cleveland's daughter Esther became the only child of a president to be born at the White House.

In 1861 the Lincolns were the first family to have their young children live in the White House. Among other antics, Tad Lincoln set up a White House refreshment stand, shot his toy cannon at the president's office door, and rode through an East Room tea party on a chair pulled by his pet goats.

Theodore and Edith Roosevelt brought their six children to the White House in 1901. These youngsters roller-skated in the East Room, "sledded" down White House staircases on serving trays, and surrounded themselves with pets—including snakes, a badger, raccoons, pigs, parrots, baby bears, and a young lion. Their father noted: "I don't think that any family has ever enjoyed the White House more than we have."

Theodore Roosevelt's youngest sons, Archie (second from right) and Quentin, liked to join the daily roll call for the White House police. Willie and Tad Lincoln (above, left, seated between their parents) were an earlier pair of brothers who roamed freely in the president's home. They knew just how to cause chaos there by ringing various bells to call White House workers.

James A. Garfield's sons had pillow fights aboard velocipedes in the East Room of the White House.

Quentin Roosevelt rode his pony, Algonquin, while growing up at the Executive Mansion. Once he brought his pet on the White House elevator so the pair could visit his brother Archie, who was laid up with measles.

Malia Obama reads *Where the Wild Things Are* with her sister, Sasha, watching, as part of the White House Easter Egg Roll activities in 2011.

The children of most presidents are already grown up or are away in college by the time their parents move into the White House. Some of these young adults have been active campaigners for their fathers. In recent decades, five presidents—John F. Kennedy, Jimmy Carter, Bill Clinton, Barack Obama, and Donald Trump—have brought younger children with them to the White House. As parents they sheltered their children from public attention while encouraging them to "just be kids" at home. Caroline Kennedy rode the grounds on her pony, Macaroni, and Amy Carter played in her own tree house, for example. Since the days of Woodrow Wilson, Secret Service agents have acted as bodyguards for children of the presidents—even out on dates! If the public spotlight ever gets too bright, presidential children can always find refuge back home in the White House.

John F. Kennedy's kids liked to visit their father in the Oval Office and hide beneath the Resolute desk (here, John Jr.).

In 1971 Tricia Nixon became the eighth and most recent presidential daughter to marry at the White House. Maria Monroe was the first in 1820.

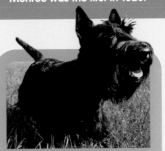

When the first family includes pets, those animals can become famous, too. Barney (above) had his own website during the presidency of George W. Bush.

Lyndon Johnson distracts grandson Patrick Lyndon (Lyn) Nugent with a lollipop while the White House barber trims his hair.

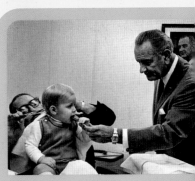

WILLIAM HOWARD TAFT
27TH PRESIDENT OF THE UNITED STATES **1909–1913**

William Howard Taft sought the presidency with the encouragement of President Theodore Roosevelt. Four years later, when the men became rivals for the post, neither of them won. Taft's career of public service concluded with his subsequent appointment as the nation's Chief Justice. No one else has been a U.S. president and served on the Supreme Court.

Taft's father had worked in the Grant and Arthur Administrations, and Taft himself would serve Presidents McKinley and Roosevelt. But his greatest love was the law. He progressed from undergraduate studies at Yale to law school at the University of Cincinnati, and by age 30 he had become a local judge. Although Taft hoped to serve someday on the Supreme Court, he repeatedly deferred that dream to fulfill other duties. He became territorial governor of the Philippine Islands at McKinley's request and directed construction of the Panama Canal for Roosevelt before easily winning the presidency in 1909.

The progressive Taft broke twice as many trusts in half the time as Roosevelt, including major monopolies in tobacco and petroleum. The Department of Labor began during his administration, and

Helen and William Howard Taft were the first presidential couple to ride in an Inaugural Parade.

Congress passed two successful amendments to the Constitution. One created the federal income tax; the other established election of U.S. senators by citizens. (Previously, state legislatures had selected them.)

Voter disapproval of other policies cost Taft his reelection bid. His poor showing set a record with only 23 percent of the popular vote and eight electoral votes. A decade later, Warren G. Harding fulfilled Taft's Supreme Court ambitions by nominating him to the bench. Taft served nine years as its Chief Justice. During this time he persuaded Congress to fund the construction of a separate building for the Court (previously it had met in the U.S. Capitol Building). Taft and his wife were the first presidential couple to be buried in Arlington National Cemetery.

NICKNAME
Big Bill

BORN
Sept. 15, 1857, in Cincinnati, OH

POLITICAL PARTY
Republican

CHIEF OPPONENT
William Jennings Bryan, Democrat (1860–1925)

TERM OF OFFICE
March 4, 1909–March 3, 1913

AGE AT INAUGURATION
51 years old

NUMBER OF TERMS
one

VICE PRESIDENT
James Schoolcraft Sherman (1855–1912)

FIRST LADY
Helen Herron Taft (1861–1943), wife (married June 19, 1886)

CHILDREN
Robert, Helen, Charles

GEOGRAPHIC SCENE
46 states

NEW STATES ADDED
New Mexico, Arizona (1912)

DIED
March 8, 1930, in Washington, DC

AGE AT DEATH
72 years old

SELECTED LANDMARKS
Cincinnati, OH (birthplace); Arlington National Cemetery, Arlington, VA

Taft, whose weight at times exceeded 330 pounds, was heavier than any other president. The story goes that he'd become stuck in the White House bathtub, and so a larger one was installed (left, workers fill the new tub). A careful review of the historical record reduces this story to an unfounded rumor, probably spread by political opponents.

PRESIDENTS AND THE SUPREME COURT
A LEGACY THAT LASTS

The cry "Oyez! Oyez! Oyez!" opens each session of the U.S. Supreme Court. The president, with the approval of Congress, determines who will sit on the bench that holds the highest authority in the judicial branch of the U.S. government. As of 2020, after 230 years of operation, only 115 individuals had ever served on it.

When a vacancy occurs on the Supreme Court, either because of death or retirement, the president nominates someone to fill the space. Nominees typically have had extensive and distinguished experience as attorneys, judges, or in political office. The Senate Judiciary Committee decides whether or not to recommend approval of a nominee by the full Senate. Most nominees win Senate confirmation, but over the years about two dozen have not. Still others fail to receive Senate consideration at all. Such was the case in 2016 when the Republican majority leader, Mitch McConnell, refused to consider an election-year nomination by the outgoing Democratic president, Barack Obama.

With the exception of Jimmy Carter and three 19th-century presidents, all other Chief Executives have appointed someone to the Supreme Court. George Washington holds the record for appointing the most justices, 10. Franklin D. Roosevelt appointed almost as many— nine—during his lengthy presidency.

Because justices serve for life and are protected from firing and salary cuts, they are expected to weigh cases free from political pressures or other influences. Even so, they often reflect the beliefs and political backgrounds of the leaders who appoint them, giving presidents a lasting legacy of influence long after they've retired from office.

The Supreme Court Building in Washington, D.C.

The size and composition of the Supreme Court (below, in 1892) has evolved since it formed in 1790 with six members. Membership ranged as high as 10 until Congress settled on its current size of nine members in 1869. The Court met for 177 years before anyone other than white men joined its bench.

The Supreme Court opens its yearly term on the first Monday of October and continues to meet until early summer. It is asked to review 7,000 to 8,000 cases each year; only about 80 are actually presented in front of the Court. Traditionally when the justices meet at the Supreme Court to undertake official business, they shake hands as a reminder of their need to remain civil even when they disagree about the law.

The Supreme Court met inside the U.S. Capitol Building for most of the first 145 years of its history. After former

William Howard Taft is the only former president to join the Supreme Court (left, during his 1921 swearing in ceremony). He served alongside two justices whom he himself had appointed to the bench.

John Roberts (above, left, with President George W. Bush) became the court's newest Chief Justice in 2005. Of the 17 people who have served as Chief Justice, John Marshall held the post the longest: 34 years (1801–1835).

president William Howard Taft became the Chief Justice in 1921, he persuaded Congress to construct a new home for the Court. Taft died before he could see the opening of the Supreme Court Building in 1935.

Each member of the court tends to bring a particular viewpoint, whether liberal or conservative, to their consideration of judicial decisions. Sometimes the judicial philosophies of members evolve over time, making their rulings less predictable. These justices can provide influential swing votes for cases that are settled by a tally of 5 to 4.

Some Supreme Court decisions merely clarify how to enforce the rule of law. Others are more monumental, such as the 1954 *Brown* v. *Board of Education* ruling that ordered the end to school segregation; they are called landmark decisions.

On two occasions, the Court has helped determine the outcome of presidential elections. After the contested election of 1876, a commission made up of five Supreme Court justices and 10 members of Congress voted 8 to 7 to hand victory to Republican candidate Rutherford B. Hayes. More recently, in 2000, the Supreme Court ruled 5 to 4 in the *Bush* v. *Gore* decision that elevated Republican George W. Bush to the presidency. In each case, justices voted in ways that supported the candidates from the political parties of the presidents who had appointed them. This alignment of party affiliation made the decisions contentious, especially for Democrats since their candidates lost in both decisions.

The Supreme Court holds the final say in government disputes. Its decisions can only be overcome in three ways: the passage of revised legislation that respects the Court's opinions, a constitutional amendment, or future rulings by the Court.

The Supreme Court reflects the influence of the presidents who nominate its members (left, shown in 2018 with members appointed during a span of three decades and five presidencies). In more recent years it has also begun to represent the diversity of the nation. The Court gained its first member of color in 1967, Thurgood Marshall, and its first female justice in 1981, Sandra Day O'Connor. Since then presidents have appointed four more women and one additional African American.

WOODROW WILSON
28TH PRESIDENT OF THE UNITED STATES 1913–1921

As president, Woodrow Wilson ushered important legislation through Congress. However, World War I became the greatest challenge of his two terms in office. When he failed to keep the United States out of the conflict, he used the nation's resources to help win it. He sought to secure lasting peace afterward with a new international governing body called the League of Nations.

Wilson grew up in the shadow of an earlier war—the Civil War. He was born in Virginia and raised in Georgia and the Carolinas. His first childhood memory was of hearing in 1860 that a war would soon begin. He watched Confederate troops march off to battle; saw soldiers die from their wounds; and, after the war, glimpsed Confederate general Robert E. Lee march through town under Union guard. His Southern heritage contributed to his support for racial segregation.

Wilson struggled with dyslexia, a

Woodrow Wilson won reelection by opposing America's entry into World War I.

learning disorder that delayed his mastery of basic skills in reading, writing, and math. He went on to graduate from the College of New Jersey (later Princeton University). Wilson practiced law, earned a graduate degree from Johns Hopkins University, and became a college professor. (Hence, his nickname.) By 1902 he was president of Princeton. Wilson stepped from that post to the White House after

NICKNAME
Professor

BORN
Dec. 29, 1856, in Staunton, VA

POLITICAL PARTY
Democratic

CHIEF OPPONENTS
1st term: Theodore Roosevelt, Progressive (1858–1919), and President William Howard Taft, Republican (1857–1930); 2nd term: Charles Evans Hughes, Republican (1862–1948)

TERM OF OFFICE
March 4, 1913–March 3, 1921

AGE AT INAUGURATION
56 years old

NUMBER OF TERMS
two

VICE PRESIDENT
Thomas Riley Marshall (1854–1925)

FIRST LADIES
Ellen Louise Axson Wilson (1860–1914), first wife (married June 24, 1885); Margaret Woodrow Wilson (1886–1944), daughter; Edith Bolling Galt Wilson (1872–1961), second wife (married Dec. 18, 1915)

CHILDREN
Born to Ellen Wilson (first wife): Margaret, Jesse, Eleanor

GEOGRAPHIC SCENE
48 states

NEW STATES ADDED
none

DIED
Feb. 3, 1924, in Washington, DC

AGE AT DEATH
67 years old

SELECTED LANDMARKS
Staunton, VA (birthplace, library, and museum); Columbia, SC (boyhood home); The President Woodrow Wilson House (museum) and Washington National Cathedral (grave), Washington, DC

By early 1917 intensified fighting in Europe had forced Wilson to change his first-term antiwar stance and enter the United States into World War I. Within 18 months some two million U.S. soldiers had joined the front lines and helped turn the tide of the Great War.

The son of a Presbyterian minister, Wilson thought it was God's will that he become president. He worked to end World War I as if he'd received a charge from heaven. His "Fourteen Points" for lasting peace (above, left), outlined in January 1918, formed the basis for the war's settlement, but Wilson wore himself out fighting for treaty ratification.

Wilson is credited with playing more golf than any other president, some 1,200 rounds.

brief service as governor of New Jersey. He was the top vote getter in the crowded presidential race of 1912 that included President William Howard Taft and former president Theodore Roosevelt.

Wilson was the first president to hold regular press conferences and to speak on the radio. He packed his first term with significant legislation that reduced import taxes, instituted wealth-based income taxes, created a Federal Trade Commission to monitor business practices, established a Federal Reserve system to manage the nation's money supply, supported the right of workers to strike, discouraged child labor, and promoted the eight-hour workday. Yet he also instituted racially biased policies, such as segregating the civil service. Wilson won reelection in part because, as his campaign slogan put it, "He Kept Us Out of War." The Great War had begun in Europe in August 1914. The United States was drawn into the fight soon after Wilson's 1916 reelection. The war ended with a truce on November 11, 1918, a date celebrated in the U.S. as Armistice Day (and later renamed Veterans Day). All told, nearly 10 million soldiers died worldwide in the four-year conflict, including 100,000 Americans. During and after the war, his administration stifled dissent and stoked fears about immigration.

Wilson became the first U.S. president to visit Europe while in office when he traveled to Paris to help establish terms for peace. The final treaty supported Wilson's idea of creating a League of Nations that would settle future disputes using words and economic influence, not weapons. Wilson could not persuade Congress to accept his plan, though, and the League formed without support from the United States. Nonetheless, in 1919 Wilson earned the Nobel Peace Prize for his efforts. The United Nations took the place of the League after World War II.

Wilson had lived through the assassinations of three presidents by the time he took office in 1913.

American cities across the country hosted victory parades (above) to honor soldiers returning home from World War I.

Woodrow and Edith Wilson set a positive example for nationwide rationing during the war by going without gas on Sundays, meat on Mondays, and wheat on Tuesdays. They even let sheep roam on the White House lawns so they could "mow" the grass naturally, saving gas and labor. Nationwide sacrifices helped make scarce resources available to U.S. soldiers overseas.

Wilson's first wife, Ellen, was a talented artist. As first lady she worked to improve housing for residents in the nation's capital. Two of the Wilsons' three daughters were wed in White House ceremonies during his first term of office. Wilson was devastated when Ellen became ill and died in 1914. He even told friends he would welcome being assassinated. The following spring Wilson was introduced to a widow. He liked her so much at first sight that he invited her to stay for tea at the White House. He married his new friend, Edith, before the end of the year.

Wilson, who had suffered for years from minor strokes, had a major stroke in October 1919, which ended his campaign to win congressional support for the League of Nations. Edith took charge of her husband's recovery. She kept details of her husband's health a secret, overruled the idea that he should resign, and controlled what official business could be brought to his attention. Although her boldness drew criticism then—and still does among historians—it helped Wilson complete his presidency.

Wilson's retirement was relatively brief, and his health remained poor. He died in 1924, six months after the death of his successor, Warren G. Harding. Both Woodrow and Edith Wilson are buried at the Washington National Cathedral. He is the only president buried in the nation's capital.

"The world must be made safe for democracy."

Woodrow Wilson, request that Congress declare war on Germany, April 2, 1917

PRESIDENTS AT WAR
SERVING AS THE COMMANDER IN CHIEF

The role of commander in chief for the nation's armed forces takes on added weight for presidents during wartime. Two of the country's earliest presidents took this duty literally. During the Whiskey Rebellion of 1794, George Washington rode at the head of more than 10,000 soldiers to silence protests over a new federal tax on liquor. Likewise, when the British threatened the nation's capital near the end of the War of 1812, James Madison actually took command of scattered troops in an attempted defense.

Since then many wartime presidents have visited troops near combat zones, even at the risk of being in harm's way. Most participate in debates about military strategy, too. All presidents receive regular national security briefings to keep them informed about the country's defense, and they help to direct the nature of the peacetime that follows.

Ironically two of the nation's most prominent wartime leaders—Woodrow Wilson and Franklin D. Roosevelt—had had no personal experience with combat because they grew up during peacetime. Including them, more than a dozen U.S. presidents never served in the military. Others include John Adams and John Quincy Adams (who were foreign diplomats instead of soldiers during the Revolutionary War), Grover Cleveland (who paid someone else to take his place during the Civil War, a legal option at the time), and Bill Clinton (who pursued his education, not military service, during the Vietnam War). Even Abraham Lincoln, one of the most important commanders in

President Washington led federal troops during the Whiskey Rebellion of 1794.

Woodrow Wilson (above, at far right) worked with leaders from France, Great Britain, and Italy to draft the peace treaty that ended World War I.

Abraham Lincoln began the practice of visiting battlefield troops in the 1860s during the Civil War.

President Truman's decision to have the *Enola Gay* (shown here) drop an atomic bomb on Japan during World War II continues to be much debated.

chief, had seen no combat while serving in a frontier territorial conflict against Native American tribes.

Nonetheless, wartime service is often seen as a measure of fitness for presidential candidates. Those with little or no experience may be criticized, particularly if it appears that service was deliberately avoided. Those with more experience are often more favorably received. A number of presidents have gained election, in part at least, because of famous military performances. They include George Washington, Andrew Jackson, Ulysses S. Grant, Theodore Roosevelt, and Dwight D. Eisenhower. Even during periods of relative international calm, the presence of someone with wartime experience can be reassuring to the public.

Presidential popularity tends to rise during times of national crisis. Approval ratings soared for Franklin D. Roosevelt after the bombing of Pearl Harbor, for Jimmy Carter during the early months of the Iran hostage crisis, and for George W. Bush following the 2001 terrorist attacks on U.S. soil. Such popularity inevitably falls if conflicts remain unresolved or if presidential leadership becomes questioned.

If presidential elections occur during times of war, voters often choose to "stay the course" instead of changing leaders. Such was the case for Franklin D. Roosevelt; he was reelected twice during World War II. George W. Bush also returned to the White House in 2004 with the help of wartime support. On the other hand, if a wartime leader is perceived to be failing as commander in chief, that issue alone can end a presidency. For example, the unpopularity of the Vietnam War forced Lyndon B. Johnson to cancel his 1968 reelection bid.

Wartime presidents often choose to reduce constitutional freedoms in the name of national defense. At the outset of the Civil War, for example, Abraham Lincoln jailed potential traitors and restricted freedom of speech. During World War II, Franklin D. Roosevelt authorized the detention in restricted camps of 120,000 Japanese Americans, most of whom were U.S. citizens. Concerns over terrorist threats prompted George W. Bush to permit greater surveillance of U.S. residents. Not all presidents have chosen this tack, however. James Madison insisted during the War of 1812 that civil liberties like free speech remain unchecked in order to demonstrate the nation's commitment to liberty.

Eleanor Roosevelt often visited World War II troops on behalf of her husband, Franklin.

Vietnam antiwar protests affected the popularity of two U.S. presidents, Lyndon B. Johnson and Richard Nixon.

Barack Obama salutes as the remains of a U.S. soldier killed in Afghanistan are returned home in 2009.

WARREN G. HARDING
29TH PRESIDENT OF THE UNITED STATES 1921–1923

When he was a young man, Warren Gamaliel Harding's friends thought he "looked like a president." Harding's presidential profile helped carry him to the White House, but it did not prepare him for the challenges of the job. Harding became the sixth president to die in office when his health failed him at midterm. His death came just as major scandals about his administration were coming to light.

Harding was born in Ohio. After graduating from Ohio Central College in Iberia, he became a newspaper publisher in the nearby town of Marion. He went on to serve in the state legislature, as lieutenant governor of Ohio, and as a U.S. senator during his climb to prominence in the Republican Party. His habit of changing his mind earned him the nickname Wobbly Warren. Harding's nomination to the party ticket of 1920 followed much behind-the-scenes, late-night dealmaking by party leaders, many of whom were heavy smokers. This strategy became known as the "smoke-filled room" approach to politics.

Harding was elected president with the greatest landslide in a century. He earned 60 percent of the popular vote in the first election in which women were able to vote nationwide. The complex responsibilities of being president began to trouble Harding midway into his term. So did hints of illegal behavior within his administration. In early 1923 an important Harding appointee fled the country because of criminal activity on the job. One of the man's co-workers committed suicide soon afterward. Then the private

Warren G. Harding embraced new technology (above, with an early recording device). He was the first Chief Executive to travel by car to his Inauguration.

secretary of Harding's scandal-plagued attorney general killed himself over a different scheme. Speculation over these events was interrupted when Harding, his health already weakened, began a cross-country trip to visit the U.S. territory of Alaska. He died suddenly during the trip while staying in San Francisco.

Warren G. Harding's presidency is consistently ranked among the worst in U.S. history because of its widespread corruption. Most notably, apparently without Harding's knowledge, his secretary of the interior had been bribed to grant oil-drilling rights on Wyoming's Teapot Dome and other federal lands, a wrongdoing dubbed the Teapot Dome affair. Recent genetic testing validates another rumored scandal: Harding fathered a child born to Nan Britton out of wedlock in 1919.

NICKNAME
Wobbly Warren

BORN
Nov. 2, 1865, in Caledonia (now Blooming Grove), OH

POLITICAL PARTY
Republican

CHIEF OPPONENT
James Middleton Cox, Democrat (1870–1957)

TERM OF OFFICE
March 4, 1921–Aug. 2, 1923

AGE AT INAUGURATION
55 years old

NUMBER OF TERMS
one (cut short by death)

VICE PRESIDENT
Calvin Coolidge (1872–1933)

FIRST LADY
Florence Kling De Wolfe Harding (1860–1924), wife (married July 8, 1891)

CHILDREN
Born to Florence Harding (wife): none; born to Nan Britton (1896–1991, mistress): Elizabeth Ann

GEOGRAPHIC SCENE
48 states

NEW STATES ADDED
none

DIED
Aug. 2, 1923, in San Francisco, CA

AGE AT DEATH
57 years old

SELECTED LANDMARKS
Harding Home and Museum and Harding Memorial (grave), Marion, OH

CALVIN COOLIDGE
30TH PRESIDENT OF THE UNITED STATES **1923–1929**

Calvin Coolidge's high standard of conduct restored trust in the presidency following the sudden death of his predecessor, Warren G. Harding. Coolidge was a calm, frugal presence in the White House during the extravagance and waste of the Roaring Twenties.

The plain style of Coolidge's presidency had its roots in his simple New England childhood. His favorite chore, as a redheaded youth in rural Vermont, was making maple syrup. He went on to graduate from Amherst College, become a lawyer, and hold more than a dozen elected posts—including governor of Massachusetts—before rising from vice president to president in 1923.

Coolidge cooperated with investigations into the Harding scandals. He removed corrupt staff members, and he chose reliable replacements for their posts. He followed a simple strategy: "When things are going along all right, it is a good plan to let them alone." This notion inspired the slogan "Keep Cool With Coolidge" during his successful election campaign in 1924.

Grace and Calvin Coolidge kept many pets at the White House, even a raccoon.

Coolidge was nicknamed Red (for his red hair), Cal (short for Calvin), and Silent Cal (because he spoke little). His habit of expressing himself with few words was famous. Once a dinner guest told Coolidge she had bet she could get three words of conversation out of him. All he replied was: "You lose." He advised his successor, Herbert Hoover, on how to handle talkative visitors: "If you keep dead still, they will run down in three or four minutes."

Coolidge retired to Massachusetts in 1929. He wrote, served as a trustee for the National Geographic Society, and worked in the insurance industry before his death in 1933. Frugal with words to the end, Silent Cal left behind a will to his estate that was only 23 words long.

NICKNAME
Silent Cal

BORN
July 4, 1872, in Plymouth, VT

POLITICAL PARTY
Republican

CHIEF OPPONENTS
1st term: none, succeeded Warren G. Harding; 2nd term: John W. Davis, Democrat (1873–1955), and Robert M. La Follette, Progressive (1855–1925)

TERM OF OFFICE
Aug. 3, 1923–March 3, 1929

AGE AT INAUGURATION
51 years old

NUMBER OF TERMS
one, plus balance of Warren G. Harding's term

VICE PRESIDENT
1st term: none; 2nd term: Charles Gates Dawes (1865–1951)

FIRST LADY
Grace Anna Goodhue Coolidge (1879–1957), wife (married Oct. 4, 1905)

CHILDREN
John, Calvin

GEOGRAPHIC SCENE
48 states

NEW STATES ADDED
none

DIED
Jan. 5, 1933, in Northampton, MA

AGE AT DEATH
60 years old

SELECTED LANDMARKS
Plymouth, VT (birthplace, homestead); Northampton, MA (library, homestead); Plymouth Notch Cemetery, Plymouth, VT

Coolidge was the last president who met with everyone who visited the White House to see its chief resident. Several hundred people often called each day. He prided himself on his speed at working through a crowd. Once, he shook hands with 1,900 visitors in only 34 minutes.

YOU'VE GOT MAIL
SWAPPING LETTERS WITH THE PRESIDENT

Ever since John Adams moved into the White House, ordinary citizens have addressed letters to the president at the Executive Mansion and waited for a reply. Whereas early correspondents wrote with quill pens and trusted the delivery of their letters to horse power, presidential communication can now take place via email or be transported by jet plane. Regardless of format and delivery, individuals continue to write to the president—and anticipate a response.

The subjects of letters may change through the years, but the motivations that inspire them remain remarkably consistent. People may write to the president to express their opinions. They may complain, ask questions, or offer help. Some correspondents request favors. Others send words of praise, thanks, or advice.

In 1860 an 11-year-old girl wrote presidential candidate Abraham Lincoln and suggested that his chances of winning the election would improve if he grew a beard. Lincoln waited until after his election victory, but then he grew his signature whiskers. As a result, he became the nation's first bearded president.

Nearly a century later, long after presidential facial hair had gone out of fashion, Harry S. Truman reached the White House. A dip into his presidential mailbox illustrates the range of correspondence he received. For example, in 1948 a 13-year-old boy from Florida wrote with an offer to

At the age of 11, Grace Bedell of New York State wrote presidential candidate Abraham Lincoln (letter shown below) and suggested his chances of winning the 1860 election would improve if he grew a beard. Facial hair had become popular, and she observed that "you would look a great deal better for your face is so thin." The future president replied promptly but suggested that people might judge him negatively if he suddenly grew a beard. By the time he took office, though, Lincoln had shed his clean-shaven look (below, left, in 1860) for a bearded one (below, right, two years after taking office).

Sometimes presidents meet their correspondents. Diego Diaz shared a letter—and a fist bump—with Barack Obama during a wished-for visit in 2011.

adopt a puppy the president had unexpectedly received. "If you don't keep him I sure would take good care of him," wrote Rusty Gilliland.

In contrast, citizens grew frustrated with Truman when a 1950 coal strike created a lack of coal fuel for home heating. They blamed the president for talking instead of acting to end the work stoppage. One wrote: "We are out of coal. Send some of your hot air out here." This correspondent, like many others, enclosed a bag of coal cinders, or ashes, with the letter.

The volume of mail sent to the White House has grown with the size and complexity of the country. By the 21st century, what was once a simple job for the president and his secretary had become a task undertaken by dozens of staffers and hundreds of volunteers. These workers process tens of thousands of emails every day plus thousands of pages of paper correspondence. Incoming mail goes through security screenings, too, to make sure no one is trying to sneak dangerous items or chemicals into the White House.

Most letters never actually reach the president today. There are just too many of them for one person to review. Even so, workers count and analyze the communication so that a president will have a sense of the public's

Mail still reaches the White House with the help of postage stamps (above, arriving by the sackful in 1938), but electronic methods work, too.

opinions. Workers answer all mail that merits a reply. These answers may be identical when addressing similar concerns or may be customized to match the specific content of the sender's message. Individual letters may appear to have been signed personally by the president but are actually signed by a machine that mimics the president's penmanship.

Each president chooses how to be kept informed about the mail received. Barack Obama, for example, decided early in his presidency that he wanted to personally read 10 letters every workday that, taken together, reflected the range of concerns addressed to his attention. His commitment to read—and in many cases respond with a handwritten reply—soon became a tradition of his presidency. Whenever presidents respond personally to a correspondent, they do so using a specific color of paper; no one else in the White House can have the same stationery.

Anyone can email the president of the United States through the White House website: whitehouse.gov/contact. Or, just as citizens young and old have done for generations, anyone can put a postage stamp on an envelope and address it to: President of the United States, The White House, 1600 Pennsylvania Avenue NW, Washington, DC 20500.

When the stock market crashed in October 1929 only a few months after Herbert Clark Hoover had taken office, the president found himself responsible for a different nation from the one he had planned to lead. The Great Depression that followed proved unstoppable and cost him the opportunity for a second term.

Hoover was a successful businessman, scientist, and public servant before becoming president. Born in Iowa and orphaned at age nine, he majored in geology at Stanford University. Hoover then began traveling the globe for the mining industry. While living in London, he received his first public service assignment—evacuating 120,000 Americans from Europe at the start of World War I. Later he helped direct relief efforts for European victims of the war. He went on to serve as secretary of commerce for Warren G. Harding and Calvin Coolidge.

Hoover carried 40 of the 48 states in the 1928 election. Although he had questioned some of the financial policies that led to the stock market crash of 1929, no one anticipated how serious the Great Depression that followed it would become. No previous economic collapse had been so far-reaching, long lasting, or severe. A desperate public blamed Hoover for their troubles and, in 1932, voted in large numbers for the Democratic candidate, Franklin D. Roosevelt.

Herbert Hoover directed European relief efforts before and after his presidency (above, in Poland, 1946). During World War I, Finnish citizens used "hoover" as a new verb meaning "to help."

Two U.S. presidents called on Hoover to perform national service near the end of his lengthy retirement. He organized post–World War II food relief in Europe for Harry S. Truman. Later he evaluated government efficiency for Truman and for Dwight D. Eisenhower. Hoover's conservative ideas on economics and the role of government influenced national politics long after his death in 1964 at age 90.

NICKNAME
Chief

BORN
Aug. 10, 1874, in West Branch, IA

POLITICAL PARTY
Republican

CHIEF OPPONENT
Alfred Emanuel Smith, Democrat (1873–1944)

TERM OF OFFICE
March 4, 1929–March 3, 1933

AGE AT INAUGURATION
54 years old

NUMBER OF TERMS
one

VICE PRESIDENT
Charles Curtis (1860–1936)

FIRST LADY
Lou Henry Hoover (1874–1944), wife (married Feb. 10, 1899)

CHILDREN
Herbert, Allan

GEOGRAPHIC SCENE
48 states

NEW STATES ADDED
none

DIED
Oct. 20, 1964, in New York, NY

AGE AT DEATH
90 years old

SELECTED LANDMARKS
Newberg, OR (boyhood home); Hoover Institution, Stanford University, Palo Alto, CA; Herbert Hoover National Historic Site (including birthplace, presidential library, museum, and grave), West Branch, IA

Hoover became a multimillionaire during his years as a geologist. He refused to be paid for his public service. Hoover acted more aggressively than any previous president to end hard times after the stock market crashed in 1929. Despite his efforts, suffering continued to spread.

FRANKLIN D. ROOSEVELT
32ND PRESIDENT OF THE UNITED STATES 1933–1945

Not since the days of Abraham Lincoln did a president face such challenges as those met by Franklin Delano Roosevelt. During what became the longest presidency in U.S. history, Roosevelt led the nation out of the Great Depression and saw it safely through the darkest days of World War II. His wife, Eleanor, was an equal partner in his political career.

Franklin D. Roosevelt was the second member of his extended family to become president of the United States. His path to the White House included many of the same political and personal steps taken decades earlier by Theodore Roosevelt, a fifth cousin. Franklin was born at his family's estate in Hyde Park, New York. He called this spot home for most of his life. Roosevelt was his parents' only child. His mother and father took seven weeks to agree upon his name. As was the custom of the era, Roosevelt was clothed in dresses and kilts until age eight. His parents took him on extended trips abroad and had him tutored at home until his teen years.

After graduating from Harvard University in 1904, Roosevelt attended Columbia Law School. He passed the bar exam and took up the practice of law. By then he had

Franklin D. Roosevelt began courting his distant cousin Eleanor Roosevelt while he was a student at Harvard University.

already married a distant relative, Anna Eleanor Roosevelt, known as Eleanor. The cousins had met for the first time in 1902, the year Eleanor turned 18 and Franklin was 20. At their wedding in 1905 the bride was given away by President Theodore Roosevelt, her uncle.

In 1910 Franklin D. Roosevelt joined the New York Senate. A few years later, Woodrow Wilson named him assistant secretary of the Navy. He ran unsuccessfully for the U.S. Senate in 1914 and left the Navy in 1920 to campaign as the running mate of the Democratic presidential nominee, James M. Cox. Illness sidelined his political career in 1921 when he was stricken suddenly with polio. Roosevelt went from being active and robust one day to being

Franklin D. Roosevelt was the only person to serve three full terms as U.S. president and be elected to a fourth. He was encouraged during his childhood to pursue public service as an adult.

NICKNAME
FDR

BORN
Jan. 30, 1882, in Hyde Park, NY

POLITICAL PARTY
Democratic

CHIEF OPPONENTS
1st term: President Herbert Hoover, Republican (1874-1964); 2nd term: Alfred Mossman Landon, Republican (1887-1987); 3rd term: Wendell Lewis Willkie, Republican (1892-1944); 4th term: Thomas Edmund Dewey, Republican (1902-1971)

TERM OF OFFICE
March 4, 1933–April 12, 1945

AGE AT INAUGURATION
51 years old

NUMBER OF TERMS
four (cut short by death)

VICE PRESIDENTS
1st & 2nd terms: John Nance Garner (1868-1967); 3rd term: Henry Agard Wallace (1888-1965); 4th term: Harry S. Truman (1884-1972)

FIRST LADY
Anna Eleanor Roosevelt Roosevelt (1884-1962), wife (married March 17, 1905)

CHILDREN
Anna, James, Elliott, Franklin, John, plus a son who died young

GEOGRAPHIC SCENE
48 states

NEW STATES ADDED
none

DIED
April 12, 1945, in Warm Springs, GA

AGE AT DEATH
63 years old

SELECTED LANDMARKS
Franklin D. Roosevelt National Historic Site (includes house that was birthplace, childhood, and adult home; presidential library; museum; grave), Hyde Park, NY; Little White House State Historic Site, Warm Springs, GA; FDR Memorial, Washington, DC

Roosevelt had the longest presidency in U.S. history. He took office in 1933 after promising to end the Great Depression. When challenges continued at home and started abroad with World War II, voters were reluctant to switch leaders. He died in office in 1945. The 22nd Amendment, which became law in 1951, prohibits anyone from serving more than two terms as president. It was written by lawmakers who were uncomfortable with Roosevelt's extended term of office.

"While it isn't written in the Constitution, nevertheless it is the inherent duty of the federal government to keep its citizens from starvation," Roosevelt observed. As president he enacted sweeping legislation, including the Social Security Act of 1935 (described at left; being signed at right).

unable to walk two days later. Eleanor encouraged her husband to fight for his recovery. Although he never regained active use of his legs, Roosevelt learned how to stand on leg braces and take limited steps with the assistance of others. Within three years he was practicing law again. Before the decade was out, he had become governor of New York.

When Roosevelt ran for president in 1932, the nation was staggering under the burden of the Great Depression—an economic crisis unlike any ever before experienced in the country. One-fourth of all workers were unemployed. Countless families had gone broke because of bank failures. More than a million people experiencing homelessness sought food and work as they roamed

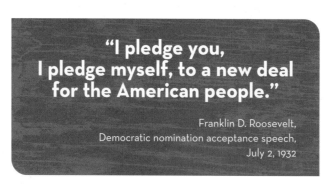

"I pledge you, I pledge myself, to a new deal for the American people."

Franklin D. Roosevelt,
Democratic nomination acceptance speech,
July 2, 1932

the country. Displaced families tacked together shacks in temporary settlements they nicknamed Hoovervilles—after President Herbert Hoover.

The grim national scene prompted voters to flock to Roosevelt and his promise of a "new deal for the American people." He earned 57 percent of the popular vote and won the electoral votes of all but six states. In the three presidential elections that followed, Roosevelt continued his streak of majority victories, earning 61 percent, 55 percent, then 53 percent of the vote.

As president, Roosevelt took charge of ending the Depression. Where Hoover had hesitated to interfere, Roosevelt plunged in. The beginning of his presidency was famous for its rush of legislation and was later

In 1943 the "Big Three" Allied leaders met in Tehran, Iran, for a wartime strategy session. Distrust ran high with Soviet Union leader Joseph Stalin (above, left). Roosevelt (above, center) won his cooperation in part by poking fun at fellow ally Winston Churchill, prime minister of Great Britain (above, right). He joked about the British, Churchill's cigars, even his moods. Soon the stern-faced Stalin was laughing along as Roosevelt teased the dictator and called him "Uncle Joe." Stalin betrayed the alliance by war's end.

Roosevelt used radio to connect with the American people in the days before television came into widespread use. His series of "fireside chats" (above), delivered in his reassuring voice, inspired the nation to face the day's challenges. He even used radio to build ties with French citizens. In 1942 he addressed them in their own language to announce the U.S. invasion of occupied French territories in North Africa. Roosevelt became the first president to appear on television with a 1939 broadcast from the New York World's Fair.

referred to as Roosevelt's Hundred Days. During this period, he signed 14 bills in all. Among other things, these new laws restored confidence in the banking industry, employed young men through a Civilian Conservation Corps, launched the construction of dams and power plants in the Tennessee River Valley, aided farmers, established loan programs, and improved working conditions. Later, Roosevelt established the Securities and Exchange Commission to help prevent future financial panics in the stock market. He also signed the Social Security Act of 1935, which established a series of cornerstone programs for public welfare that, among other benefits, ensured retirement incomes for senior citizens and temporary financial support for the unemployed. Many of these New Deal programs endure as essential elements of the American way of life.

In 1932 voters were asked to "Kick Out Depression With a Democratic Vote." Four years later they agreed overwhelmingly to "Follow Through With Roosevelt." In

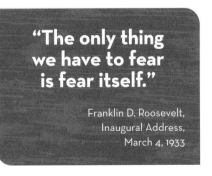

"The only thing we have to fear is fear itself."

Franklin D. Roosevelt, Inaugural Address, March 4, 1933

1940 they supported Roosevelt's third presidential campaign because he pledged that unless the U.S. was attacked, he would stay out of the war that was spreading around the globe. The next year Japan bombed the U.S. naval base at Pearl Harbor, Hawaii. Roosevelt predicted that the date, December 7, would "live in infamy," and he asked Congress to declare war on Japan. Declarations against Germany and Italy followed. For the rest of his life, the world would be at war.

Roosevelt took seriously his role as commander in chief during World War II. He plotted military strategy, appointed key field commanders, and authorized the secret development of the atomic bomb. He formed partnerships with Winston Churchill from Great Britain and, later, with Joseph Stalin of the Soviet Union. The "Big Three" discussed strategies for war and peace, including Roosevelt's idea for starting the United Nations. In 1944, with war raging full tilt, Roosevelt agreed to serve for a fourth term as president. Voters decided not to "change horses in

Roosevelt's mother (back row, center) was a central figure in his family life along with his wife, Eleanor, and their five children.

Eleanor (above, in 1936) became known as the first lady of the world for her work with the United Nations after her husband's death. She was part of the first U.S. delegation to that body, chaired its Commission on Human Rights, and helped write its Universal Declaration of Human Rights. She was the first president's wife to fly abroad.

midstream" and returned him to the White House once more.

During the early years of her husband's presidency, Eleanor Roosevelt tried to broaden the reach of the New Deal to African Americans, working women, children, labor unions, and immigrants. She wrote a daily national newspaper column and met weekly with women reporters. When war took center stage, she shifted her focus to it. Eleanor toured factories, launched battleships, and visited troops around the world. She represented her husband beyond the nation's capital, while he focused on diplomatic and military planning.

In the spring of 1945 President Roosevelt made a visit to the "Little White House," his retreat at Warm Springs, Georgia. Twelve years had passed since his first Inauguration, and it was almost three months since his fourth. (Beginning in 1937, presidents were inaugurated on January 20 instead of March 4.) Other commitments kept Eleanor

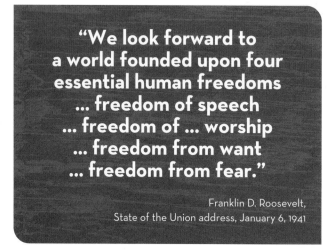

"We look forward to a world founded upon four essential human freedoms ... freedom of speech ... freedom of ... worship ... freedom from want ... freedom from fear."

Franklin D. Roosevelt,
State of the Union address, January 6, 1941

from making the trip, but among those joining the president was Lucy Page Mercer Rutherford. More than 30 years earlier, Lucy and Roosevelt had shared a romantic relationship while she served as Eleanor's secretary. Roosevelt ended their affair after his wife discovered it, but the pair secretly renewed their friendship later on. During the visit to Georgia, Roosevelt suddenly fell ill while being sketched for a portrait. He reached for his head and observed: "I have a terrific headache." He was having a stroke. Roosevelt never spoke again and died within hours.

The nation was plunged into grief. Roosevelt was the only president whom many people had ever known, and he had helped them survive some of the country's toughest challenges. Roosevelt's combination as "Dr. New Deal" and "Dr. Win the War" had cured the Great Depression. Within months of his death, World War II would end, too. His pattern of federal involvement in national issues became the norm for future leaders. In 1997 Roosevelt became the fifth president

U.S. soldiers fought battles around the globe after the United States joined the fighting of World War II in 1941. U.S. servicemen were part of the Allied forces who stormed the coast of Normandy, France, on D-Day, June 6, 1944 (above), in their march to free Europe from Nazi Germany.

This musician wept as he played at Roosevelt's memorial service. Some of Roosevelt's wartime policies—such as the fear-based detention of 120,000 Japanese Americans, most of whom were U.S. citizens—have been discredited as mistakes, but he remains one of the nation's most acclaimed presidents overall.

Conquest of Pacific islands, including Japan's Iwo Jima in early 1945, helped turn the tide of battle in the Pacific. Later this battle was recalled in the U.S. Marine Corps War Memorial (above).

to earn a national monument in Washington, D.C. Prior memorials honored George Washington, Thomas Jefferson, Abraham Lincoln, and Theodore Roosevelt. In 2020 President Dwight D. Eisenhower was similarly recognized.

THE FIRST LADIES
PARTNERS, HOSTESSES, AND ADVOCATES

The tradition of male presidents being supported in their work by female partners is a practice that will invite reinvention when the first spouse is not a woman. New customs will emerge after a "first gentleman" settles into the Executive Mansion. Patterns have varied at other times in history, too. Not all wives have played the expected role of White House hostess, either because of poor health, lack of interest, or death. In such cases other female relatives or friends have stepped in to help plan and host social occasions.

Early on, these presidential partners were addressed with titles such as "Lady," or "Mrs. President." The term "first lady" became popular by the early 20th century; it recalled a role for women in the home that was seen as first in importance to the nation.

For more than 100 years the chief duty of the first lady was to serve as hostess at White House events. However, many of these women, such as Dolley Madison, were more than gracious entertainers; they were shrewd students of politics, too. They knew just how to soothe upset guests and win support for their husbands.

Entertaining was the focus for First Lady Martha Washington.

Early first ladies came to the White House with the same background in domestic life as other women of their day. Until the mid-19th century, few had even attended school. Abigail Fillmore was the first president's wife to have held a job of her own (as a schoolteacher).

Eleanor Roosevelt expanded the role of the president's wife during her 12 years as first lady. Because her husband's mobility was limited by polio, she traveled and spoke extensively on his behalf. She pursued her own interests, too—from civil rights to family welfare to benefits for laborers.

In recent decades, each first lady has focused national attention on issues that might otherwise have been

Edith Wilson stepped in to deal with administrative details in 1919 after a stroke left her husband partially paralyzed. Critics charged that she had become too involved in presidential matters, but her work helped her husband complete his term.

A variety of roles have occupied first ladies during their partnerships with U.S. presidents. Louisa Adams kept her husband, John Quincy Adams, company in 1828 by winding silk from her own silkworms while he worked nearby.

Lucretia Garfield helping in the kitchen, 1881

Melania Trump visits a classroom in Tulsa, Oklahoma, as part of her Be Best outreach for children.

Hillary Clinton proved that first ladies could hold elected office by becoming a U.S. senator in 2000. Twice she ran for president (below, her 2016 bid). She is the first woman ever nominated for that office by a major party.

neglected. Jacqueline Kennedy restored historical spaces inside the White House, while her successor, Lady Bird Johnson, worked to beautify the landscape in the nation's capital and beyond. Barbara Bush and her daughter-in-law Laura Bush each promoted the cause of literacy. Many first ladies have sought to improve public health and civic engagement through such causes as increased volunteerism (Pat Nixon), better care for handicapped children (Betty Ford), more support for the mentally ill (Rosalynn Carter), avoidance of illegal drug use (Nancy Reagan), streamlined delivery of health care (Hillary Clinton), better childhood nutrition (Michelle Obama), and reduced cyber-bullying (Melania Trump).

Jacqueline Kennedy coaxes a smile out of Soviet Union premier Nikita S. Khrushchev.

Laura Bush stands shoulder to shoulder with members of the armed services in a show of wartime support.

Fitness advocate Michelle Obama leads hundreds of children in jumping jacks on the way to setting a Guinness world record.

Eleanor Roosevelt visits with mine workers.

SEEKING STABILITY IN THE ATOMIC AGE

1945–1989

The challenges faced by presidents increased in complexity as the 20th century progressed. Leaders struggled to fight wars, end poverty, preserve democracy, extend equality, survive energy shortages, and heal national wounds. They led citizens through the tragedies of presidential deaths and scandals, too. Much of the era was dominated by the uneasy balance of power between the rivals of the atomic age—the United States and the Soviet Union. Presidents sought to offset the troubles of the times with hopes for a promising future.

1946
The first programmable electronic computer weighed 30 tons and used some 18,000 bulky vacuum tubes to transfer information. By 1952 computers were calculating election results.

1957
Racial tensions mounted in Little Rock, Arkansas, after the governor ignored the 1954 Supreme Court ruling on the integration of public schools, *Brown* v. *Board of Education*.

1962
Labor advocates César Chávez and Dolores Huerta (above, during a national grape boycott) established what became the United Farm Workers union to promote safety and fair pay for migrant farm workers.

1967
Widespread protest of U.S. involvement in the Vietnam War developed during the late 1960s, particularly among young people (above, a protester fills gun barrels with flowers).

A mushroom cloud marks the devastating impact of the atomic bomb dropped by an American aircraft on Hiroshima, Japan, on August 6, 1945. Three days later, the U.S. destroyed Nagasaki, Japan, with another atomic bomb. Soon after, Japan agreed to surrender, bringing an end to World War II. Nuclear weapons have never again been used in combat.

1969
On July 20, humans set foot on the moon for the first time. A series of six Apollo lunar missions carried 12 U.S. astronauts to the moon between 1969 and 1972.

1973
Some 200 members of the American Indian Movement occupied Wounded Knee on South Dakota's Pine Ridge Reservation to protest broken treaties and tribal misman-agement. Two died during the 71-day armed siege.

1981
A new technology company named Microsoft helped launch the personal computer industry with its MS-DOS operating system. It quickly became a leader in the field (above, floppy disks, 1993).

1989
Berlin citizens marked the end of the Cold War by tearing down the wall that had divided their city into separate zones. East reunited with West in a new democracy.

HARRY S. TRUMAN
33RD PRESIDENT OF THE UNITED STATES **1945–1953**

When Vice President Harry S. Truman became president after the sudden death of Franklin D. Roosevelt, he was stunned. "I felt like the moon, the stars, and all the planets had fallen on me," he said. Issues such as the use of atomic weapons, tensions with the Soviet Union, and war in Korea dominated his administration.

Truman was no stranger to challenge when he became president. He grew up on a farm in Missouri, and tight family finances made him the only 20th-century president who did not attend college, although he later went to law school. Truman's meandering career included work as a railroad timekeeper, a farmer, a World War I artillery captain, and a clothing store owner. He entered politics in 1922 as a local administrator; eventually he spent 10 years in the U.S. Senate.

Harry S. Truman's whistle-stop campaign of 1948

In 1944 President Franklin D. Roosevelt persuaded Senator Truman to join his fourth-term reelection ticket.

Only months after becoming vice president, Truman found himself taking the presidential oath of office because President Roosevelt had died. Soon after that, World War II ended in Europe. But the war with Japan continued. Truman decided to use a secret weapon—the atomic bomb—to end it and to stop further U.S. combat losses. His strategy worked, but 200,000 Japanese civilians were immediately killed or wounded in the nuclear attacks that led to Japan's

Truman married Elizabeth "Bess" Wallace when he was 35; the couple met in Sunday school when he was six. Truman's middle initial did not stand for a middle name; his parents used the letter to honor their own fathers, each of whom had a name that started with *S*.

NICKNAME
Give 'Em Hell Harry

BORN
May 8, 1884, in Lamar, MO

POLITICAL PARTY
Democratic

CHIEF OPPONENT
1st term: none, succeeded Franklin D. Roosevelt; 2nd term: Thomas Edmund Dewey, Republican (1902–1971)

TERM OF OFFICE
April 12, 1945–Jan. 20, 1953

AGE AT INAUGURATION
60 years old

NUMBER OF TERMS
one, plus balance of Franklin D. Roosevelt's term

VICE PRESIDENT
1st term: none; 2nd term: Alben William Barkley (1877–1956)

FIRST LADY
Elizabeth (Bess) Virginia Wallace Truman (1885–1982), wife (married June 29, 1919)

CHILDREN
Margaret

GEOGRAPHIC SCENE
48 states

NEW STATES ADDED
none

DIED
Dec. 26, 1972, in Independence, MO

AGE AT DEATH
88 years old

SELECTED LANDMARKS
Lamar, MO (birthplace); Grandview, MO (family farm); Key West Little White House Museum, Key West, FL; Harry S. Truman National Historic Site (adult home) and Harry S. Truman Library and Museum (and grave), Independence, MO

surrender. By then worldwide combat casualties had reached an estimated 15 million, more than 400,000 of them Americans. At least another 45 million civilians had died, including more than 10 million who perished in the Nazi genocide known as the Holocaust.

International events dominated Truman's presidency. He supported the creation of the United Nations and favored the formation of Israel. He used the

Marshall Plan to rebuild war-torn Europe and helped form the North Atlantic Treaty Organization (NATO) to fortify the security of Western Europe, the United States, and Canada. In particular, he sought to discourage the expanding influence of the Soviet Union and its political system of communism. Communism—a program of government control over citizens, industries, and finances—was at odds with the U.S. system of democracy, freedom, and market-based capitalism. A Cold War—one with limited fighting but much hostility, mistrust, and stockpiling of nuclear weapons—developed between the United States, the Soviet Union, and their allies.

As tensions grew between these two "blocs" of countries, Truman, with his Truman Doctrine, committed the United States to "support free peoples who are resisting" conquest. When the Soviet Union restricted access to West Berlin in 1948, Truman organized a massive airlift of supplies into the city. When war broke out in 1950 between communist North Korea and democratic South Korea, Truman developed an international army through the United Nations to "contain" the spread of communism. When anticommunist citizens asked for U.S. assistance in Vietnam, Truman sent aid.

A fear of communism at home developed at the same time as these international worries. U.S. senator Joseph McCarthy exploited this anxiety by conducting congressional investigations of suspected communists. Among those who eventually joined his efforts was a

Truman took delight in a newspaper headline that mistakenly announced the victory of his opponent in 1948. His whistle-stop campaign effort helped clinch his victory. It took him to six million people during a 31,000-mile train journey. "Give 'em hell, Harry!" yelled supporters when Truman criticized the uncooperative Congress.

Truman met with Allied leaders in July 1945.

The nation enjoyed a postwar boom during Truman's presidency. Couples wed in record numbers and started a "baby boom" of soaring births. Thousands of veterans found ladders into the middle class through federal support of education and housing with the G.I. Bill of Rights, but these opportunities were not shared equally with minorities.

future president, Senator Richard Nixon. McCarthy's Red Scare (named after the symbolic communist color) lasted until 1954, when other senators put a stop to the discredited hearings.

Truman won election in his own right in 1948. As president he tried to extend Roosevelt's New Deal of federal programs with his own 21-point Fair Deal, but most proposals failed to take hold. His efforts to integrate all races in the armed forces met with both favor and controversy.

"The buck stops here."

Motto on Harry S. Truman's desk

Challenged by so many difficult issues, Truman left the White House with the lowest approval rating for a president up to that time. In later years, respect for Truman's handling of tough times increased; since 1962 historians have consistently ranked him among the top 10 presidents.

Truman and his wife retired to Independence, Missouri. Bess Truman lived to age 97—longer than any other first lady. She died in 1982, 10 years after her husband.

After World War II, Germany and its capital city of Berlin were divided in half; the Soviet Union assumed control over eastern sections, and the United States, France, and Great Britain oversaw western territories. When the Soviet Union cut off access to West Berlin in June 1948, Western allies delivered necessary supplies to stranded residents (left). Planes landed as often as every few minutes during the Berlin airlift. The Soviet blockade lasted until May 1949.

Truman knew nothing about the development of the atomic bomb until after he became president near the end of World War II. As commander in chief he followed the war's progress by visiting the White House Map Room (left).

After the war Truman supported the European recovery plan devised by Secretary of State George C. Marshall (far right). The Marshall Plan shared $12 billion over three years with such countries as Great Britain, France, and West Germany. It boosted the American economy and helped create democracies throughout Europe. "Peace, freedom, and world trade are indivisible," noted Truman.

POLLSTERS AND POLLING
SIZING UP PUBLIC OPINION

One of the first recorded public opinion surveys—conducted in 1824 by a newspaper in Pennsylvania—suggested that Andrew Jackson would win the election. He did not. (His strong showing among voters failed to earn him the support he needed in the Electoral College.) Informal measures of public opinion, often called straw polls, continue to this day. So do complex polls conducted by professional researchers, although even these efforts can lead to false predictions.

The scientific research methods used by modern pollsters originated in 1935 through the work of statisticians such as George Gallup and Elmo Roper. They competed in 1936 with *Literary Digest*, a magazine known for its respected polls, to predict whether or not Franklin D. Roosevelt would be reelected for a second term of office. Gallup and Roper each predicted victory for Roosevelt, while *Literary Digest* forecast that Alfred Landon would win. Landon, in fact, lost decisively, establishing Gallup and Roper as trustworthy pollsters.

Analysis of the *Literary Digest* poll revealed unintended bias in the magazine's choice of whom to survey. By targeting people listed as owners of cars and telephones, they had inadvertently surveyed individuals who matched the more affluent background of Republican voters. Instead, Gallup and Roper deliberately had interviewed people chosen to represent the mix of the overall population.

Over the years pollsters have worked to improve

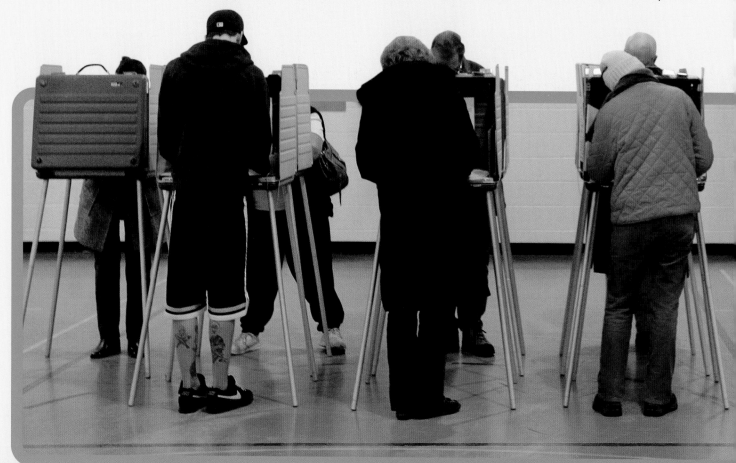

the accuracy of their results. They learned to survey a large number of people, often 1,000 or more individuals. They worked to create questions free from unintended pressures on how best to answer them. Pollsters tried to account for people who might give misleading answers, too. Someone who objected to candidates for personal reasons—such as their gender or race—might be reluctant to admit that prejudice to an interviewer, for example. Polling results typically include a margin of error percentage that can be applied to the survey's results.

George Gallup, political pollster

Even so, pollsters make mistakes. In 1948 they failed to predict the victory of Harry S. Truman over Republican challenger Thomas E. Dewey. Polling firms concluded they had missed late-breaking trends by discontinuing their surveys several weeks before Election Day.

Pollsters have struggled in recent years to predict the results of presidential races. Neither the 2016 nor the 2020 elections played out as forecast. In 2016 the projected loser—Donald Trump—actually won the race.

In an effort to make accurate predictions, some organizations conduct daily tracking polls to chart a candidate's level of support over time. Other polls measure voter opinions at specific moments during the campaign season, such as after a presidential debate or major political event. Polling continues even on Election Day with interviews of voters. These so-called exit polls help news organizations predict the outcome of the day's results even as the ballots are still being counted. Only after reviewing the final tallies can pollsters breathe a sigh of relief or—as they have done more recently—determine what went wrong and identify better methods for use during the next election season.

Pollsters conduct surveys by mail, telephone, online, and in person (above, in Florida). Answers are tabulated in an effort to gauge support for policy proposals, track the standing of political candidates, and identify trends. The accuracy of polls that predict support for particular political candidates is put to the test on Election Day when citizens cast their ballots (left). The forecasts of pollsters are measured against the final results.

DWIGHT D. EISENHOWER
34TH PRESIDENT OF THE UNITED STATES **1953–1961**

Like Generals George Washington and Ulysses S. Grant, Gen. Dwight David Eisenhower became president thanks to his popularity as a war hero. Eisenhower—the man who helped bring victory to Europe during World War II—sought to keep peace at home and abroad after becoming president. His moderate political views earned the Republican Party new respect.

Although born in Texas, Eisenhower was raised in Abilene, Kansas, where his father worked in a creamery. He learned lessons about war and peace at an early age while growing up there with five brothers. The boys, all of whom took turns using the nickname Ike, never hesitated to come to blows among themselves or with others when arguments arose. Even as a youngster, Eisenhower enjoyed studying military history. He went on to graduate from the U.S. Military Academy at West Point in 1915 and take

up a career in the Army. Later that year he met Marie "Mamie" Doud; the couple married soon afterward.

For the next 26 years, Eisenhower's Army duties took him to bases throughout the United States as well as to the Panama Canal Zone and the Philippines. Along the way he finished first in his class at officer training school and did desk duty at war offices in Washington, D.C. Much to his regret he missed out on World War I combat; he was instead assigned to train others to fight.

By the time of World War II, however, Eisenhower's leadership skills and organizational talents earned him key military appointments. He commanded the combined Allied forces that overran enemy

The Eisenhowers on their wedding day

Dwight D. Eisenhower played football at West Point until a knee injury ended his athletic career. His skills as a military leader helped carry him to the White House years later.

NICKNAME
Ike

BORN
Oct. 14, 1890, in Denison, TX

POLITICAL PARTY
Republican

CHIEF OPPONENT
1st and 2nd terms: Adlai Ewing Stevenson, Democrat (1900–1965)

TERM OF OFFICE
Jan. 20, 1953–Jan. 20, 1961

AGE AT INAUGURATION
62 years old

NUMBER OF TERMS
two

VICE PRESIDENT
Richard Nixon (1913–1994)

FIRST LADY
Marie (Mamie) Geneva Doud Eisenhower (1896–1979), wife (married July 1, 1916)

CHILDREN
John, plus a son who died young

GEOGRAPHIC SCENE
48 states

NEW STATES ADDED
Alaska, Hawaii (1959)

DIED
March 28, 1969, in Washington, DC

AGE AT DEATH
78 years old

SELECTED LANDMARKS
Eisenhower Birthplace State Historic Site, Denison, TX; Eisenhower National Historic Site, Gettysburg, PA (retirement home); Eisenhower Center (including presidential library, museum, family home, and grave), Abilene, KS; Dwight D. Eisenhower Memorial, Washington, DC

General Eisenhower served as supreme commander of all Allied forces during the World War II campaigns that liberated North Africa and Europe from German and Italian occupation forces. In June 1944 Eisenhower urged members of the U.S. 101st Airborne Division (left) to accomplish their mission during the impending D-Day invasion of France. Later on, Eisenhower toured so many countries as president—27 in all—that his travels were written up in *National Geographic*.

Republicans reclaimed the White House after a 20-year absence thanks to the popular appeal of Eisenhower as the party's nominee. During his presidency, "Ike" authorized construction of the nation's interstate highway system and collaborated with Canada to create the St. Lawrence Seaway linking the Great Lakes with the Atlantic Ocean. By the end of his administration, citizens could chant: "Ike is nifty, Ike is nifty; started out with 48; ended up with 50," because Alaska and Hawaii had joined the Union.

Broadway songwriter Irving Berlin wrote a catchy tune to popularize Eisenhower's 1952 campaign slogan.

troops in North Africa, Sicily, Italy, and northern Europe. Before the end of the war he had risen to the Army's highest rank—five-star general. One soldier who spotted the rows of stars on Eisenhower's uniform exclaimed: "Cripes! The whole Milky Way!"

After the war Eisenhower served as chief of staff for the Army, president of Columbia University, and commander of international troops in Europe. As early as 1943 people had suggested that

> "What counts is not necessarily the size of the dog in the fight—it's the size of the fight in the dog."
>
> Dwight D. Eisenhower, January 31, 1958

Eisenhower run for president with either political party. Happy with Army life, he dismissed the idea.

Finally, in 1952, he agreed to mount a campaign as a Republican. Eisenhower faced the same opponent that year and four years later—Adlai Stevenson. Eisenhower's signature grin, victory wave, and record of wartime service encouraged voters to proclaim: "We like Ike!" They proved it by awarding Eisenhower a sizable majority of votes in each election.

Challenges from the Truman Administration carried over into Eisenhower's presidency. Peace talks finally ended the fighting in Korea in 1953. The conflict had killed or wounded more than three million people, including 34,000 Americans. Relations with the Soviet Union remained tense. Although Eisenhower urged the Soviets to consider nuclear disarmament, or the reduction of atomic weapons, neither

President-elect Eisenhower (far left) visited U.S. troops in Korea during 1952 as part of his efforts to end U.S. military involvement there.

Senator Joseph McCarthy continued to inflame U.S. fears of communism at home until fellow senators shut down his high-profile congressional hearings (above) in 1954. The domino theory—the idea that communism could spread from one vulnerable country to the next like a row of tumbling dominoes—led the president to develop his Eisenhower Doctrine. This policy fostered increased U.S. assistance for anticommunist efforts in Vietnam during his administration.

Dwight and Mamie Eisenhower were a popular presidential couple. Mamie acted as a traditional hostess during her years as first lady. She restored the custom, discontinued during World War II, of holding an annual White House Easter Egg Roll. Eisenhower renamed the presidential retreat in Maryland Camp David to honor their grandson. Franklin D. Roosevelt had originally called it Shangri-La.

side seemed willing to trust the other. In 1957 the Soviets launched the world's first satellite, Sputnik. Americans feared it might be armed with nuclear weapons. Three years later, the Soviets were equally alarmed when they captured a U.S. pilot flying a U-2 spy plane over their country.

Although Eisenhower didn't consider ending segregation in the United States a priority, he took modest steps to advance racial integration. When laws changed, he considered it his constitutional duty to uphold them. The president sent federal troops to Little Rock, Arkansas, to enforce the Supreme Court's *Brown* v. *Board of Education* ruling. This landmark decision called for public schools to be desegregated, or open to children of all races. He also bolstered civil rights by signing new voting laws.

In 1961 Eisenhower and his wife retired to a farm they had purchased in 1950 near Gettysburg, Pennsylvania. Because Eisenhower's career had kept them forever on the go (they moved 28 times during their marriage), this was the first home they ever owned. Although several heart attacks threatened the former president's health, he enjoyed writing his memoirs, playing golf, painting landscapes, and keeping a finger in politics. He died in 1969. Mamie died 10 years later.

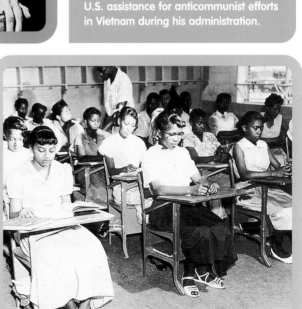

When Eisenhower became president, Black children and white children in the United States were routinely educated in separate schools. The Supreme Court ruled such segregation illegal in 1954.

JOHN F. KENNEDY
35TH PRESIDENT OF THE UNITED STATES **1961–1963**

John Fitzgerald Kennedy was elected by the narrowest popular vote margin in history—fewer than 120,000 votes nationwide—and served as president for only about 1,000 days before he was assassinated. Yet he remains a central figure of the American presidency. His eloquent calls for peace, justice, and national service inspired action among countless citizens during his presidency and beyond.

After his death, the Kennedy Administration was compared to Camelot, the legendary ancient realm of the fair-minded King Arthur. Kennedy's birth to a privileged family was the perfect place to begin the comparison. His father hoped one of his four sons would become president; eventually three of them campaigned for that office. John (nicknamed Jack, and later JFK) attended prestigious schools and graduated with honors from Harvard University. Although plagued by a string of childhood illnesses, he was athletic, playful, and handsome.

John F. Kennedy (perched on a scooter) with his mother, Rose, and siblings (left to right) Eunice, Kathleen, Rosemary, and Joe Jr.

A decorated World War II naval officer, Kennedy took up the family's presidential hopes after his older brother, Joseph, died in combat.

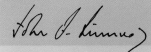

NICKNAMES
JFK, Jack

BORN
May 29, 1917, in Brookline, MA

POLITICAL PARTY
Democratic

CHIEF OPPONENT
Richard Nixon, Republican (1913–1994)

TERM OF OFFICE
Jan. 20, 1961–Nov. 22, 1963

AGE AT INAUGURATION
43 years old

NUMBER OF TERMS
one (cut short by assassination)

VICE PRESIDENT
Lyndon B. Johnson (1908–1973)

FIRST LADY
Jacqueline Lee Bouvier Kennedy (1929–1994), wife (married Sept. 12, 1953)

CHILDREN
Caroline, John, plus a daughter and son who died young

GEOGRAPHIC SCENE
50 states

DIED
Nov. 22, 1963, in Dallas, TX

AGE AT DEATH
46 years old

SELECTED LANDMARKS
Brookline, MA (birthplace); Hammersmith Farm, Newport, RI ("summer White House"); Sixth Floor Museum, Dallas, TX; John F. Kennedy Library and Museum, Boston, MA; Arlington National Cemetery, Arlington, VA

Kennedy (above) became a World War II hero after the patrol torpedo boat (PT-109) under his command was destroyed by a Japanese warship (left). Kennedy swam with the surviving crew members to safety several miles away, towing one injured sailor by clamping the man's life jacket strap in his teeth. When asked later how he became a hero, Kennedy replied: "It was easy— they sank my boat."

Jacqueline Kennedy was an active first lady while mothering the Kennedys' young children, Caroline and John Jr. (below, with the president on vacation in Hyannisport, Massachusetts).

Kennedy (above, right, as a U.S. senator in 1957 with his younger brother Robert, center), brought Bobby into his administration as his attorney general and close adviser.

Cold War tensions were reduced shortly before Kennedy's death when the U.S. signed a nuclear test ban treaty with the Soviet Union and the United Kingdom, outlawing atomic explosions in the atmosphere, in space, and underwater.

Military arsenals for the Soviet Union and the United States grew in the 1960s (above, Kennedy reviews the preparedness of U.S. ally West Germany).

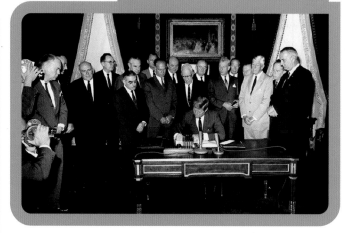

Kennedy met Jacqueline Bouvier during his six years as a U.S. congressman from Massachusetts. Jackie was sophisticated, charming, and beautiful. The pair were married in 1953, soon after he became a U.S. senator. Kennedy sought the Democratic presidential nomination in 1960. "We stand today on the edge of a New Frontier," he proclaimed after winning the nomination. Kennedy narrowly defeated Richard Nixon in a tight race. A surge in support among African Americans in key states like Texas and Illinois may have helped seal his victory. Kennedy was the first Catholic to become president.

Conflicts in the Cold War dominated much of Kennedy's presidency. First, the U.S. government secretly tried to overthrow Cuba's new communist dictator, Fidel Castro, by helping Cuban exiles invade their homeland at the Bay of Pigs. U.S. involvement proved embarrassing when the mission failed. Then tensions flared when the Soviet Union built a wall dividing East and West Berlin in Germany. Next the two superpowers narrowly avoided nuclear war during the Cuban missile crisis, a tense standoff resulting from the U.S. discovery of Soviet warheads in Cuba. Secretly, Kennedy fought the spread of communism elsewhere by continuing U.S. support of anticommunists in Vietnam. Publicly he urged Americans to win the "space race" against the Soviets by sending astronauts to the moon and back. Cold War tensions eased somewhat in 1963 after the two nations signed a treaty banning most nuclear testing.

Kennedy visited coal miners as part of his presidential campaign in 1960.

Near the end of the Kennedy Administration, more than 200,000 people took part in the March on Washington for Jobs and Freedom. This event occurred during the 100th anniversary of Abraham Lincoln's Emancipation Proclamation. Martin Luther King, Jr., delivered his famous "I Have a Dream" speech from the steps of the Lincoln Memorial during the massive peaceful protest for Black equality.

Kennedy was the youngest man ever elected president. (Teddy Roosevelt was the youngest president by succession, not election.) Kennedy was also the youngest one to die, when an assassin shot him in a motorcade just three years after his election. Jacqueline Kennedy modeled her husband's funeral after Abraham Lincoln's. Kennedy's casket lay in state at the U.S. Capitol on the same platform that was used for Lincoln.

Civil rights, including the freedom for all citizens regardless of race to vote, was a dominant issue, too. At first Kennedy relied on the Justice Department, headed by his younger brother Robert, to aid this cause. Later the president publicly supported racial equality. Much of the civil rights legislation Kennedy favored became law in tribute to him after his assassination.

Kennedy was shot and killed on November 22, 1963, while touring Dallas, Texas, in a presidential motorcade. More than a hundred nations sent representatives to his funeral in Washington, D.C. Anyone who could find a television "attended" the event, too. All were moved by the solemn processions, by Jackie's dignity, and by the composure of their children. Hearts broke as three-year-old John-John saluted his father's coffin.

The identity of Kennedy's assassin remains a subject of speculation. Gunman Lee Harvey Oswald was charged with the death but was himself murdered before he could be tried. Repeated investigations have failed to confirm theories that others may have helped Oswald kill the president.

Kennedy's presidency remains highly ranked despite facts that have emerged in the years since (such as the extent of the covert, or secret, support his administration gave to anticommunists in Vietnam, and his extramarital affairs while in office). The president's brother Bobby became a U.S. senator; he was assassinated in 1968 while running for president. His youngest brother, Edward, served five decades as a U.S. senator; he sought his party's nomination for president in 1980.

Jackie remarried five years after her husband's death. She died from cancer in her mid-60s and was buried beside her husband at Arlington National Cemetery.

> "Ask not what your country can do for you—ask what you can do for your country."
>
> John F. Kennedy,
> Inaugural Address, January 20, 1961

PRESIDENTS WHO DIED IN OFFICE
THE MYSTERIOUS 20-YEAR CURSE

Eight of the nation's presidents have died before completing their terms of office. Half of these people were victims of illnesses; the others were assassinated. Oddly, seven of these deaths have occurred in a regular pattern. The winner of every fifth election from 1840 to 1960 died before completing his final term. This peculiar circumstance has been called the 20-year curse even though the deaths are not exactly 20 years apart.

The first president to die in office was William Henry Harrison. He became ill after his Inauguration and died one month later on April 4, 1841. Abraham Lincoln's first term began 20 years after Harrison's. Lincoln died on April 15, 1865, within weeks of the beginning of his second term and the ending of the Civil War. His assassin supported the defeated South.

Twenty years after Lincoln's first election, James A. Garfield took office. He was shot on July 2, 1881, by a deranged former political supporter. The president died two and a half months later.

President William McKinley was shot 20 years afterward. Early in his second term, a disgruntled factory worker fired on him in a receiving line. McKinley died eight days later, on Sept. 14, 1901.

The next two sitting presidents to die five terms apart were victims of natural causes. Warren G. Harding died suddenly on Aug. 2, 1923. Doctors think he may have had a heart attack. Franklin D. Roosevelt was killed by a stroke, a brain injury caused by improper

President Kennedy lies in state, 1963.

Mourners hung ribbons (far left) in their windows following the assassination of Abraham Lincoln. Future president Theodore Roosevelt, as a child in New York City, was among the countless citizens who viewed Lincoln's coffin when it traveled through key cities (left, Washington, D.C.) on its way to burial in Illinois.

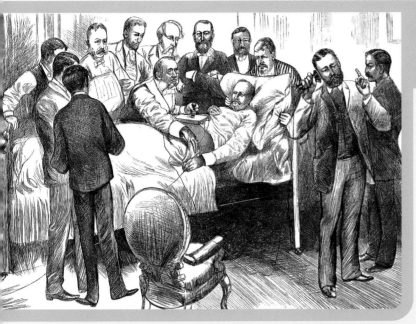

In 1881 Alexander Graham Bell tried to find the bullet lodged in James A. Garfield by an assassin's gun. Bell's early metal detector failed, and Garfield died of blood poisoning.

Presidential deaths make front-page news.

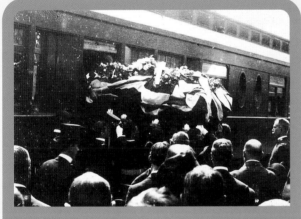

The death of a president brings shock and sorrow to the entire nation, not just to relatives and political supporters. Mourners bade farewell to William McKinley as his coffin was loaded onto his funeral train.

John F. Kennedy's family observed his funeral procession while millions of citizens watched via live television broadcast.

blood flow in the head. He died a few months into his fourth term of office on April 12, 1945.

John F. Kennedy, the most recent president to die in office, was assassinated on November 22, 1963, in Dallas, Texas. His term had begun 20 years after the beginning of Roosevelt's presidency. Zachary Taylor was the only serving president who died outside of the 20-year cycle. His death occurred after a short illness on July 9, 1850.

Ronald Reagan finally broke the 120-year history of cyclical presidential deaths. Even so, his life was threatened by an assassination attempt in 1981. Prompt modern medical attention saved his life.

Other assassination attempts were made against presidents Andrew Jackson, Harry S. Truman, and Gerald R. Ford. An assassin threatened president-elect Franklin D. Roosevelt, too. No vice presidents have been assassinated, but seven have died in office.

Often the bodies of fallen presidents—even those who die after leaving office—lie in state. During this honor, the casket is displayed on the same catafalque, or platform, that was used for Lincoln. Visitors file past in tribute. Sometimes the casket is open; at other times it is closed and covered with the U.S. flag. Seven presidents have lain in state in the White House East Room; 12 have rested in the Rotunda of the U.S. Capitol. George H. W. Bush was the most recent president to receive this honor. Abraham Lincoln was the first.

LYNDON B. JOHNSON
36TH PRESIDENT OF THE UNITED STATES 1963–1969

Lyndon Baines Johnson channeled energy from the nation's grief over the sudden death of John F. Kennedy into the creation of a living memorial to the slain leader. Johnson called this legacy the Great Society. He envisioned a nation that offered opportunity, prosperity, and fairness to all citizens. His tireless efforts for this cause brought considerable improvement to the lives of racial minorities and the poor. These accomplishments became overshadowed, however, by escalating U.S. involvement in an increasingly controversial war in Vietnam.

"No words are sad enough to express our sense of loss," President Johnson observed two days after the funeral of John F. Kennedy. "No words are strong enough to express our determination to continue the forward thrust of America that he began." Johnson, a veteran politician, was uniquely prepared to lead that effort.

LBJ and Lady Bird by the U.S. Capitol

The son of a farmer and legislator, Johnson grew up in rural Texas. His childhood mixed hard times and endless chores with breaks for marble games and a memorable visit to the Alamo. After finishing high school, he drifted around California for two years doing odd jobs. Later he enrolled at Southwest Texas State Teachers College; he graduated in

Lyndon B. Johnson became the only U.S. president to take the oath of office on an airplane when he was sworn in aboard Air Force One two hours after the assassination of John F. Kennedy. The plane was preparing to take him back to Washington, D.C., along with Kennedy's body. Johnson was flanked by his wife (on his right) and Kennedy's widow. Jacqueline Kennedy still wore the clothes stained during the shooting of her husband.

NICKNAME
LBJ

BORN
Aug. 27, 1908, near Stonewall, TX

POLITICAL PARTY
Democratic

CHIEF OPPONENT
1st term: none, succeeded John F. Kennedy; 2nd term: Barry Morris Goldwater, Republican (1909–1998)

TERM OF OFFICE
Nov. 22, 1963–Jan. 20, 1969

AGE AT INAUGURATION
55 years old

NUMBER OF TERMS
one, plus balance of John F. Kennedy's term

VICE PRESIDENT
1st term: none; 2nd term: Hubert Horatio Humphrey (1911–1978)

FIRST LADY
Claudia Alta (Lady Bird) Taylor Johnson (1912–2007), wife (married Nov. 17, 1934)

CHILDREN
Lynda, Luci

GEOGRAPHIC SCENE
50 states

DIED
Jan. 22, 1973, near San Antonio, TX

AGE AT DEATH
64 years old

SELECTED LANDMARKS
Lyndon B. Johnson National Historical Park, Stonewall, TX, and Johnson City, TX (includes visitor center, reconstructed birthplace, school, boyhood home, Johnson Settlement, "Texas White House," LBJ Ranch, and grave); Lyndon Baines Johnson Library and Museum, University of Texas, Austin, TX

1930. Johnson met his future wife, Claudia "Lady Bird" Taylor, while working for a U.S. congressman. Her nickname gave the couple the same initials after they were married. In future years, their daughters, their Texas ranch, and even a family dog bore names that yielded the trademark LBJ initials.

Johnson was elected to the House of Representatives six consecutive times beginning in 1937. He received a Silver Star for World War II service while on leave from Congress. He earned the nickname Landslide Lyndon in 1948 when he won his first U.S. Senate seat by nothing like a landslide—just 87 votes. He was reelected overwhelmingly six years later. In 1960 Kennedy asked the influential senator to be his running mate. (He had just defeated Johnson in a spirited contest for their party's presidential nomination.) Johnson's southern background helped secure their victory that fall.

After the assassination of President Kennedy three years later, Johnson sought to create a so-called Great Society to commemorate the slain leader. Using skills from his years as a powerful U.S. senator, Johnson influenced Congress to pass sweeping laws. Among other things, this legislation secured fair voting rights for Blacks and other minorities, funded education programs, battled poverty and crime, encouraged

Johnson was famous for giving "the treatment" (left)—intense verbal and physical communication—to anyone whose support he needed. "You really felt as if a St. Bernard had licked your face for an hour, had pawed you all over," explained one recipient. Johnson worked two shifts a day while president. He slept a few hours at night and took a break to nap in his pajamas during the day.

> "Let this session of Congress be known as the session which did more for civil rights than the last hundred sessions combined."
>
> Lyndon B. Johnson, State of the Union address, January 8, 1964

fair housing practices, strengthened access to health care, aided environmental cleanup and conservation, and established federal programs such as the Public Broadcasting Service. No president has ever been more successful at ushering legislation through Congress.

Johnson won outright election to the presidency in the midst of this burst of legislation. Voters agreed to go "All the Way With LBJ" in 1964. He truly was Landslide Lyndon by then, earning 16 million more votes than his opponent. This edge gave him 61 percent of the popular vote.

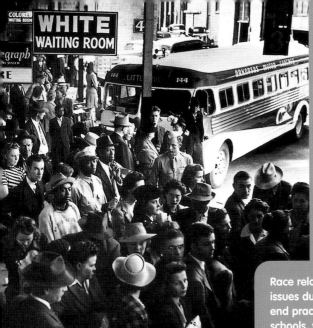

Johnson appointed the first African American to the Supreme Court in 1967—Thurgood Marshall. The president's commitment to civil rights led many southern whites to abandon the Democratic Party.

Race relations and civil rights were dominant issues during Johnson's presidency. He sought to end practices of discrimination that remained in schools, waiting rooms, and other public areas (left) by signing legislation to protect human rights regardless of race (above).

The Johnsons enjoyed the beauty of the Hill Country (left) in their native Texas. During their years together in the White House, Lady Bird promoted legislation to limit unsightly billboards along highways, and she encouraged better landscaping of public areas in the nation's capital and elsewhere. Later she promoted the study and cultivation of wildflowers around the country.

Sticking with the Cold War instincts of earlier presidents, Johnson insisted that the Vietnam War had to be won to prevent the spread of communism throughout Southeast Asia. He secretly sent more and more aid to anticommunist South Vietnam until, by the end of his presidency, more than half a million U.S. soldiers were on duty there.

The Vietnam War undercut Johnson's domestic triumphs. Before his administration was over, the United States had dropped more tons of bombs over the divided countries of North and South Vietnam than it had used in Europe during all of World War II. Yet, despite these efforts, North Vietnamese communists were more committed than ever in the fight to reunite North with South. Widespread opposition developed to the war among U.S. citizens, particularly as the growing level of their nation's involvement became fully known.

Public protests about the Vietnam War forced Johnson to abandon thoughts of running for reelection in 1968. Instead, he pledged to seek peace between the North and South Vietnamese. His efforts were unsuccessful; the two sides had difficulty even agreeing what shape to make their negotiating table.

In 1969 Johnson retired with Lady Bird to the LBJ Ranch near Johnson City, Texas. He wrote his memoirs, managed his farm, and regretted the bitter end of his presidency. Johnson had had a severe heart attack years earlier while a U.S. senator; he suffered two more during his retirement. The last one proved fatal. After lying in state at the U.S. Capitol, President Johnson's body was buried at his family ranch. In the decades following her husband's death, Lady Bird Johnson worked tirelessly for her favorite causes. She died in 2007 at the age of 94.

RICHARD NIXON
37TH PRESIDENT OF THE UNITED STATES 1969–1974

Richard Milhous Nixon was forced to resign from office after the public learned how he had encouraged the use of illegal activity to support his bid for reelection. He is the only U.S. president who resigned from the job. All others completed their terms or died in office. The importance of Nixon's official accomplishments in office are diminished by his serious abuses of presidential power.

Throughout his long political career, Nixon made much of his humble origins. He grew up in Southern California, where his family struggled against poverty and ill health. Two of his four brothers had died by the time he was 20. Nixon paid for his education at nearby Whittier College by working long hours as manager of the vegetable section in his father's grocery store. Later he graduated from Duke University Law School in North Carolina and opened a law practice back home. He met his future wife, Thelma "Pat" Ryan, when they acted together in a local play. He served as a noncombat naval officer in the Pacific during World War II.

Nixon, who served in the U.S. Navy during World War II, contributed to a growing public mistrust of government during his presidency. The more often he used his trademark phrase, "Let me make one thing perfectly clear," the less sure citizens became that they were hearing the truth. This "credibility gap" had begun after World War II as the public realized government actions did not always match government claims.

Vice President Richard Nixon and family (from left, Julie, Tricia, and Pat) with their dog Checkers in 1953.

Nixon won seats in the U.S. House in 1946 and the U.S. Senate in 1950. By then, people were calling him Tricky Dick because of the dirty tricks (including illegal campaign funding and sensational character attacks) he used to get elected. He won notice for his part in Senator Joseph McCarthy's "Red Scare" search for communists. Then Nixon became Dwight D. Eisenhower's vice president. He lost the 1960 presidential race to John F. Kennedy and the 1962 California governor's race before being elected president in 1968.

In the White House at last, Nixon was eager to mark his place in history. At home he tried to improve welfare, protect the environment, and reduce crime. He fought

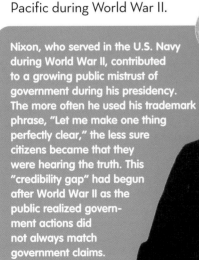

NICKNAME
Tricky Dick

BORN
Jan. 9, 1913, in Yorba Linda, CA

POLITICAL PARTY
Republican

CHIEF OPPONENTS
1st term: Hubert Horatio Humphrey, Democrat (1911–1978), and George Corley Wallace, American Independent (1919–1998); 2nd term: George Stanley McGovern, Democrat (1922–2012)

TERM OF OFFICE
Jan. 20, 1969–Aug. 9, 1974

AGE AT INAUGURATION
56 years old

NUMBER OF TERMS
two (cut short by resignation)

VICE PRESIDENTS
1st term & 2nd term (partial): Spiro Theodore Agnew (1918–1996); 2nd term (balance): Gerald (Jerry) R. Ford (1913–2006)

FIRST LADY
Thelma Catherine (Pat) Ryan Nixon (1912–1993), wife (married June 21, 1940)

CHILDREN
Patricia, Julie

GEOGRAPHIC SCENE
50 states

DIED
April 22, 1994, in New York, NY

AGE AT DEATH
81 years old

SELECTED LANDMARKS
Nixon Presidential Library and Museum (includes birthplace and grave), Yorba Linda, CA

Nixon spoke with U.S. astronauts in space after their successful landing on the moon on July 20, 1969.

Nixon toured the country with enthusiasm whether he was campaigning or appearing as president. Nixon appeared on 55 covers of *Time* magazine, more than anyone else in history. During his administration the nation's voting age was lowered from 21 to 18 by constitutional amendment.

In 1972 Nixon became the first sitting U.S. president to visit China. Nixon helped reduce hostilities between the two nations by meeting with communist leaders and visiting landmarks like the Great Wall (with his wife, Pat). Three months later he met with communist leaders in the Soviet Union.

double-digit inflation caused by large military budgets and shortages in oil and gas. He often ignored or stretched laws that met with his disapproval (from those that regulated wiretapping procedures to those that funded Native American education programs). Federal courts often overruled him.

Abroad, Nixon improved relations between the United States and the communist nations of China and the Soviet Union. He made celebrated trips to each country, and he signed new agreements limiting the spread of nuclear weapons. Although Nixon entered the White House with a pledge to end the Vietnam War, the task proved difficult. Even as he brought more troops home, fighting spread to nearby countries. North Vietnam took control of South Vietnam in 1975, two years after the nations made "peace" and U.S. troops had withdrawn. Many Americans were bitter about the war's costs: 58,000 U.S. lives and $110 billion since America joined the effort in 1956.

Nixon expanded on his use of "dirty tricks" while president. He and other staff members broke laws in their efforts to discover embarrassing information about his rivals and enemies (a list of more than 40,000 names). They hired people to commit burglaries and tap phones in their search for "dirt." They silenced their helpers with "hush money," spent federal campaign funds improperly, made illegal use of government records, and filed false income tax reports.

In 1972 Nixon's associates hired men to burglarize Democratic Party offices at the Watergate building in Washington, D.C. (They hoped to gain insider information there that would help Nixon be reelected later that year.) The Watergate scandal that ended Nixon's presidency began after the burglars were caught. The investigation of the break-in did not progress quickly enough, though, to prevent Nixon's landslide reelection in 1972.

For more than two years, Nixon and others tried to hide their involvement in the crime. They denied that Nixon was involved in planning the caper or its cover-up. Newspaper reporters and members of Congress led increasingly intense investigations into possible crimes. Eventually the Supreme Court forced Nixon to release secret tape recordings he had made of his White House conversations. The tapes confirmed that Nixon had lied about his innocence in planning illegal activities and covering them up.

> "Those who hate you don't win unless you hate them. And then you destroy yourself."
>
> Richard Nixon, parting speech, August 9, 1974

On August 9, 1974, Nixon resigned from office. Otherwise he faced the likelihood of impeachment by the House of Representatives and removal from office through a trial in the U.S. Senate. More than 20 other people, including top White House staff members, a former attorney general, and a former secretary of commerce, were found guilty of crimes, fined, and/or sent to jail.

Nixon had two vice presidents. His first, Spiro Agnew, resigned amid his own scandal in 1973. The recently ratified 25th Amendment required Nixon to fill the vacant post. The man he appointed, Gerald R. Ford, later succeeded him as president.

One of Ford's first acts was to pardon his predecessor, a gesture that sparked controversy because it protected Nixon from further prosecution. Even so the former leader was permanently disgraced, and historians have consistently judged his presidency harshly. Classified documents from his administration continue to be made public, allowing scholars to further evaluate his reputation and legacy.

Pat Nixon earned her nickname for being born near St. Patrick's Day. As first lady she traveled widely and promoted volunteer work. She is shown here with daughters Julie (far left) and Tricia.

Nixon announced his plans to resign from office during a televised address on August 8, 1974 (below).

Scandals resulting from the bungled 1972 burglary of Democratic Party offices in the Watergate building (left) eventually led to calls for Nixon's removal from office (above). In 1952 Nixon preserved his spot as vice president on Dwight D. Eisenhower's ticket by denying, during a televised speech, his illegal use of campaign funds. His remarks became known as the "Checkers speech" because he admitted that the family dog, Checkers, had been a political gift.

Raymond Kinstler

GERALD R. FORD
38TH PRESIDENT OF THE UNITED STATES 1974–1977

Gerald Rudolph Ford is the only person to serve as president and vice president without being elected to either office. Following provisions of the newly ratified 25th Amendment, President Richard Nixon appointed Ford to fill a vice presidential vacancy. Ford assumed the presidency after Nixon resigned to avoid impeachment. President Ford worked to restore the confidence of citizens in the leadership of the nation.

Ford came to the presidency after serving 25 years as one of Michigan's representatives to Congress. A native of Nebraska, he was a graduate of the University of Michigan and Yale University Law School. During World War II, he earned 10 battle stars for combat duty in the Navy. Gerald "Jerry" Ford married Elizabeth "Betty" Bloomer Warren, a former professional dancer, in 1948.

Ford, who joined Congress in 1949, became vice president in 1973. He was appointed to the post by then President Nixon after Vice President Spiro T. Agnew was forced by scandals to resign from office. When the scandal-plagued Nixon himself resigned in disgrace some eight months later, Ford became president. "This is an hour of history that troubles our minds and hurts our hearts," Ford noted. Yet he praised the soundness of the nation for its successful transfer of power from Nixon to himself. "Our Constitution works; our great Republic is a government of laws and not of men. Here the people rule," he said.

With words like these and with honest behavior, the new president

Gerald R. Ford rejected offers to play professional football after college and went to law school instead. Years later, Lyndon B. Johnson joked that Ford had "played football too long without a helmet." Ford replied by showing up at a public event with an old helmet that no longer fit. "Heads tend to swell in Washington," he joked.

began restoring citizen trust in the government. His efforts to resolve other challenges—such as double-digit inflation, high unemployment, and economic recession—were less successful. Ford drew criticism, too, for granting Nixon a full pardon for crimes committed while president. In a close contest in 1976, Ford lost his chance to gain outright election. He lived to see five others hold the office of president.

NICKNAME
Jerry

BORN
July 14, 1913, in Omaha, NE

POLITICAL PARTY
Republican

CHIEF OPPONENT
none; succeeded Richard Nixon

TERM OF OFFICE
Aug. 9, 1974–Jan. 20, 1977

AGE AT INAUGURATION
61 years old

NUMBER OF TERMS
one (partial)

VICE PRESIDENT
Nelson Aldrich Rockefeller (1908–1979)

FIRST LADY
Elizabeth (Betty) Bloomer Warren Ford (1918–2011), wife (married Oct. 15, 1948)

CHILDREN
Michael, John, Steven, Susan

GEOGRAPHIC SCENE
50 states

DIED
Dec. 26, 2006

AGE AT DEATH
93 years old

SELECTED LANDMARKS
Omaha, NE (birthplace); Gerald R. Ford Library, Ann Arbor, MI; Gerald R. Ford Museum (and grave), Grand Rapids, MI

Public distrust of the presidency carried over from Nixon's term in office to Ford's.

173

THE ELECTORAL COLLEGE
GATEKEEPER OF THE PRESIDENCY

I n most countries, presidential elections are straight-forward affairs. Eligible voters mark their preferences on a ballot, and victors are determined based on the tabulated results.

Citizens of the United States participate in a more complex, two-part system. The first one, the popular vote, is the tally of all ballots cast by registered voters as part of Election Day. These votes are used to determine who participates in the second step of the system, the Electoral College. The U.S. Constitution entrusts these electors with the ultimate responsibility for selecting the country's president and vice president.

The quantity of each state's electors is equivalent to its total number of members of Congress. The District of Columbia has electoral votes, too, even though it lacks full representation in Congress. U.S. territories are represented indirectly. The country's first Electoral College had 69 members. Today it has more than 500. At least one more

ELECTORAL VOTES BY STATE

The makeup of the Electoral College is determined every 10 years by the U.S. census. The 2010 census allocated 538 votes between the states and the nation's capital (see map). It guided presidential elections through 2020. The 2020 head count will determine the number and distribution of electoral votes for the 2024 and 2028 elections.

After the contested election of 2000 (above, protests at the Supreme Court), people began an effort to reduce the Electoral College to a ceremonial body. So far more than a dozen state legislatures have joined the National Popular Vote effort. If a majority of electors become governed by this system, their votes must match the national popular vote results.

than half of the total number of electors must support a candidate for that person to win.

The Founding Fathers established the Electoral College to ensure that the president and vice president would be selected by an elite group of learned and well-qualified individuals, fairly distributed among the states. At the time, few people had the right to vote, and members of the Electoral College were either appointed by governors or selected by state legislatures. The earliest members of the Electoral College voted independently, based on their individual judgments.

States began to let citizens select their electors in the 1820s after more people gained the right to vote. This system continues today. The choices voters make for president are linked to unnamed individuals who stand ready to serve as electors. All but two states practice a "winner-take-all" formula to determine which electors advance to the Electoral College. When a candidate wins a majority of a state's popular votes, that candidate's electors join the group. The District of Columbia uses the same allocation system. Maine and Nebraska choose their electors based on the popular vote outcomes in each state's congressional districts.

Members of the Electoral College vote during separately held state meetings on an appointed day in December, and their votes are tabulated in front of a joint session of Congress in early January. If controversies arise when votes are tallied, Congress is empowered to

intervene. Otherwise the selection process for president and vice president is complete.

Thus every presidential election has two sets of results, the popular vote and the Electoral College vote. In most cases, the winner of the popular vote is victorious in the Electoral College as well. However, five of the nation's presidential elections have brought victory to candidates who failed to win the popular vote.

Three of these elections occurred during the 19th century. Inconclusive voting by the Electoral College in 1824 prompted the House of Representatives to award the presidency to John Quincy Adams. Rutherford B. Hayes became president following the election of 1876 when disputes over the selection of electors forced Congress to refer the decision to a special commission. In 1888 Benjamin Harrison defeated Grover Cleveland without dispute in the Electoral College yet failed to win a majority of popular votes.

The long absence of further discrepancies between popular and electoral voting led many to view the Electoral College as a largely ceremonial body. Then, unexpectedly, two of the first five elections of the 21st century resulted in Electoral College victories without majority support in the popular vote. In each case Republicans triumphed over Democrats, first in 2000 with the victory of George W. Bush and then in 2016 with Donald Trump's win. These outcomes have pushed campaigns to concentrate on the Electoral College race.

JIMMY CARTER
39TH PRESIDENT OF THE UNITED STATES **1977–1981**

James Earl Carter, Jr., was the first person elected president from the Deep South since Zachary Taylor in 1848. Economic troubles at home combined with other challenges from abroad (including American citizens being taken hostage in Iran) cost him his bid for a second term of office. Carter returned to the world stage after his presidency ended, serving as an advocate for international peace. In 2002 he became the third U.S. president to earn a Nobel Peace Prize.

Carter liked his nickname, Jimmy, so much that he was sworn in as president by that name. As a child growing up in Georgia, Carter had been known by another nickname, too: Hot, short for Hot Shot. Carter helped with chores on his father's sizable peanut farm, attended schools segregated by race, and played with children both Black and white. He graduated 59th out of the 820 students in his class at the U.S. Naval Academy

The Carters on their wedding day

at Annapolis. He married the best friend of one of his sisters and took up a career in the U.S. Navy.

After his father's sudden death in 1953, Carter left the Navy and his post as a nuclear submarine engineer to manage the family farm. Later he served in the Georgia Senate. As governor of the state

NICKNAME
Jimmy

BORN
Oct. 1, 1924, in Plains, GA

POLITICAL PARTY
Democratic

CHIEF OPPONENT
President Gerald R. Ford, Republican (1913–2006)

TERM OF OFFICE
Jan. 20, 1977–Jan. 20, 1981

AGE AT INAUGURATION
52 years old

NUMBER OF TERMS
one

VICE PRESIDENT
Walter Frederick (Fritz) Mondale (1928–present)

FIRST LADY
Rosalynn Smith Carter (1927–present), wife (married July 7, 1946)

CHILDREN
John, James, Donnel, Amy

GEOGRAPHIC SCENE
50 states

SELECTED LANDMARKS
Plains Nursing Center, Inc., Plains, GA (birthplace); Jimmy Carter National Historic Site, Plains, GA; the Carter Center and the Jimmy Carter Library, Atlanta, GA (includes a museum)

Jimmy Carter (left, meeting with his Cabinet) was nicknamed Jimmy Cardigan after he wore a sweater instead of a suit when he addressed the nation during a televised fireside chat in 1977. Carter dispensed with other formal precedents, too. Bands stopped playing "Hail to the Chief" for his public entrances. He sent his daughter, Amy, to public schools. Sometimes he even carried his own suitcase and stayed at private homes when he traveled.

Carter broke with precedent during his Inaugural Parade in 1977. Instead of riding in a motorcade, he walked from the U.S. Capitol toward the White House with his daughter, Amy; his wife, Rosalynn; and other family members. As first lady, Rosalynn sat in on Cabinet meetings, represented the nation abroad, and spoke out in favor of mental health care.

The risks of generating nuclear energy became apparent during the Carter presidency after a serious accident occurred in 1979 at the Three Mile Island nuclear power plant near Harrisburg, Pennsylvania (left). Carter encouraged scientists to develop new forms of energy using such renewable resources as the sun and the wind.

during the early 1970s Carter criticized racial discrimination, the practice of favoring whites over Blacks and other races. Carter entered the presidential contest of 1976 almost completely unknown to the rest of the country. His tireless campaigning won him the Democratic Party nomination and, in what became a tight race, the presidency.

Carter was elected in part because voters liked the fact that he was an outsider—someone who was not part of national politics and the recent Watergate scandal. Being an outsider turned into a drawback after Carter became president. Because he ignored the political strategies of Congress, legislators on Capitol Hill regularly refused to pass his bills. The economy did not cooperate either. Years of extravagant government spending and a new wave of energy shortages sent prices higher than ever. Citizens were literally stranded at empty gas pumps in their search for fuel.

Although these issues proved troublesome to solve, Carter took other significant actions. He pardoned citizens who had illegally avoided fighting in the Vietnam War, appointed people from diverse backgrounds to key posts, reduced the rules that governed national

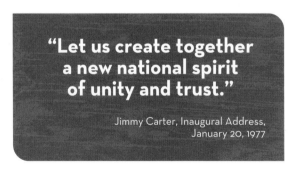

"Let us create together a new national spirit of unity and trust."

Jimmy Carter, Inaugural Address,
January 20, 1977

transportation systems, increased protection of the environment, and promoted research into alternative forms of energy. He also established a Department of Energy and a separate Department of Education.

Carter emphasized respect for human rights in his relations with other nations. He withheld U.S. foreign aid from countries with unjust governments. Carter arranged for Panama to assume control of the canal that the United States had built through its territory decades earlier. He expanded relations with China. He tried to further limit the spread of nuclear weapons. He organized international protests, including a controversial boycott of the 1980 Summer Olympics in Moscow, after the Soviet Union invaded nearby Afghanistan.

Carter's greatest foreign policy challenge began in 1979 when anti-American rebels stormed the U.S. Embassy in Tehran, Iran, and seized 52 hostages. All efforts to free the Americans failed during his tenure, including an attempted military rescue. Only after he left office were the captives released.

Carter helped negotiate important treaties between Egyptian president Anwar Sadat (above, left) and Israel's Prime Minister Menachem Begin (above, right) in 1978. Their Camp David Accords were reached with Carter's help at the presidential retreat in Maryland. These agreements renewed hopes for peace in the Middle East, a region plagued by wars and terrorism.

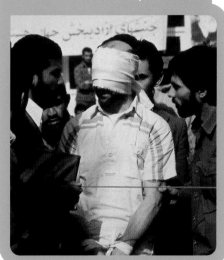

The most difficult challenge Carter faced in his presidency was the Iranian hostage crisis. Fifty-two Americans were held prisoner by Iranian militants for 444 days (below). They were finally set free just after Carter left office in January 1981.

Carter, who was only 56 years old at the end of his presidency, went on to distinguish himself in the decades that followed as a global peacemaker and monitor of democratic elections. His public service after leaving office earned him the Nobel Peace Prize (right) in 2002 at age 78.

As president, Carter's popularity ranged from very high to very low. It shifted depending on the state of the economy, the status of the hostage crisis, and his success at restoring confidence in government. He lost his reelection bid by a wide margin.

Just 56 years old, Carter began what would become the longest presidential retirement in U.S. history. He used that time to write more than 30 books, many of them best sellers. His greatest focus, however, became the Carter Center, which he founded in Atlanta, Georgia, with his wife, Rosalynn, soon after his presidency ended.

Working through the center, Carter helped negotiate peace agreements between nations, collaborated on efforts to verify that countries have fair elections, and directed efforts to improve health in developing lands. These and his other efforts to increase world peace earned him the Nobel Peace Prize in 2002. Only three other presidents—Theodore Roosevelt, Woodrow Wilson, and Barack Obama—have been so honored. Carter's prize was the only one of the four to recognize postpresidential achievements.

RONALD REAGAN
40TH PRESIDENT OF THE UNITED STATES **1981–1989**

No one older had ever become president when the 69-year-old Ronald Wilson Reagan took office. Yet this former Hollywood actor and governor of California brought a youthful optimism to his work. The "Great Communicator" strengthened support for the Republican Party and filled federal courts with conservative judges. He helped force the end of the Cold War through record spending on national defense, but his policies created financial challenges for future presidents.

Reagan ended his presidential career near the end of the 20th century, having been born during a simpler era when the century was just beginning. He grew up in small towns in northern Illinois, particularly Dixon. His family called him Dutch, short for "fat little Dutchman." He enjoyed playing sports and was a popular actor at the public schools he attended and at Eureka College in Eureka, Illinois.

After graduation he worked as a radio sports announcer in the Midwest. In 1937 Reagan moved to Hollywood. He made 53 movies and hosted two television shows during the next three decades. Even his World War II service involved making training films for the armed forces. Reagan "lived" so many lives through

Nancy Davis met her future husband, Ronald Reagan, when both of them were acting in Hollywood. They married three years later (above). She appeared in a total of 11 films. As first lady she encouraged children to "Just Say No" to illegal drugs.

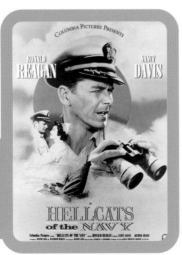

Ronald Reagan and his second wife, Nancy Davis, appeared together in the 1957 World War II drama *Hellcats of the Navy.*

the parts he played in movies that sometimes he recalled combat scenes from his films with the conviction of someone who had actually lived through the experiences. Reagan married twice; both of his wives had been Hollywood actresses. He was the first president who had a marriage end in divorce.

Reagan's experiences as a union labor leader in Hollywood, public speaker, and political volunteer helped interest him in running for office. Although he had grown up loyal to the Democratic Party, he began supporting

NICKNAME
Dutch

BORN
Feb. 6, 1911, in Tampico, IL

POLITICAL PARTY
Republican

CHIEF OPPONENTS
1st term: President Jimmy Carter, Democrat (1924–present), and John Bayard Anderson, Independent (1922–2017); 2nd term: Walter Frederick (Fritz) Mondale, Democrat (1928–present)

TERM OF OFFICE
Jan. 20, 1981–Jan. 20, 1989

AGE AT INAUGURATION
69 years old

NUMBER OF TERMS
two

VICE PRESIDENT
George H. W. Bush (1924–2018)

FIRST LADY
Nancy Davis Reagan (1921–2016), second wife (married March 4, 1952)

OTHER MARRIAGES
Jane Wyman (1914–2007), married 1940, divorced 1949

CHILDREN
Born to Jane Wyman (first wife): Maureen, Michael; born to Nancy Reagan (second wife): Patricia, Ronald

GEOGRAPHIC SCENE
50 states

DIED
June 5, 2004, in Los Angeles, CA

AGE AT DEATH
93 years old

SELECTED LANDMARKS
Tampico, IL (birthplace); Dixon, IL (boyhood home); Ronald Reagan Presidential Library and Center for Public Affairs (and grave), Simi Valley, CA

The Reagan Administration drew criticism because of the Iran-contra scandal: secret foreign policy dealings by high-level government officials, including Lt. Col. Oliver North (right), that contradicted official policy.

Reagan fired 13,000 air traffic controllers in 1981 when they went out on strike. His action led others to challenge the power of unionized workers, too.

Republicans during the Eisenhower era. He officially joined the Republican Party in 1962. In 1966 Californians elected him to the first of two terms as governor. Reagan sought his party's presidential nomination twice (in 1968 and 1976) before earning it in 1980. Citizens voted "yes" to elect Reagan as president because they generally answered "no" to his query about their lives during the Carter presidency: "Are you better off than you were four years ago?" He was reelected four years later.

In an effort to improve the economy, Reagan cut taxes, reduced federal spending in some areas, and increased government spending on defense by $1.5 trillion over seven years. He proposed the first trillion-dollar federal budget. His economic program came to be known as Reaganomics or supply-side economics. It suggested that if the wealthy received economic benefits such as tax cuts, a portion of this windfall would "trickle down" to less affluent citizens. The concept remained popular with Republicans for decades despite limited evidence of success.

American embassy workers held hostage after Iranians stormed their compound in 1979 gained their freedom on the first day of Reagan's presidency. Jimmy Carter's team had negotiated the release, but credit often falls to Reagan because of the timing.

A lone gunman attempted to assassinate Reagan in Washington, D.C., a few months after he took office. Prompt emergency care saved his life. During his recovery he joked to hospital staffers, "If I had had this much attention in Hollywood, I'd have stayed there."

During his presidency, Reagan had the opportunity to place three justices on the U.S. Supreme Court, including Sandra Day O'Connor, its first female member (below, being sworn in on September 25, 1981). Reagan appointed new judges to half of the nation's federal court seats, too, allowing him to embed elements of his own judicial philosophy in the courts throughout the land.

Reagan's plan of increased spending on national defense put a strain on the U.S. economy and added to the national debt. His program was even tougher on the Soviet Union. America's old Cold War foe simply could not afford to keep up in the military arms race anymore. Mikhail Gorbachev (above, right), a more moderate Soviet leader, sought to reduce Cold War tensions through his glasnost initiative. In 1987 Reagan and Gorbachev signed an agreement to reduce stockpiles of nuclear missiles for the first time.

Although inflation and unemployment eventually improved during his administration, new problems developed. The collapse of the savings and loan industry, sizable annual budget deficits, and a growing national debt became costly concerns for future presidents.

A series of scandals unfolded during the Reagan Administration. The greatest one, the Iran-contra scandal, involved illegal sales of arms to the Middle Eastern nation of Iran. Profits from the sales were secretly diverted to support rebel forces in Nicaragua, a country in Central America. Upper-level administrators encouraged the activity. Other charges of illegal behavior forced the resignations of President Reagan's secretary of labor, his attorney general, and senior staff members at the Environmental Protection Agency, the Central Intelligence Agency, the Defense Department, and the Department of Housing and Urban Development.

Reagan remained popular despite the scandals and criticisms of his presidency. Some credited this success to his Hollywood

Reagan's death in 2004 brought the nation its first presidential state funeral in more than 20 years. At one point during the weeklong series of events, his casket was moved by horse-drawn caisson to the U.S. Capitol for public viewing. When Nancy Reagan died in 2016, she was laid to rest beside her husband on the grounds of his presidential library in California.

looks and his skill as the Great Communicator. Others called him the "Teflon President" because, just like the nonstick pan surface, nothing bad ever "stuck" to his image.

Reagan was 77 years old when he retired with his wife, Nancy, to Los Angeles. In 1994 he was diagnosed with Alzheimer's, a devastating memory loss disease. He led an increasingly secluded life for the next 10 years. His death in 2004 prompted tributes on both coasts. After lying in state at the U.S. Capitol and being honored by a state funeral, his body was flown home to California for a sunset burial.

> **"What I'd really like to do is go down in history as the President who made Americans believe in themselves again."**
>
> Ronald Reagan, 1981

PATHWAYS FOR A NEW MILLENNIUM

1989–PRESENT

The thawing of the Cold War sparked an era of shifting global alliances for the new millennium. Regional wars erupted and acts of terrorism increased within borders and beyond. People, trade goods, and even disease became more mobile on a planet where information instantaneously circles the globe. Rising income inequality, economic uncertainty, and the climate crisis have placed additional pressures on countries during debates over how to balance their self-interests within an increasingly interdependent world.

1992
The North American Free Trade Agreement (NAFTA) enhanced the flow of goods between the U.S., Canada, and Mexico. A 2020 update sought to reduce the related loss of American jobs.

2001
On September 11 members of the al Qaeda terror network crashed hijacked jets into the World Trade Center in New York City and other targets. The towers were destroyed and more than 2,700 people died.

2004
Online social media use soared after the launch of Facebook by Mark Zuckerberg and fellow students from Harvard University. By 2012 the platform had more than one billion global users.

2008
Irresponsible investment strategies triggered a collapse of the U.S. housing market. The global financial hardships that followed were severe but did not match the Great Depression.

For all the changes in the world, some things stay constant: The White House remains home base for the nation's presidents.

2012
After the federal government started using drones to patrol U.S. borders (above) and conduct military missions, local governments and businesses began imagining peaceful uses for the unmanned aircraft.

2018
Students nationwide united to fight school gun violence after 17 were shot in Parkland, Florida. Thousands rallied on March 24 in the nation's capital (above, left, Parkland survivor Emma González).

2019
What began as an individual protest about the climate crisis by Swedish student activist Greta Thunberg (above, with her famous school strike sign), turned into a worldwide youth movement.

2020
The spillover of the novel coronavirus from wild animals to humans set off the global COVID-19 pandemic. It disrupted health, travel, commerce, education, recreation, and financial security worldwide.

185

GEORGE H. W. BUSH
41ST PRESIDENT OF THE UNITED STATES 1989–1993

George Herbert Walker Bush presided over his party's continuing shift toward conservative ideas, but his own beliefs were more moderate than those of Republican successors. American forces took part in two military actions during his presidency; at the same time the Soviet Union collapsed. A sagging economy undercut Bush's wartime popularity and spoiled his reelection bid. Later, his eldest son became president.

Bush brought years of varied government service and a distinguished background with him to the White House. The son of a wealthy banker turned U.S. senator, he attended elite private schools. Bush enlisted in the military after high school as the Navy's youngest pilot and went on to earn a Distinguished Flying Cross. He was the last veteran of World War II to become president.

George H. W. Bush played baseball for Yale University. He was named after a grandfather, George Herbert Walker, who was known as Pop. Bush was called Little Pop or Poppy into adulthood.

After the war, Bush graduated with honors from Yale University. He worked in the oil business in Texas for 18 years before seeking his first public office. He lost a 1964 U.S. Senate bid, but he gained a seat in the U.S. House of Representatives two years later. After two terms he made a second unsuccessful run for the Senate. Over the next 10 years, he was appointed by Republican presidents Richard Nixon and Gerald R. Ford to a series of prominent posts: U.S. ambassador to the United Nations, chairman of the Republican National Committee, top U.S. diplomat in China, and director of the Central Intelligence Agency.

Bush married Barbara Pierce while on leave from World War II service. The couple had met two years before during an earlier shore leave. Both claim to have fallen in love at first sight.

NICKNAMES
Poppy, 41

BORN
June 12, 1924, in Milton, MA

POLITICAL PARTY
Republican

CHIEF OPPONENT
Michael Stanley Dukakis, Democrat (1933–present)

TERM OF OFFICE
Jan. 20, 1989–Jan. 20, 1993

AGE AT INAUGURATION
64 years old

NUMBER OF TERMS
one

VICE PRESIDENT
James Danforth (Dan) Quayle III (1947–present)

FIRST LADY
Barbara Pierce Bush (1925–2018), wife (married Jan. 6, 1945)

CHILDREN
George, Robin (died young), John (Jeb), Neil, Marvin, Dorothy

GEOGRAPHIC SCENE
50 states

DIED
November 30, 2018, in Houston, TX

AGE AT DEATH
94 years old

SELECTED LANDMARKS
George Bush Presidential Library (and grave), Texas A&M University, College Station, TX

As first lady, Barbara Bush promoted literacy and other education programs. Entertainers were among those attending the third national literacy awards she hosted at the White House (above). The color of Barbara Bush's hair turned to a distinctive silver at an unexpectedly early age following the death of their three-year-old daughter to leukemia.

American soldiers wore gas masks and special clothing when they invaded Iraq in early 1991. Their protective gear was designed as defense against poisonous chemical weapons.

In 1989 the *Exxon Valdez* oil tanker ran aground off Alaska. The accident resulted in one of the largest oil spills in the nation's history. Almost 11 million gallons of oil polluted more than 1,000 miles of shoreline and killed hundreds of thousands of birds and other animals. The disaster destroyed the local fishing industry despite an extensive and costly cleanup effort.

Bush eyed the vice presidency in 1968 and 1974, and he sought the Republican presidential nomination in 1980. Instead, he earned eight years of experience as Ronald Reagan's vice president before gaining the presidency himself in the election of 1988.

Bush inherited from Reagan a national and world scene that was in transition. Most notable was the rapid transformation of the Soviet Union from a Cold War superpower into a splintered collection of former communist states. First Poland, then East Germany, Czechoslovakia, Hungary, Yugoslavia, Bulgaria, Albania, and, finally, the Soviet Union itself, rejected the communist form of government. The Soviet Union dissolved, and Russia emerged as its most powerful descendant. Most of the momentum for these changes came from within the region itself, but the Bush Administration supported these moves toward democracy. The only remaining strongholds of communism by the end of the Bush presidency were China, Cuba, Laos, North Korea, and Vietnam.

In 1989 Bush ordered U.S. troops to invade Panama. Their mission was to seize Manuel Noriega, the country's military leader, and bring him to the United States so he could stand trial on charges of drug trafficking. He was captured four days later. (Eventually he was tried, convicted, and imprisoned for his illegal activity.) The invasion caused significant property damage, left 500 Panamanians dead, and cost the lives of 23 Americans.

Thirteen months later American soldiers were fighting again. Iraq's 1990 invasion of neighboring Kuwait, a tiny oil-rich nation on the Persian Gulf, provoked

Bush and his four sons in 1970 (from left to right: Neil, John (Jeb), George W., and Marvin). Two sons tried to follow their father to the White House. George W., the eldest, succeeded in 2000 while serving as governor of Texas. His younger brother Jeb, a former Florida governor, failed to win the 2016 Republican Party presidential nomination.

President Bush, in his role as commander in chief, reviewed a ceremonial guard in 1989.

Four years after his presidency, Bush made his first parachute jump since World War II (right). He repeated the feat in 2014 at age 90.

worldwide outrage. The United States led an international fight in the region several months later that liberated Kuwait and severely damaged Iraq's military defenses. Iraq's leader, Saddam Hussein, remained in command of his nation, but other governments agreed to enforce sanctions, or restrictions, on Iraq until the nation could prove it no longer possessed weapons of mass destruction. The war, which lasted only a few months, cost more than $60 billion, a sum that many nations helped pay. The United States lost 148 lives during the war. As many as 100,000 Iraqis died, most of them civilians.

These international events often overshadowed domestic policy during the Bush Administration. Nonetheless, the president worked to

rescue the bankrupt savings and loan industry, fought rising unemployment, signed a new Clean Air Act, and agreed to legislation that promoted equal rights of access for the disabled. Enormous budget deficits continued to swell the national debt. They forced Bush to break his 1988 campaign promise—"Read my lips: No new taxes."

This change and a worsening economy cost him his reelection bid in the three-way race of 1992. It was the worst incumbent defeat since 1912.

The Bushes enjoyed one of the longest marriages in presidential history—73 years. After their son George became president, the similarly named men were sometimes referenced by the numbers of their administrations, 41 and 43.

> "Out of these troubled times ... a new world order can emerge: a new era, freer from the threat of terror, stronger in the pursuit of justice, and more secure in the quest for peace."
>
> George H. W. Bush, September 12, 1990

IN THE PRESIDENT'S SHADOW
SECURITY, THE MEDIA, AND PRESIDENTIAL PERKS

Today's presidents may share the same residence as their predecessors, but their work and lifestyles are vastly different. The first presidents handled much of their own paperwork, for example. They met freely with citizens who dropped by the White House, too. As the nation and its government grew in size, so did the complexity of the job for its presidents.

Now presidents travel by jet and limousine, not horse and buggy. The size of their staffs has grown from a handful to hundreds. The cost of running the White House has kept a parallel pace. The risks and realities of presidential assassinations have tightened the presidents' freedom of movement. Gone are the days when John Quincy Adams could walk alone from the White House to the Potomac River and swim there in the nude.

Presidential planes date to the era of Franklin D. Roosevelt. Travel by jet began with Dwight D. Eisenhower.

Now dozens of Secret Service agents take turns guarding the president and family members around the clock. Other staff members help manage the president's busy calendar, assist with speechwriting, and advise the president on everything from foreign policy to party politics.

As a result, today's presidents are more isolated than ever before from ordinary life. William Henry Harrison once strolled beyond the White House gates to do a little grocery shopping. Ulysses S. Grant took off by himself on speeding buggy rides. But no president sets foot beyond the grounds of the White House today just on a whim or all alone.

However, even as the lives of presidents have

Secret Service agents began guarding the life of the U.S. president following the assassination of William McKinley in 1901.

Secret Service agents protect the presidential limousine (right, Donald Trump's Inaugural Parade, 2017) and safeguard other movements by the president and family members. Whether the Chief Executive wants to buy a gift, browse through a bookstore, or go for a jog, Secret Service agents ensure that the outing is safe and sound.

Presents may escape White House routines by visiting the nearby Camp David presidential retreat in Maryland (left, Barack Obama joins the 2011 pool party for his youngest daughter's birthday), but members of the news media are never far away (below, with Obama in the White House press briefing room).

Technically the term Air Force One refers to the aircraft currently in use by the president, but it's commonly considered the name for the president's jet. The presidential helicopter (right) is called Marine One.

become more controlled, their activities have grown in national visibility. Expanding media coverage by newspapers, radio, television, social media, and the internet ensures that the public knows more than ever about what a president says and does. All major news outlets assign one or more people to cover the president's activities. There can be as many as 2,000 or more members of the presidential press corps.

This many reporters could not possibly follow every single move of the president. Instead, small groups of them—a few dozen or so at a time—take turns with the work. They are called the press pool because they pool, or collect, their reports, then share them with everyone in the press corps.

One representative of each day's press pool writes an eyewitness summary of the day's events. These reports are filled with colorful details so that other reporters will be able to visualize and write vivid news accounts. Additional members of the pool make still photos, video footage, and audio recordings to share with the press corps. The reports

of the press pool form the basis for the hundreds of news stories seen by the public.

Today's presidents balance the demands and scrutiny of their jobs with many impressive perks, or benefits. For starters, they receive an annual salary of $400,000. (George Washington earned $25,000 a year.) They have free housing at the White House as well as at the presidential retreat of Camp David, in nearby Maryland.

These homes offer many luxuries that cushion the impact of their isolation. Presidents may enjoy swimming, bowling, horseback riding, skeet shooting, and woodland walks without ever leaving home. They can screen movies in a private theater and read the latest books in a private library, too.

When it's time to travel, presidents may choose between a fleet of limousines, a jet known as Air Force One, a helicopter, even an armored motor coach nicknamed Ground Force One. Yet at the end of the day, they tread the same stairs to bed as have all the presidents since John Adams.

BILL CLINTON
42ND PRESIDENT OF THE UNITED STATES 1993–2001

William Jefferson Clinton brought the Democratic Party its first two-term presidency since the era of Franklin D. Roosevelt. Clinton earned respect internationally for his leadership and work for world peace. At home he balanced the federal budget for the first time in decades and reduced the national debt. These professional successes were undercut by bitter partisan political fighting over real and alleged scandals. Impeached by the House of Representatives on charges of misconduct, Clinton was tried and acquitted by the U.S. Senate.

William "Bill" Clinton was the first U.S. president born after World War II. He grew up in Hot Springs, Arkansas, where he did well in school. As a youth, Clinton joined the Boy Scouts, sang in the church choir, and raced to complete crossword puzzles. Later he graduated from Georgetown University in Washington,

Bill Clinton's 1963 handshake with President John F. Kennedy helped cement his childhood ambition to be president. Clinton was known until age 16 by the birth name he shared with his natural father, William Jefferson Blythe, who died before Bill was born. Later, he adopted his stepfather's last name.

D.C., and studied as a prestigious Rhodes Scholar at England's Oxford University before turning his attention to law. He met his future wife, Hillary Rodham, while the two of them were law students at Yale University.

NICKNAME
Comeback Kid

BORN
Aug. 19, 1946, in Hope, AR

POLITICAL PARTY
Democratic

CHIEF OPPONENTS
1st term: President George H. W. Bush, Republican (1924–2018), and Henry Ross Perot, Independent (1930–2019); 2nd term: Robert Joseph Dole, Republican (1923–present), and Henry Ross Perot, Reform (1930–2019)

TERM OF OFFICE
Jan. 20, 1993–Jan. 20, 2001

AGE AT INAUGURATION
46 years old

NUMBER OF TERMS
two

VICE PRESIDENT
Albert (Al) Arnold Gore, Jr. (1948–present)

FIRST LADY
Hillary Diane Rodham Clinton (1947–present), wife (married Oct. 11, 1975)

CHILDREN
Chelsea

GEOGRAPHIC SCENE
50 states

SELECTED LANDMARKS
William J. Clinton Presidential Library and Museum, Little Rock, AR; home, Fayetteville, AR

During his youth, Clinton played the saxophone in a jazz trio called the Three Blind Mice; sunglasses completed the musicians' attire. During presidential campaigns he performed twice on nationally televised talk shows. Clinton jammed with other musicians at a White House jazz festival (left).

With Russian leader Boris Yeltsin, Clinton worked to reduce arms and improve international relations.

Throughout his presidency, Clinton (center) tried to foster peaceful relations. In meetings with Israeli and Palestinian leaders, he sought to improve understanding between people of different religions.

During the last six years of President Clinton's administration, Kenneth Starr (center) led a series of investigations into possible illegal behavior by the president and his associates. These proceedings became ensnared in bitter partisan, or political party, disputes. Republicans accused Democrats of hiding the truth, while Democrats accused Republicans of trying to undermine the Clinton presidency with false charges.

After graduating, Clinton taught law at the University of Arkansas and took up politics. By 1978, at age 32, he had become the nation's youngest governor. Although unseated in the next election, Clinton became known as the Comeback Kid after he regained his post as governor of Arkansas in 1982. He went on to be reelected three times. As a presidential candidate in 1992, Clinton portrayed himself as a moderate Democrat, one who understood the perspective of a majority of Americans. Clinton and his vice presidential nominee, Tennessee senator Albert "Al" Gore, became the youngest national ticket ever elected; they were the first all-southern ticket since the Jackson Administration of 1828. The two men were reelected four years later. Clinton went on to become one of only five presidents in the century to complete two terms of office.

As president, Clinton (helped by a booming economy) began balancing the federal budget for the first time in four decades. He created free trade between the United States, Canada, and Mexico with the North American Free Trade Agreement (NAFTA), and he normalized U.S. trade relations with China. As his presidency progressed, Clinton worked to improve relations with Russia and promoted peace and human rights in such places as Northern Ireland, the Middle East, Haiti, Bosnia, and Kosovo.

Clinton lived up to his image as the Comeback Kid during a presidency that was challenged by party politics, international instability, and personal scandal. In 1994 Republicans captured control of Congress for the first time in 40 years. Clinton struggled to focus attention on the nation's business as partisan lawmakers scrutinized his administrative and personal choices. He battled with members of Congress over how to manage the budget, taxes, health care, and trade while he labored to define the role of the United States as a peacemaker in a post–Cold War world.

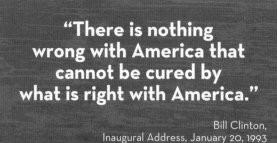

"There is nothing wrong with America that cannot be cured by what is right with America."

Bill Clinton,
Inaugural Address, January 20, 1993

194

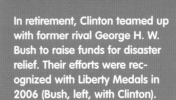

In retirement, Clinton teamed up with former rival George H. W. Bush to raise funds for disaster relief. Their efforts were recognized with Liberty Medals in 2006 (Bush, left, with Clinton).

The former president campaigned on behalf of his wife's two presidential bids (above, in 2008).

In 1998 Kenneth Starr, an independent prosecutor, accused Clinton of breaking laws to conceal a romantic affair he had had with a White House intern. With Republicans in control of Congress, the House considered Starr's charges and, for only the second time in history, approved articles of impeachment against a president. Clinton stood accused of lying under oath and obstructing justice. After the Senate examined the charges and the question of whether to remove him from office, a majority of senators voted for his acquittal on February 12, 1999, including all Democrats and a few Republicans.

Clinton remained a popular president, and his policies helped broaden his party's base. Many past supporters of the Republican Party, particularly a wide variety of voters from middle-income levels, began to favor the Democratic Party instead. But the taint of personal scandal surrounding Clinton by the end of his administration limited how effectively he could support the presidential bid of his own vice president in 2000.

Hillary Clinton assumed a broader range of responsibilities as first lady than any other president's wife since Eleanor Roosevelt. She headed an effort to reform the nation's health care system, traveled extensively on behalf of her husband, promoted the rights of women and children, and wrote a weekly newspaper column. She protected the privacy of her teenage daughter and supported her husband during the scandals that plagued his presidency. While still serving as first lady, she won election to the U.S. Senate, the first presidential spouse to seek and win elected office. Her subsequent service as secretary of state for Barack Obama was bookended by two unsuccessful attempts to become the nation's first female president.

President Clinton shared the spotlight during the celebration of his Inauguration in 1997 with his wife, Hillary, and the couple's teenage daughter, Chelsea. During his second term, opinion polls showed that most citizens supported Clinton's performance as president even though the House of Representatives was recommending that he be removed from office.

GEORGE W. BUSH
43RD PRESIDENT OF THE UNITED STATES **2001–2009**

George Walker Bush became the first president in more than a century to reach the White House without carrying the nation's popular vote. Only John Quincy Adams, Rutherford B. Hayes, and Benjamin Harrison did likewise. Unlike these predecessors, Bush was reelected four years later. Not since the Adamses had a father and his son each become president of the United States.

A family tradition of elected public service began while George W. Bush was growing up in Texas. He was six years old when his grandfather became a U.S. senator. Twelve years later his father made his first bid for elected office. As a child Bush played baseball and dreamed of becoming a star athlete. However, he shadowed his father's rise to political life by attending the same private high school as his father and the same college, Yale University. He graduated in 1968 with a major in history. Bush served in the Air Force National Guard during the Vietnam

Two future presidents were captured in this family snapshot from 1955. George H. W. Bush, the nation's 41st Chief Executive, holds his young son, George W. Bush, who became the nation's 43rd president in 2001. Wife, mother, and future first lady Barbara Bush looks on. During the son's presidency, the similar names of the men were distinguished by the use of the son's middle initial, W., a letter that had become his nickname as well. Some people referred to them by the numbers of their administrations: 41 and 43, or Bush 41 and Bush 43.

War and learned how to fly an F-102 fighter jet. Later he earned a degree from Harvard Business School.

In 1975 Bush returned to Texas and, like his father, found work in the oil industry. He married Laura Welch in 1977, just three months after they had met. The next year Bush made an unsuccessful bid for election to the U.S. House of Representatives. Later he became an owner and manager of the Texas Rangers baseball team. He was elected governor of Texas in 1994 and was reelected four years later.

During the Vietnam War, George W. Bush joined the Air Force National Guard (left). Questions over unfinished service requirements became a campaign issue during his presidential bids.

NICKNAMES
Dubya (W.), 43

BORN
July 6, 1946, in New Haven, CT

POLITICAL PARTY
Republican

CHIEF OPPONENTS
1st term: Albert (Al) Arnold Gore, Jr., Democrat (1948-present), and Ralph Nader, Green (1934-present); 2nd term: John Kerry, Democrat (1943-present), and Ralph Nader, Independent (1934-present)

TERM OF OFFICE
Jan. 20, 2001-Jan. 20, 2009

AGE AT INAUGURATION
54 years old

NUMBER OF TERMS
two

VICE PRESIDENT
Richard (Dick) Bruce Cheney (1941-present)

FIRST LADY
Laura Welch Bush (1946-present), wife (married November 5, 1977)

CHILDREN
Jenna, Barbara (twins)

GEOGRAPHIC SCENE
50 states

SELECTED LANDMARKS
George W. Bush Presidential Center (includes presidential library and museum), Dallas, TX

The terrorist attacks of September 11, 2001, became a rallying point for the Bush Administration. His leadership drew praise at first, particularly after his dramatic visit to ground zero (right) at the site of the collapsed twin towers from New York's World Trade Center. Public opinion grew more divided later on.

Bush is the only president to be the father of twins (above, with his newborn daughters in 1981).

First Lady Laura Bush and her husband (above, visiting with children in Romania) emphasized their commitment to faith and family during his presidency.

The first lady (above, walking in a wintry White House Rose Garden) promoted literacy during her husband's administration.

Bush campaigned for the presidency in 2000 against the sitting vice president, Al Gore. Their contest ended with a hotly disputed debate over how to count election returns in Florida, a state governed by Bush's younger brother John (Jeb). Intervention by the U.S. Supreme Court some five weeks after Election Day secured the presidency for Bush even though he trailed Gore nationally by more than 500,000 popular votes. Bush took office with only a narrow margin of Republican control in the House of Representatives and the first ever equally divided U.S. Senate.

The Bush presidency featured many advisers who had served during his father's administration, including Vice President Richard Cheney, who was secretary of defense for the elder Bush and a staff member during the Nixon and Ford presidencies. Within months of taking office, Bush was forced to shift his focus from domestic concerns to international affairs. The catastrophic series of terrorist attacks on September 11, 2001, prompted the president and his advisers to renew security concerns about the Middle East that had arisen during the administration of Bush's father.

The president's popularity soared as the United States invaded Afghanistan in an effort to capture those responsible for the attacks, including al Qaeda terrorist leader Osama bin Laden. The decision to attack Iraq in 2003 as a protective necessity met with general support at first, but public opinion splintered after reasons justifying the action proved unfounded. Critics also charged that missteps during the invasion helped to prolong the conflict and destabilize other countries in the Middle East. The administration's wartime use of torture further undermined support.

Bush sought to strengthen national defense through the creation of a Department of Homeland Security. The lack of further attacks on the U.S. and a willingness among many Americans to "stay the course" helped Bush secure reelection in 2004 against his Democratic Party challenger, Senator John Kerry.

Bush faced challenges both foreign and domestic during his two-term presidency, most notably with international conflicts (right, meeting with advisers in advance of the Iraq war).

The Bush Administration was criticized for its halting response to the impact of Hurricane Katrina on the Gulf Coast in 2005 (left, Bush visits the region).

During his retirement years, the president is collaborating with First Lady Laura Bush on outreach through the Bush Institute, a component of the presidential center in Dallas that includes his presidential library, which opened in 2013. Areas of focus include public education, democracy, global health, and economic prosperity.

During his second term the death of the Supreme Court's Chief Justice and the resignation of another justice enabled Bush to place two judicial conservatives on the nation's highest court. These appointments allowed him to preserve the conservative tilt of the Court.

As president, Bush succeeded at implementing some domestic policy initiatives, such as his No Child Left Behind program for education reform, but he failed to win congressional support for others, including Social Security modification and the reform of immigration laws. Charges of improper influence over the government by political appointees, especially those in the White House and Justice Department, led to a series of high-profile investigations.

Growing public dissatisfaction with the Bush Administration helped fuel midterm election victories in 2006 that put Democrats in control of the House and Senate for the first time in 14 years. Bush, determined to succeed in his so-called War on Terror,

sent additional U.S. troops to Iraq in 2007. His decision was heavily criticized but did help stabilize the country. Peace never fully returned, however, making it impossible for the American military to leave the region even during subsequent presidencies.

The administration's consistent support for tax cuts earned praise among conservatives, but it was later seen as contributing to a dramatic rise in budget shortfalls. U.S. involvement in wars in Iraq and Afghanistan became costly, too. The growing unbalance in the federal budget, sluggish economic growth, soaring oil prices, and reduced government control of the housing and banking systems contributed to a worldwide economic crisis near the end of Bush's presidency. This hardship persisted during the administration of his successor. It came to be known as the Great Recession.

> "America was targeted for attack because we're the brightest beacon for freedom and opportunity in the world. And no one will keep that light from shining."
>
> George W. Bush,
> September 11, 2001

BARACK OBAMA
44TH PRESIDENT OF THE UNITED STATES 2009–2017

Barack Hussein Obama became the nation's first African-American president in the historic election of 2008. Worldwide economic uncertainties, continuing wars, and random acts of terrorism presented him with dizzying challenges in a nation increasingly polarized by political disagreements. His eight-year administration included the implementation of landmark legislation on health care.

The son of a white mother born in Kansas and a Black father from Africa, Obama spent most of his childhood in Hawaii, where he was raised by his mother and her parents. He was the first president born there and the first born to a nation of 50 states. He attended Occidental College in Los Angeles, completed his undergraduate degree at New York's Columbia University, and, after working with disadvantaged residents of Chicago, earned a law degree from Harvard. After winning election to the Illinois State Senate in 1996, Obama advanced to the U.S. Senate and the White House. He was the first senator since John F. Kennedy to become president and, in 2012, became the first Chief Executive since Ronald Reagan to win back-to-back elections with majority support.

Obama assumed office during an economic crisis that stirred memories of the Great Depression; many called it the Great Recession. Concerted action by the president, Congress, and the Federal Reserve

During his studies at Harvard Law School (above), Barack Obama became the first African American to head the prestigious *Harvard Law Review*. His father's enrollment at Harvard years earlier had separated him from his family when his son was only two. With the exception of a month-long visit when Obama was 10, the father and son never saw each other again. The future president spent four years of his childhood living in Asia when his mother, then divorced, married an Indonesian. Obama has a half sister from that union.

halted the nation's economic nosedive and ultimately fueled the longest streak of job creation in American history. Some regions and segments of the population rebounded better than others, though, and unease spread as an elite class of ultra-wealthy citizens prospered while others, especially minorities, did not. A divide widened in the political landscape, too, as the growth of the 24-hour news cycle, partisan cable channels, and social media fed more conflict than compromise. Although Democrats held nominal control of the House and Senate,

NICKNAME
Barry

BORN
August 4, 1961, in Honolulu, HI

POLITICAL PARTY
Democratic

CHIEF OPPONENTS
1st term: John McCain, Republican (1936–2018);
2nd term: Mitt Romney, Republican (1947–present)

TERM OF OFFICE
Jan. 20, 2009–Jan. 20, 2017

AGE AT INAUGURATION
47 years old

NUMBER OF TERMS
two

VICE PRESIDENT
Joseph (Joe) R. Biden, Jr. (1942–present)

FIRST LADY
Michelle Robinson Obama (1964–present), wife (married October 3, 1992)

CHILDREN
Malia, Sasha

GEOGRAPHIC SCENE
50 states

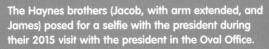

The Haynes brothers (Jacob, with arm extended, and James) posed for a selfie with the president during their 2015 visit with the president in the Oval Office.

On a dozen occasions, Obama ordered flags set to half-staff to commemorate victims of mass shootings, more frequently than any predecessor (below, consoling mourners after a 2015 shooting at a historically Black church in Charleston, South Carolina). Such attacks occurred almost once every three months during his administration. Legislative proposals aimed at curbing gun violence failed due to opposition from advocates for the Second Amendment right to bear arms.

To monitor the military mission that killed Osama bin Laden in 2011, Obama gathered in the White House Situation Room with his advisers, including Vice President Joe Biden (on sofa), and Hillary Clinton, his secretary of state (opposite Obama).

Republicans flexed their minority party muscle in ways that slowed, diminished, or defeated many of the Democratic president's efforts.

Nonetheless, there were legislative successes, including the repeal of the ban against gays serving in the military, greater regulation of the financial industry, increased fuel efficiency standards for vehicles, and enhanced support for the rights of women to equal pay for their work. Obama's signature achievement, the Affordable Care Act of 2010, passed without a single Republican vote. The program, which took effect in 2014, achieved a long-sought Democratic goal: guaranteed access to health care for all Americans. The law withstood multiple legal challenges as well as dozens of attempted repeals; it expanded health insurance coverage to more than 10 million citizens.

In 2010 a deeply conservative Tea Party movement gained influence in the Republican Party, pushing it further right in opposition to Obama. Its candidates helped Republicans gain control of the Senate that year and the House in 2015. Legislation ground to a virtual standstill, so political power shifted to other branches of government. Obama used the power of presidential executive orders to advance key elements of his policy agenda, from regulations for cleaner air, to a strengthening of worker rights, to a ban against torture during

First Lady Michelle Obama displayed a style, grace, and example of good works that influenced everything from fashion to health. Her Let's Move initiative emphasized the importance of childhood nutrition and fitness. She promoted the value of fresh foods by starting the White House Kitchen Garden (right) as a living laboratory and source of produce for family members, area residents, and state guests.

military interrogations, to the expansion of protected wilderness. In the judicial branch, liberals benefited from some Supreme Court decisions, but conservatives made gains, too, with rulings that created new avenues for funding political campaigns and made it easier to restrict voting rights.

Growing instability in the Middle East kept U.S. forces engaged in that region throughout Obama's presidency. Almost 7,000 American soldiers died in Iraq and Afghanistan during his tenure and his predecessor's, and more than 50,000 were wounded. Gains made fighting the al Qaeda terrorist network—most notably the death at American hands of its leader Osama bin Laden—were undercut by the development of a new terrorist threat, the so-called Islamic State, sometimes referred to as ISIS or ISIL. Obama, who in 2009 became the fourth U.S. president to earn a Nobel Peace Prize, overcame long-standing international animosities to end an embargo against Cuba that had stood since before his

Global instability sparked the largest international refugee crisis since World War II (above, refugees reach Greece after fleeing war-torn regions of the Middle East).

Critics condemned health care reform as Obamacare, creating a term the president and supporters soon embraced (advocates outside the Supreme Court in 2012).

The White House was lit with a symbolic rainbow when the Supreme Court issued its marriage equality ruling on June 26, 2015. The 5–4 decision eliminated all barriers to same-sex marriage nationwide in a hard-fought victory for members and allies of the LGBTQ community. The court's landmark ruling left conservative Americans shocked and dismayed.

excessive force by police officers against people of color, a Black Lives Matter movement emerged to demand change.

When two vacancies opened on the Supreme Court during his first two years of office, Obama replaced retiring male justices with women. His action placed the first person of Latino heritage on the high court and raised the number of female justices on the court to three, a record. The death of Justice Antonin Scalia, a conservative icon, early in the president's final year of office gave him an unexpected opportunity to reshape the court's judicial direction. Alarmed Republicans refused to consider Obama's moderate nominee, justifying their inaction by the fact that it was an election year. Although high court nominations had become complicated during previous election years, none had ever before failed to receive at least a hearing. The resulting vacancy became the longest in Supreme Court history.

By delaying, Republicans hoped to win back the White House and restore the court's conservative majority, a strategy that worked with the victory of Donald Trump. Trump's defeat of Obama's preferred successor, his former secretary of state Hillary Clinton, followed a long-standing pattern. Only once since World War II has a two-term president—Ronald Reagan—been succeeded by a member of the same party.

birth. His administration helped broker the first U.S. treaty with Iran since the presidency of Jimmy Carter, one that limited Iran's ability to develop nuclear weapons. Obama's team advanced global efforts to reduce climate change, too, culminating in Paris during 2015 with a bold international agreement for action.

Many had viewed Obama's historic election as a sign of growing unity between races in America, but instead it seemed to expose deeply buried divisions. The Republican Party's white male conservative leadership rebuffed the administration's attempts to find policy compromises. At the same time the rise of social media platforms and the development of cell phone cameras directed the nation's attention to long-standing issues of racial injustice. After personal videos repeatedly documented the use of

> "For as long as I live, I will never forget that in no other country on Earth is my story even possible."
>
> Barack Obama,
> March 18, 2008

DONALD TRUMP
45TH PRESIDENT OF THE UNITED STATES **2017–2021**

Donald John Trump chose to ignore two centuries of presidential norms and traditions while in office. This approach earned him almost equal measures of celebration and condemnation in an increasingly divided country. His actions and leadership served to widen the gulf between Americans who applauded his brash style of governance and those who regarded it as a threat to democracy itself. Trump's inconsistent leadership during 2020 in the face of a devastating global pandemic helped to erode his support and limit him to a single term in office.

Even Trump's background broke norms. He was the first Chief Executive without any experience in the military, elected office, or appointed government service. Instead he attracted support as a business executive with legendary dealmaking skills. Trump, the son of a successful New York City real estate developer, earned his high school diploma at the New York Military Academy. He then attended Fordham University before completing his education in business and finance at what is now known as the Wharton School of the University of Pennsylvania. He went on to invest in real estate, entertainment, and other ventures, amassing a global empire that made the Trump name synonymous with wealth and power.

During his 2016 presidential campaign, Trump promised to "Make America Great Again." He prevailed in a crowded Republican primary field that included John "Jeb" Bush, the son and brother of former presidents. The general election

Donald Trump's 2016 presidential bid built on his fame as a reality TV show host (on the set of *The Apprentice* in 2007). His first wife gave him a lasting nickname: The Donald.

contest was rocked by surprises, including evidence that the Russian government worked to sway the results in Trump's favor. His competitor was Hillary Clinton, a former first lady, U.S. senator, and cabinet secretary from the administration of Trump's predecessor, Barack Obama. Although Clinton surpassed Trump by nearly three million ballots in the popular vote, he prevailed in the Electoral College and gained the presidency.

When Trump took office at age 70, he was the oldest person ever to assume the post. He enjoyed the advantage of Republican majorities in both chambers of Congress and used this power to enact elements of his promised agenda. Key legislative initiatives

NICKNAME
The Donald

BORN
June 14, 1946, in Queens, NY

POLITICAL PARTY
Republican

CHIEF OPPONENT
Hillary Clinton, Democrat (1947–present)

TERM OF OFFICE
Jan. 20, 2017–Jan. 20, 2021

AGE AT INAUGURATION
70 years old

NUMBER OF TERMS
One

VICE PRESIDENT
Michael (Mike) R. Pence (1959–present)

FIRST LADY
Melania Knauss Trump (1970–present), third wife (married Jan. 22, 2005)

OTHER MARRIAGES
Ivana Zelníčková Winklmayr Trump (1949–present), married 1977, divorced 1992; Marla Maples (1963–present), married 1993, divorced 1999

CHILDREN
Born to Ivana Trump (first wife): Donald, Ivanka, Eric; born to Marla Maples (second wife): Tiffany; born to Melania Trump (third wife): Barron

GEOGRAPHIC SCENE
50 states

President Trump and First Lady Melania Trump are the most recent couple to raise a child in the White House. Their son, Barron (with his parents in 2019), was 10 years old when his father became president.

Supporters in 2016 chanted "Build that wall" at Trump campaign rallies because they shared his interest in restricting immigration along the nation's southern border. Although the president only added a limited amount of wall (left, a new section in Yuma, Arizona), his executive orders made it harder than it had been in decades to move to the U.S.

Trump (above, with phone) was the first president to announce changes in staffing and policy on social media. Previous administrations had generally shared such developments through the news media first. Trump's system allowed him greater control of the news cycle by letting him divert attention to particular stories.

> ## "From this moment on, it's going to be America First."
>
> Donald Trump,
> Inaugural Address, January 20, 2017

included a $1.5 trillion tax cut, the First Step Act for criminal sentencing and prison reform, increased military spending, and a new trade agreement between the U.S., Mexico, and Canada (USMCA). When Congress refused to allocate money for wall construction along the border with Mexico, Trump declared a national emergency and redirected U.S. defense funds for this purpose. Although Republicans had promised to repeal and replace the Affordable Care Act (nicknamed Obamacare), the signature health care program of the previous administration, they failed to muster the votes to do so. In frustration Trump followed President Obama's example and frequently set policy through executive and administrative action—often reversing the initiatives of his Democratic predecessor in the process.

President Trump promoted his protectionist "America First" outlook and withdrew the United States from international agreements related to climate, trade, nuclear proliferation, and global cooperation. He used executive orders to limit the entry of immigrants to the U.S., undermine Obamacare, boost fossil fuel production, roll back environmental protections, reduce other government regulations, and generally advance the goals of his conservative base. Trump further satisfied supporters by filling three Supreme Court vacancies and numerous other federal court seats with conservative appointees.

Although federal judges often overturned or curtailed Trump's executive actions, many initiatives prevailed.

As a candidate, Trump had gained notoriety—and political support—by making controversial statements at rallies or through social media. Many assumed he would adopt a more presidential tone after reaching the White House, but typically he did not. Trump's opponents were horrified, but his supporters appreciated his unusual and at times shocking leadership style. As a result, even disapproving fellow Republicans rarely criticized him for fear of angering the president's loyal base of voters.

Trump's administration revealed how the institution of the presidency largely relied on norms and traditions rather than constitutional directives and national laws. Unlike previous presidents, who had generally sought to unite the country after an election, Trump continued to favor his own voters. He refused to share his tax returns or divest himself from his vast family businesses, which made it hard for the public to know if he was personally enriching himself while in office. He asked family members to serve as official advisers and government representatives—a form of nepotism, or favoritism, that is frowned upon in democracies because it can lead to corruption. He ignored the advice of career officials in national and foreign policy when it disagreed with his

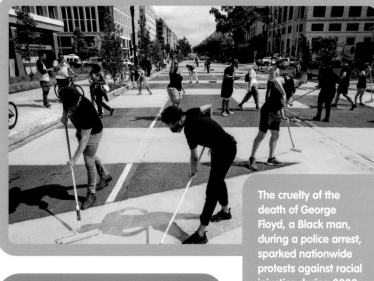

During a 2018 meeting in Helsinki, Finland (with Russian President Vladimir Putin, at right), Trump publicly accepted Putin's assurances that Russia had not meddled in the 2016 presidential election. Trump's embrace of Putin's word over those of U.S. intelligence officials—who had documented the interference—alarmed the president's critics. Many wondered if Trump was beholden to Putin through past business deals. The exchange even prompted rare words of criticism from the president's Republican allies in Congress.

The cruelty of the death of George Floyd, a Black man, during a police arrest, sparked nationwide protests against racial injustice during 2020. Americans of diverse ages, races, and backgrounds insisted that Black Lives Matter. In Washington, D.C., the mayor permitted advocates to paint the phrase in giant letters within sight of the White House.

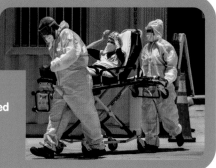

Whereas most countries mounted a national strategy to fight COVID-19, President Trump preferred a decentralized approach. The diverse plans of the various states made it harder to contain the virus (right, transporting a patient in Florida).

own instincts. He dismissed criticism by the press as "fake news," and misstated the truth to an unprecedented degree, making thousands of false statements.

Controversies from the 2016 election carried over into Trump's administration when independent prosecutor Robert Mueller investigated his campaign's ties to Russia. This work led to convictions for several Trump associates but left the president largely untarnished. Then Trump ignited new concerns after he seemed to seek reelection assistance from the president of Ukraine. Democrats, who had regained control of the House in 2019, voted to impeach him for abuse of power and obstructing Congress. When the Republican-led Senate considered the charges in early 2020, Democrats unanimously found Trump guilty. Mitt Romney, a Republican and former presidential nominee, became the only senator in presidential impeachment history to vote to convict a fellow party member when he supported the abuse of power charge. Total votes fell far short of the two-thirds majority required for removal from office.

This acquittal and the nation's strong economy gave Trump a solid case for reelection in early 2020, but the emergence of the COVID-19 virus upended those prospects. Despite unprecedented action by Congress,

the pandemic disrupted the financial health of the nation in ways that rivaled the Great Depression. More than 20 million people lost their jobs, with millions remaining unemployed for months. Millions became ill, too, including the president, and by Election Day more than 230,000 had died. The country was further roiled in 2020 after Trump objected to nationwide protests against racial injustice. Despite the fact that the actions were almost all peaceful, he accused protesters of promoting violence and urged Americans to stand on the side of "law and order."

Trump is the only president in the history of polling who failed to earn a majority of approval in public opinion surveys by the time of a reelection bid. Although he maintained a loyal core of supporters throughout his presidency, he was unable to achieve victory in 2020. Americans voted in such numbers that they surpassed all levels of presidential election participation since 1900. Former Obama vice president Joe Biden prevailed in the contest, winning both the Electoral College and the popular vote. Trump became one of only five presidents in a hundred years to lose a reelection bid. The others were Herbert Hoover, Gerald R. Ford, Jimmy Carter, and George H. W. Bush.

ELECTION 2020
CHOOSING A PRESIDENT DURING A PANDEMIC

Decades of campaign tradition and strategy became irrelevant during 2020 after the emergence of a foe more ferocious than any political opponent: COVID-19. The new, highly contagious virus triggered a global pandemic that transformed not just the style of the year's presidential race but the very issues that drove its results. Donald Trump, the Republican incumbent, had expected to secure his reelection based on the strong economy of his first three years in office. But restrictions necessary for combating COVID-19 turned this fiscal success into one of the nation's gravest financial nightmares. Because the health crisis made it risky for crowds to gather safely, traditional political campaign strategies were disrupted, too. These circumstances combined to make it challenging for Trump, who himself contracted the disease, to make a winning case for reelection.

The president faced a formidable political challenger in Joe Biden, a career politician who had served for two terms as Barack Obama's vice president. Biden represented a Democratic Party that was determined to limit Trump to a single term in office. More than two dozen candidates, including six women, had vied for the party's nomination in the most diverse group ever assembled for a presidential race. The field included Black, Asian, and Latino Americans, and the first prominent candidate to be openly gay. Biden acknowledged the importance of diversity by naming Kamala D. Harris his running mate. As the daughter of immigrants from India and Jamaica, she is the first woman of color ever chosen for the post. The pair campaigned on an increasingly progressive campaign platform, in contrast to the president's conservative one.

The 2020 race made history in other ways, too. Voters had never before been presented with presidential candidates of such advanced ages. Trump's 2016 victory had made him, at age 70, the oldest person to become president. Four years later, his opponent was poised to

In 2020 President Donald Trump sought a second term alongside his vice president, Mike Pence (far right, after accepting his renomination to the Republican ticket). The president (near right) rarely wore a protective face mask in public even though scientists recommended them. Pence and many supporters followed his example.

Millions of 2020 voters avoided polling-place exposure to COVID-19 by returning ballots via the U.S. mail or at designated drop boxes (left, a box in Connecticut).

U.S. senator Kamala D. Harris became only the third female nominee for vice president in major party history when she joined Joe Biden's ticket in August 2020 (shown demonstrating mask safety during the announcement). The pair pitched their Democratic Party campaign against President Donald Trump as a "Battle for the Soul of the Nation."

top that record by eight years. Neither faced the typical grueling pace of the campaign season, though, because COVID-19 so disrupted the usual practices and traditions. The ongoing risk of contagion made it advisable for campaigns to adjust travel plans, reconfigure summer nominating conventions, scale back rallies, and avoid handshakes and selfies. Even the traditional fall series of televised presidential debates had to be adjusted: One of the three events was canceled after the president was infected with the virus.

As a result the two campaigns relied more than ever on outreach through news interviews, social media, televised speeches, video promotions, mailings, and advertisements. Supporters followed the pattern of past elections and flooded both campaigns with contributions. Each side received billions of dollars in support.

The continuing threat of COVID-19 influenced when and how Americans chose to vote. For the first time ever, most people cast their ballots before Election Day. More than 100 million voted early—either in person, with mailed ballots, or by using drop boxes. Election officials embraced the trustworthiness of these options despite the president's unfounded claims that they were vulnerable to fraud. Trump encouraged his supporters to vote on Election Day, and most of them did. A majority of Democrats voted earlier.

These preferences were reflected in the vote tallies that emerged after polls closed on Tuesday, November 3. Results of same-day voting were evident within hours and showed Trump ahead. But, during the time-consuming work of counting the flood of early votes, the president's lead steadily shrank. On Saturday—four days after the election—Biden's lead widened so decisively that he was declared the Electoral College winner. In modern times, only two presidential election outcomes, in 1916 and 2000, have taken longer to determine. President Trump disputed the accuracy of the tallies in multiple states but failed to produce evidence supporting his claims.

In the popular vote, Biden set a record for the most presidential ballots ever received. He won a majority of all votes cast, something accomplished in only half of the previous eight presidential elections. In the 21st century, only his former boss, Barack Obama, earned a wider margin of victory in the popular vote.

Protests against racial injustice filled the election year after a series of deadly police encounters with Black Americans. Almost all demonstrations were peaceful, but the activism became politicized after a few events turned violent. President Trump promoted law enforcement while Joe Biden pushed for racial reconciliation. Activists (left) marched peacefully through the newly designated Black Lives Matter Plaza near the White House in June.

Concerns about the spread of COVID-19 forced Democrats and Republicans to reconfigure their summer nominating conventions, but the parties' approaches varied greatly. Democrats staged their finale in a parking lot (left) where spectators could safely distance themselves from one another in separate vehicles. The Republican convention concluded with a large crowd and few masks on the South Lawn of the White House (above). Previous presidents had believed it inappropriate—and even illegal—to use the People's House for reelection activities.

JOE BIDEN
46TH PRESIDENT OF THE UNITED STATES **2021–PRESENT**

Few presidents have entered the White House facing as many simultaneous challenges as the country's newest president, Joseph Robinette Biden, Jr. The lack of a shared vision for the nation's future rivaled what Abraham Lincoln encountered after his election in 1860. Debates about voting results recalled the controversies of Rutherford B. Hayes's election. The nation's economic hardships mirrored those that confronted Herbert Hoover and Franklin D. Roosevelt during the Great Depression. And hovering ever present was the added danger of the most serious global pandemic since the era of Woodrow Wilson.

His election made Joseph "Joe" Biden the nation's oldest president ever, at age 78. He was the only one born between the Great Depression and the end of World War II. Biden, a Democrat, was the eldest of four children in a Catholic family that had fallen on hard times. When he was in third grade, the Bidens moved from his hometown of Scranton, Pennsylvania, to Delaware, which became his lifelong home. Biden struggled to overcome his childhood stutter by reciting memorized speeches to his reflection and planning conversations in advance. He achieved greater recognition on the football field than in the classroom but went on to graduate from the University of Delaware and earn a law degree in New York State from Syracuse University.

Biden soon turned to politics and at age 29 became one of the youngest U.S. senators ever elected. Just days before his swearing in, his wife and year-old daughter were killed in an automobile

"Amtrak Joe" Biden earned his nickname for commuting by rail as a U.S. senator. He campaigned on trains, too (with family in 1987 during his first White House bid).

accident. The couple's two young sons were seriously injured. Biden took his Senate seat with reluctance but went on to serve 36 years. A respected bipartisan legislator, he gained both praise and criticism for his work in such areas as judicial appointments, criminal justice, and foreign affairs. During this time he remarried and with Jill Biden added a daughter to their family. Senator Biden made two unsuccessful attempts to become president before joining the ticket of Barack Obama in 2008. He is one of only nine vice presidents to serve two terms in that office and one of only six former vice presidents to win the presidency outright.

NICKNAME
Amtrak Joe

BORN
November 20, 1942, in Scranton, PA

POLITICAL PARTY
Democratic

CHIEF OPPONENT
President Donald Trump, Republican (1946–present)

TERM OF OFFICE
Jan. 20, 2021–present

AGE AT INAUGURATION
78 years old

NUMBER OF TERMS
one (ongoing)

VICE PRESIDENT
Kamala Devi Harris (1964–present)

FIRST LADY
Jill Jacobs Biden (1951–present), second wife (married June 17, 1977)

OTHER MARRIAGE
Neilia Hunter Biden (1942–1972), married August 27, 1966

CHILDREN
Born to Neilia Biden (first wife): Joseph ("Beau," deceased), Hunter, Naomi (deceased); born to Jill Biden (second wife): Ashley

GEOGRAPHIC SCENE
50 states

Biden, who served under the nation's first Black president, chose as his own deputy the first Black person and the first woman to hold that post, Kamala D. Harris (speaking at their victory celebration, November 7, 2020).

FORMER PRESIDENTS
EXPERIENCED ELDERS WITH A LASTING INFLUENCE

For U.S. presidents, it's only a matter of time before their job comes to an end. No matter how popular they may be or how much they relish their responsibilities, four or eight years after taking office, they're out of work.

Presidents have completed their administrations when they were as young as 50 (Theodore Roosevelt) and as old as 77 (Ronald Reagan). Some have enjoyed lengthy retirements. Jimmy Carter broke Herbert Hoover's record of 31 years in 2012. Other retirements are very brief, such as James K. Polk's (three months).

Usually the nation has at least one living former president at any given time, but on five occasions there have been none. Richard Nixon was president during the last such period. There have never been more than five former presidents alive at once.

Some former presidents have continued in public service after leaving the White House. John Quincy Adams and Andrew Johnson joined the U.S. Congress. William Howard Taft was appointed Chief Justice of the United States. Others, like Herbert Hoover and Jimmy Carter, have played less formal roles but have

assisted in government studies, peacemaking, or international humanitarian efforts. Carter earned a Nobel Peace Prize for his postpresidential work.

Other former presidents have kept busy by writing and speaking about their lives, by teaching, with travel, or by just having fun. George W. Bush took up portrait painting, for example. In recent decades former presidents have spent considerable time working with their presidential libraries, too.

In a show of respect, Chief Executives continue to be addressed as president even after they leave office. The earliest ones departed the White House with little more than this title. Not until 1958 did Congress begin

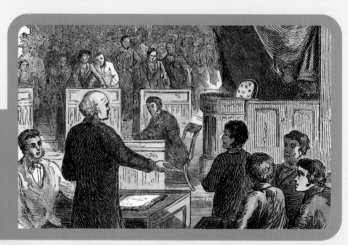

Two years after his presidential retirement, John Quincy Adams won election to the U.S. House of Representatives. He served there for 17 years (right) until his death near the House chamber at age 80.

Bill Clinton, like many former presidents, wrote his autobiography after leaving office.

William Howard Taft, who had always wanted to serve on the Supreme Court, earned that distinction (first row, center), eight years after his presidency by becoming Chief Justice.

appropriating money for presidential retirement funds. Harry S. Truman received the first such pension; it totaled $25,000 a year. Presidential widows were granted pensions of $10,000; later their sum was increased to $20,000.

Today presidents earn an annual retirement salary of about $200,000. In addition they receive office support, health care benefits, some paid travel expenses, free U.S. postage, and assistance with their presidential libraries. All former presidents are entitled to receive lifetime protection for themselves and their spouses by members of the Secret Service. Their children are similarly protected through age 15.

Although presidents have no formal role in the government after leaving the White House, they often remain influential figures. Sitting presidents may seek their advice and gather with them for important events, such as state funerals. By tradition, retiring presidents are encouraged to withdraw from the public stage when their terms conclude. That way the new Chief Executive can lead the nation without being undercut by commentary from old political rivals. When election season rolls around, past presidents frequently offer endorsements of support for new candidates for the office.

Former presidents often find that their popularity fluctuates with time. Even those who may not have been well regarded on leaving office can gain public support later on, as did Jimmy Carter, for example. Reputations continue to evolve and shift, even after the presidents' deaths.

The death of a former president starts off a period of national mourning and recognition. U.S. flags fly at half-staff for 30 days. Some presidents request simple burial services. Others prefer more elaborate events, such as state funerals in the nation's capital. Whether simple or complex, funeral plans are prepared after each president leaves office, then saved until the former leader's death.

"Now is the best time of all," Jimmy Carter once said about retirement. For over three decades he combined recreational pursuits—from fly-fishing to time with his grandchildren—with writing, teaching, and community service (at right, volunteering with his wife, Rosalynn, on a Habitat for Humanity construction site).

The death of a president brings together surviving peers. Four former presidents joined President George W. Bush (front row, far left) to mourn the passing of Ronald Reagan in 2004. Those in attendance with their wives were (second row, from left) George H. W. Bush, Jimmy Carter, Gerald R. Ford, and (front row, second from right) Bill Clinton.

Election Year	Number of Presidency	Name of President, Years of Office, and Chief Opponents	Name of Political Party	Name of Vice President	Percentage of Popular Vote	Electoral Vote
1789	1	George Washington, 1789–1797	Federalist	John Adams		69
		John Adams	Federalist			34
		Others				35
1792		George Washington, 1789–1797	Federalist	John Adams		132
		John Adams	Federalist			77
		George Clinton	Federalist			50
		Others				5
1796	2	John Adams, 1797–1801	Federalist	Thomas Jefferson		71
		Thomas Jefferson	Democratic-Republican			68
		Thomas Pinckney	Federalist			59
		Aaron Burr	Democratic-Republican			30
		Others				48
1800	3	Thomas Jefferson, 1801–1809	Democratic-Republican	Aaron Burr		73
		Aaron Burr	Democratic-Republican			73
		John Adams	Federalist			65
		Charles C. Pinckney	Federalist			64
		John Jay	Federalist			1
1804		Thomas Jefferson, 1801–1809	Democratic-Republican	George Clinton		162
		Charles C. Pinckney	Federalist			14
1808	4	James Madison, 1809–1817	Democratic-Republican	George Clinton		122
		Charles C. Pinckney	Federalist			47
		George Clinton	Democratic-Republican			6
1812		James Madison, 1809–1817	Democratic-Republican	Elbridge Gerry		128
		DeWitt Clinton	Federalist			89
1816	5	James Monroe, 1817–1825	Democratic-Republican	Daniel D. Tompkins		183
		Rufus King	Federalist			34
1820		James Monroe, 1817–1825	Democratic-Republican	Daniel D. Tompkins		231
		John Quincy Adams	Democratic-Republican			1
1824	6	John Quincy Adams, 1825–1829	Democratic-Republican	John C. Calhoun	30.5%	84
		Andrew Jackson	Democratic-Republican		43.1%	99
		William Crawford	Democratic-Republican		13.1%	41
		Henry Clay	Democratic-Republican		13.2%	37
1828	7	Andrew Jackson, 1829–1837	Democratic	John C. Calhoun	56.0%	178
		John Quincy Adams	National Republican		44.0%	83
1832		Andrew Jackson, 1829–1837	Democratic	Martin Van Buren	54.9%	219
		Henry Clay	National Republican		42.4%	49
		Others			2.6%	18
1836	8	Martin Van Buren, 1837–1841	Democratic	Richard M. Johnson	50.9%	170
		William Henry Harrison	Whig		36.6%	73
		Others			12.4%	51

Election Year	Number of Presidency	Name of President, Years of Office, and Chief Opponents	Name of Political Party	Name of Vice President	Percentage of Popular Vote	Electoral Vote
1840	9	William Henry Harrison, 1841	Whig	John Tyler	52.8%	234
		Martin Van Buren	Democratic		46.8%	60
		James G. Birney	Liberty		0.3%	0
	10	John Tyler, 1841–1845	Whig	None		
1844	11	James K. Polk, 1845–1849	Democratic	George M. Dallas	49.6%	170
		Henry Clay	Whig		48.1%	105
		James G. Birney	Liberty		2.3%	0
1848	12	Zachary Taylor, 1849–1850	Whig	Millard Fillmore	47.4%	163
		Lewis Cass	Democratic		42.5%	127
		Martin Van Buren	Free-Soil		10.1%	0
	13	Millard Fillmore, 1850–1853	Whig	None		
1852	14	Franklin Pierce, 1853–1857	Democratic	William R. D. King	50.9%	254
		Winfield Scott	Whig		44.1%	42
		John P. Hale	Free-Soil		5.0%	0
1856	15	James Buchanan, 1857–1861	Democratic	John C. Breckinridge	45.3%	174
		John C. Frémont	Republican		33.1%	114
		Millard Fillmore	Know-Nothing		21.6%	8
1860	16	Abraham Lincoln, 1861–1865	Republican	Hannibal Hamlin	39.8%	180
		Stephen A. Douglas	Democratic		29.5%	12
		John C. Breckinridge	Democratic		18.1%	72
		John Bell	Constitutional Union		12.6%	39
1864		Abraham Lincoln, 1861–1865	Republican	Andrew Johnson	55.0%	212
		George B. McClellan	Democratic		45.0%	21
	17	Andrew Johnson, 1865–1869	Democratic	None		
1868	18	Ulysses S. Grant, 1869–1877	Republican	Schuyler Colfax	52.7%	214
		Horatio Seymour	Democratic		47.3%	80
1872		Ulysses S. Grant, 1869–1877	Republican	Henry Wilson	55.6%	286
		Horace Greeley	Democratic		43.9%	0
1876	19	Rutherford B. Hayes, 1877–1881	Republican	William A. Wheeler	48.0%	185
		Samuel J. Tilden	Democratic		51.0%	184
1880	20	James A. Garfield, 1881	Republican	Chester A. Arthur	48.5%	214
		Winfield S. Hancock	Democratic		48.1%	155
		James B. Weaver	Greenback-Labor		3.4%	0
	21	Chester A. Arthur, 1881–1885	Republican	None		
1884	22	Grover Cleveland, 1885–1889	Democratic	Thomas A. Hendricks	48.5%	219
		James G. Blaine	Republican		48.2%	182
		Others			3.3%	0
1888	23	Benjamin Harrison, 1889–1893	Republican	Levi P. Morton	47.9%	233
		Grover Cleveland	Democratic		48.6%	168
		Others			3.5%	0
1892	24	Grover Cleveland, 1893–1897	Democratic	Adlai E. Stevenson	46.1%	277
		Benjamin Harrison	Republican		43.0%	145
		James Weaver	Populist		8.5%	22
		John Bidwell	Prohibition		2.2%	0
1896	25	William McKinley, 1897–1901	Republican	Garret A. Hobart	51.1%	271
		William J. Bryan	Democratic		47.7%	176

Election Year	Number of Presidency	Name of President, Years of Office, and Chief Opponents	Name of Political Party	Name of Vice President	Percentage of Popular Vote	Electoral Vote
1900		William McKinley, 1897–1901	Republican	Theodore Roosevelt	51.7%	292
		William J. Bryan	Democratic/Populist		45.5%	155
		John C. Woolley	Prohibition		1.5%	0
	26	Theodore Roosevelt, 1901–1909	Republican	None		
1904		Theodore Roosevelt, 1901–1909	Republican	Charles W. Fairbanks	56.4%	336
		Alton B. Parker	Democratic		37.6%	140
		Eugene V. Debs	Socialist		3.0%	0
		Silas C. Swallow	Prohibition		1.9%	0
1908	27	William Howard Taft, 1909–1913	Republican	James S. Sherman	51.6%	321
		William J. Bryan	Democratic		43.1%	162
		Eugene V. Debs	Socialist		2.8%	0
		Eugene W. Chafin	Prohibition		1.7%	0
1912	28	Woodrow Wilson, 1913–1921	Democratic	Thomas R. Marshall	41.9%	435
		Theodore Roosevelt	Progressive		27.4%	88
		William H. Taft	Republican		23.2%	8
		Eugene V. Debs	Socialist		6.0%	0
		Eugene W. Chafin	Prohibition		1.5%	0
1916		Woodrow Wilson, 1913–1921	Democratic	Thomas R. Marshall	49.4%	277
		Charles E. Hughes	Republican		46.2%	254
		Others			4.4%	0
1920	29	Warren G. Harding, 1921–1923	Republican	Calvin Coolidge	60.4%	
		James M. Cox	Democratic		34.2%	127
		Eugene V. Debs	Socialist		3.4%	0
		P. P. Christensen	Farmer-Labor		1.0%	0
	30	Calvin Coolidge, 1923–1929	Republican	None		
1924		Calvin Coolidge, 1923–1929	Republican	Charles G. Dawes	54.0%	382
		John W. Davis	Democratic		28.8%	136
		Robert M. La Follette	Progressive		16.6%	13
1928	31	Herbert Hoover, 1929–1933	Republican	Charles Curtis	58.2%	444
		Alfred E. Smith	Democratic		40.9%	87
1932	32	Franklin D. Roosevelt, 1933–1945	Democratic	John N. Garner	57.4%	472
		Herbert Hoover	Republican		39.7%	59
		Norman Thomas	Socialist		2.2%	0
1936		Franklin D. Roosevelt, 1933–1945	Democratic	John N. Garner	60.8%	523
		Alfred M. Landon	Republican		36.5%	8
		William Lemke	Union		1.9%	0
1940		Franklin D. Roosevelt, 1933–1945	Democratic	Henry A. Wallace	54.8%	449
		Wendell Willkie	Republican		44.8%	82
1944		Franklin D. Roosevelt, 1933–1945	Democratic	Harry S. Truman	53.5%	432
		Thomas E. Dewey	Republican		46.0%	99
	33	Harry S. Truman, 1945–1953	Democratic	None		
1948		Harry S. Truman, 1945–1953	Democratic	Alben W. Barkley	50%	303
		Thomas E. Dewey	Republican		49.9%	189
		J. Strom Thurmond	States' Rights		2.4%	39
		Henry A. Wallace	Progressive		2.4%	0
1952	34	Dwight D. Eisenhower, 1953–1961	Republican	Richard Nixon	55.1%	442
		Adlai E. Stevenson	Democratic		44.4%	89

Election Year	Number of Presidency	Name of President, Years of Office, and Chief Opponents	Name of Political Party	Name of Vice President	Percentage of Popular Vote	Electoral Vote
1956		Dwight D. Eisenhower, 1953–1961	Republican	Richard Nixon	57.6%	457
		Adlai E. Stevenson	Democratic		42.1%	73
1960	35	John F. Kennedy, 1961–1963	Democratic	Lyndon B. Johnson	49.9%	303
		Richard Nixon	Republican		49.6%	219
	36	Lyndon B. Johnson, 1963–1969	Democratic	None		
1964		Lyndon B. Johnson, 1963–1969	Democratic	Hubert H. Humphrey	61.1%	486
		Barry M. Goldwater	Republican		38.5%	52
1968	37	Richard Nixon, 1969–1974	Republican	Spiro T. Agnew	43.4%	301
		Hubert H. Humphrey	Democratic		42.7%	191
		George C. Wallace	American Independent		13.5%	46
1972		Richard Nixon, 1969–1974	Republican	Spiro T. Agnew	60.6%	520
				Gerald R. Ford		
		George S. McGovern	Democratic		37.5%	17
	38	Gerald R. Ford, 1974–1977	Republican	Nelson A. Rockefeller		
1976	39	Jimmy Carter, 1977–1981	Democratic	Walter F. Mondale	50.1%	297
		Gerald R. Ford	Republican		47.9%	240
1980	40	Ronald Reagan, 1981–1989	Republican	George H. W. Bush	50.9%	489
		Jimmy Carter	Democratic		41.2%	49
		John B. Anderson	Independent		7.9%	0
1984		Ronald Reagan, 1981–1989	Republican	George H. W. Bush	59.0%	525
		Walter F. Mondale	Democratic		41.0%	13
1988	41	George H. W. Bush, 1989–1993	Republican	James Danforth Quayle, III	53.4%	426
		Michael S. Dukakis	Democratic		45.6%	111
1992	42	Bill Clinton, 1993–2001	Democratic	Albert A. Gore, Jr.	43.0%	370
		George H. W. Bush	Republican		37.0%	168
		H. Ross Perot	Independent		19.0%	0
1996		Bill Clinton, 1993–2001	Democratic	Albert A. Gore, Jr.	49.0%	379
		Robert J. Dole	Republican		41.0%	159
		H. Ross Perot	Reform		8.0%	0
2000	43	George W. Bush, 2001–2009	Republican	Richard B. Cheney	48.0%	271
		Albert A. Gore, Jr.	Democratic		48.5%	266
		Ralph Nader	Green		2.7%	0
		Others			0.8%	0
		Abstained				1
2004		George W. Bush, 2001–2009	Republican	Richard B. Cheney	51.0%	274
		John Kerry	Democratic		48.0%	252
		Ralph Nader	Independent		1.0%	0
2008	44	Barack Obama, 2009–2017	Democratic	Joe Biden	52.5%	365
		John McCain	Republican		46.3%	173
2012		Barack Obama, 2009–2017	Democratic	Joe Biden	51.0%	332
		Mitt Romney	Republican		48.0%	206
2016	45	Donald Trump, 2017–2021	Republican	Michael R. Pence	46.1%	304
		Hillary Clinton	Democratic		48.2%	227
		Others			5.7%	7
2020*	46	Joe Biden, 2021–present	Democratic	Kamala D. Harris	50.8%	290
		Donald Trump	Republican		47.5%	214
		Others			1.7%	0

* Tallies reflect popular vote percentages as determined by the Associated Press when this book went to press. The 34 Electoral College votes from Alaska, Georgia, and North Carolina had not yet been awarded. Electoral College vote allocations are provisional until confirmed by electors in December.

FIND OUT MORE

BOOKS

Allen, Thomas B. *George Washington, Spymaster: How the Americans Outspied the British and Won the Revolutionary War.* Washington, D.C.: National Geographic, 2004, 2007 (paperback).

Bausum, Ann, *Denied, Detained, Deported: Stories from the Dark Side of American Immigration.* Washington, D.C.: National Geographic, 2009, 2019 (revised edition).

___. *Unraveling Freedom: The Battle for Democracy on the Home Front During World War I.* Washington, D.C.: National Geographic, 2010.

___. *With Courage and Cloth: Winning the Fight for a Woman's Right to Vote.* Washington, D.C.: National Geographic, 2004.

Blumenthal, Karen. *Hillary Rodham Clinton: A Woman Living History.* New York: Feiwel and Friends, 2016; Square Fish, 2017 (revised paperback edition).

Denenberg, Barry. *Lincoln Shot: A President's Life Remembered.* New York: Feiwel and Friends, 2008; Square Fish, 2011 (paperback).

DuMont, Brianna. *Weird But True Know-It-All: U.S. Presidents.* Washington, D.C.: National Geographic Kids, 2017.

Harness, Cheryl. *Abe Lincoln Goes to Washington, 1837–1865.* Washington, D.C.: National Geographic, 1997, 2008 (paperback).

___. *George Washington.* Washington, D.C.: National Geographic, 2000, 2006 (paperback).

___. *The Remarkable Rough-Riding Life of Theodore Roosevelt and the Rise of Empire America.* Washington, D.C.: National Geographic, 2007.

___. *The Revolutionary John Adams.* Washington, D.C.: National Geographic, 2003, 2006 (paperback).

___. *Thomas Jefferson.* Washington, D.C.: National Geographic, 2004, 2007 (paperback).

___. *Young Abe Lincoln: The Frontier Days, 1809–1837.* Washington, D.C.: National Geographic, 1996, 2008 (paperback).

Johnston, Robert D. *The Making of America: The History of the United States From 1492 to the Present.* Washington, D.C.: National Geographic, 2010.

Kerley, Barbara. Edwin Fotheringham, illustrator. *Eleanor Makes Her Mark.* New York: Scholastic Press, 2020.

McClafferty, Carla Killough. *Buried Lives: The Enslaved People of George Washington's Mount Vernon.* New York: Holiday House, 2018.

___. *The Many Faces of George Washington: Remaking a Presidential Icon.* Minneapolis, Minn.: Carolrhoda Books, 2011.

McGill, Erin. *If You Want a Friend in Washington: Wacky, Wild and Wonderful Presidential Pets.* New York: Schwartz & Wade, 2020.

Meacham, Jon. *Thomas Jefferson: President and Philosopher* (illustrated edition). New York: Crown Books for Young Readers, 2014; Yearling, 2016 (paperback).

Provensen, Alice. *The Buck Stops Here.* New York: Browndeer Press, Harcourt Brace, 1997; Viking Books for Young Readers, 2010 (anniversary edition).

Schanzer, Rosalyn. *George vs. George: The American Revolution as Seen From Both Sides.* Washington, D.C.: National Geographic, 2004, 2007 (paperback).

Swanson, James L. *"The President Has Been Shot!": The Assassination of John F. Kennedy.* New York: Scholastic Press, 2013.

___. *Chasing Lincoln's Killer.* New York: Scholastic Press, 2009.

St. George, Judith. *So You Want to Be President?* New York: Philomel, 2004 (revised edition).

Walker, Diana. *Public & Private: Twenty Years Photographing the Presidency.* Washington, D.C.: National Geographic, 2002.

VIDEOS AND TELEVISION PROGRAMS

Air Force One. National Geographic, 2005.

Inside the White House. National Geographic, 2003.

On Board Marine One. National Geographic, 2009.

The Presidents. American Experience (series), Public Broadcasting Service. pbs.org/wgbh/americanexperience/collections/presidents

U.S. Secret Service: On the Front Line. National Geographic, 2019.

WEBSITES

"Electoral College," National Archives and Records Administration archives.gov/electoral-college

"First Ladies," the White House whitehouse.gov/about-the-white-house/first-ladies

National Popular Vote nationalpopularvote.com

"The Presidency," Miller Center, University of Virginia millercenter.org/the-presidency

"Presidential Campaign Commercials, 1952–present," Museum of the Moving Image livingroomcandidate.org

"Presidential Libraries," National Archives and Records Administration archives.gov/presidential-libraries

"Presidential Speeches," Miller Center, University of Virginia millercenter.org/the-presidency/presidential-speeches

"Presidents," the White House whitehouse.gov/about-the-white-house/presidents

"Slavery in the President's Neighborhood," White House Historical Association whitehousehistory.org/spn/introduction

Smithsonian National Museum of American History americanhistory.si.edu

White House Historical Association whitehousehistory.org

PLACES TO VISIT

"The American Presidency," permanent exhibit, National Museum of American History, Smithsonian Institution, Washington, D.C.

The White House, Washington, D.C.

See also each president's fact box.

BIBLIOGRAPHY

Resources cited here formed the foundation of research during the creation of the first edition of *Our Country's Presidents* (2001). Subsequent editions have been published every four years. Each one is thoroughly reviewed and updated using additional resources such as government documents, the work of journalists, institutional internet sites, presidential biographies, and other scholarly studies. Information presented is current through the most recent presidential election.

Aikman, Lonnelle. *The Living White House.* Washington, D.C.: White House Historical Association and National Geographic Society, 1996 (10th edition).

___. *We, the People: The Story of the United States Capitol—Its Past and Its Promise.* Washington, D.C.: The United States Capitol Historical Society and National Geographic Society, 1991 (14th edition).

Boller, Paul F., Jr. *Presidential Anecdotes.* New York: Oxford University Press, 1981.

___. *Presidential Wives.* New York: Oxford University Press, 1988.

Brinkley, Alan and Davis Dyer, editors. *The Reader's Companion to the American Presidency.* Boston: Houghton Mifflin, 2004.

Caroli, Betty Boyd. *First Ladies.* New York: Oxford University Press, 1995 (expanded edition).

DeGregorio, William A. *The Complete Book of U.S. Presidents.* New York: Wings Books, Random House, 2005 (sixth edition, revised).

Freidel, Frank. *The Presidents of the United States of America.* Washington, D.C.: White House Historical Association and National Geographic Society, 1995 (14th edition).

Gibbs, Nancy and Michael Duffy. *The Presidents' Club: Inside the World's Most Exclusive Fraternity.* New York: Simon & Schuster, 2012.

Graff, Henry F., editor. *The Presidents: A Reference History.* New York: Charles Scribner's Sons, 1996 (second edition).

Hamilton, Alexander, James Madison, and John Jay. *The Federalist Papers.* New York: New American Library, 1961.

Kane, Joseph Nathan. *Facts About the Presidents: A Compilation of Biographical and Historical Information.* New York: H. W. Wilson Company, 2001 (seventh edition), with new co-authors: Janet Podell and Steven Anzovin.

Keyssar, Alexander. *The Right to Vote: The Contested History of Democracy in the United States.* New York: Basic Books, 2000.

Klapthor, Margaret Brown. *The First Ladies.* Washington, D.C.: White House Historical Association and National Geographic Society, 1999 (ninth edition).

Kruh, David and Louis Kruh. *Presidential Landmarks.* New York: Hippocrene Books, Inc., 1992.

Pearce, Lorraine. *The White House: An Historic Guide.* Washington, D.C.: White House Historical Association and National Geographic Society, 1999 (20th edition).

Purcell, L. Edward, editor. *Vice Presidents: A Biographical Dictionary.* New York: Checkmark Books, Facts On File, 2001.

Schaefer, Peggy. *The Ideals Guide to Presidential Homes and Libraries.* Nashville: Ideals Press, 2002.

The World Almanac and Book of Facts. New York: World Almanac Books, 2004.

ANN BAUSUM is the author of 16 nonfiction history titles. *Ensnared in the Wolf's Lair* (2021) is her latest work for teen readers. Her books for young people have received numerous awards, including a Sibert Honor, the Jane Addams Children's Book Award, the SCBWI Golden Kite Award, and the Carter G. Woodson Award (twice). The Children's Book Guild of Washington, D.C., recognized the body of her work by naming her the 2017 recipient of its nonfiction award, a coveted distinction for children's authors. Notable titles from her writing career include *The March Against Fear; Stubby the War Dog; Marching to the Mountaintop; Denied, Detained, Deported; Freedom Riders; With Courage and Cloth; Stonewall;* and *Viral.* The daughter of a history professor, Bausum grew up with a love of research and American history. She tackled each presidency as its own assignment, immersing herself in reference volumes, historical documents, and period anecdotes. Finding the facts she knows kids will love is her favorite part of research. A graduate of Beloit College, she makes her home in Wisconsin. Bausum's website is annbausum.com.

Consultant **ROBERT D. JOHNSTON** is professor of history and director of the Teaching of History Program at the University of Illinois at Chicago. He is also the author of National Geographic's *The Making of America: The History of the United States From 1492 to the Present,* which was named a *School Library Journal* Best Book of the Year. Johnston lives in Chicago with his wife, Anne.

ILLUSTRATIONS CREDITS

AL = Alamy Stock Photo; GI = Getty Images; LOC = Library of Congress Prints and Photographs Division; NGIC = National Geographic Image Collection; SS = Shutterstock; WHC = White House Collection; WHHA = White House Historical Association

FRONT COVER: (George Washington), WHC/WHHA; (antique flag), Triff/SS; (Joe Biden), David Lienemann/The White House; (Franklin Delano Roosevelt) WHC/WHHA; (Ronald Reagan), WHC/WHHA; (Abraham Lincoln), WHC/WHHA; (Barack Obama), Pete Souza/The White House; **SPINE:** Lunamarina/Dreamstime; **BACK COVER:** (presidential seal), Vladislav Gurfinkel/GI; (the White House), S.Borisov/SS; **FLAPS:** (rippling flag), Vlada Young/SS

FRONT MATTER: 1, Larry Downing/GI; 2-3, ESB Professional/SS; 5, Ashley Werter/Dreamstime; 6, Brooks Kraft LLC/Corbis Premium Historical/GI; 8 (UP), Vladislav Gurfinkel/GI; 8 (LO), Stock Montage/GI; 9 (UP LE), Universal History Archive/GI; 9 (UP RT), Bettmann/GI; 9 (LO), LOC; 10, Jupiterimages/GI; **THE PRESIDENCY AND HOW IT GREW:** 12-13, WHHA; 12 (A), National Archives; 12 (B), ukartpics/AL; 12 (C), Granger, All Rights Reserved; 12 (D), Granger, All Rights Reserved; 13 (A), Art Reserve/AL; 13 (B), Science History Images/AL; 13 (C), Granger, All Rights Reserved; 13 (D), North Wind Picture Archives/AL; 14, WHC/WHHA; 15 (UP), Granger, All Rights Reserved; 15 (LO), LOC; 16 (UP LE), Bequest of Grace Wilkes, 1922/Metropolitan Museum of Art; 16 (UP RT), LOC; 16 (LO), Gift of John Stewart Kennedy, 1897/Metropolitan Museum of Art; 17 (LE), Ian Dagnall/AL; 17 (RT), LOC; 18 (UP), Bettmann Archive/GI; 18 (LO), Granger, All Rights Reserved; 19 (UP), LOC; 19 (LO LE), Bequest of William Nelson, 1905/Metropolitan Museum of Art; 19 (LO RT), Granger, All Rights Reserved; 20, WHC/WHHA; 21 (UP), Adams National Historical Site/NPS/Bob Allnut; 21 (LO), Granger, All Rights Reserved; 22 (UP), Everett Collection Historical/AL; 22 (LO), Lisa Biganzoli/NGIC; 23 (LE), Granger, All Rights Reserved; 23 (RT), Glasshouse Images/AL; 24 (UP), Sean Pavone/SS; 24 (CTR), LOC; 24 (LO), Granger, All Rights Reserved; 25 (UP), Tom Freeman 2004/WHHA; 25 (LO), NGIC; 26, WHC/WHHA; 27 (LE), LOC; 27 (RT), The U.S. National Archives and Records Administration; 28 (UP), GL Archive/AL; 28 (LO), Everett Collection Historical/AL; 29 (UP), Marie-Louise Brimberg/NGIC; 29 (LO), MPI/GI; 30 (UP), Authur Lidov/NGIC; 30 (LO), Vlad Kharitonov/NGIC; 31 (UP), Linda Bartlett/NGIC; 31 (LO LE), Linda Bartlett/NGIC; 31 (LO RT), WHC/WHHA; 32, WHC/WHHA; 33 (UP), WHC/WHHA; 33 (LO), Eastern National Park & Monument/NGIC; 34 (UP), LOC; 34 (CTR), North Wind Picture Archives/AL/AL; 34 (LO), Niday Picture Library/AL; 35 (UP LE), Everett Collection/SS; 35 (UP RT), William Woodward, artist. 2009. Courtesy the Montpelier Foundation; 35 (LO), LOC; 36 (UP), amadeustx/SS; 36 (LO LE), Brendan Smialowski/AFP/GI; 36 (LO RT), AP/Rex Features/SS; 37 (UP), The U.S. National Archives and Records Administration; 37 (LO), Everett Collection/SS; 38, WHC/WHHA; 39, Pierre Mion/NGIC; 40, Carl Rakeman/Federal Highway Administration; 41 (UP), LOC; 41 (CTR), Bettmann/GI; 41 (LO), WHC/WHHA; 42, WHC/WHHA; 43, Granger, All Rights Reserved; 44 (UP), Olivier Douliery-Pool/GI; 44 (LO), Chip Somodevilla/GI; 45 (UP LE), Martin H. Simon-Pool/GI; 45 (UP RT), Brendan Smialowski/AFP/GI; 45 (LO), Michelle LaVaughn Robinson Obama by Amy Sherald, oil on linen, 2018. National Portrait Gallery, Smithsonian Institution. The National Portrait Gallery is grateful to the following lead donors for their support of the Obama portraits: Kate Capshaw and Steven Spielberg; Judith Kern and Kent Whealy; Tommie L. Pegues and Donald A. Capoccia; 46, WHC/WHHA; 47 (UP), LOC; 47 (LO), Granger, All Rights Reserved; 48 (UP LE), LOC; 48 (UP RT), Peter Newark American Pictures/Bridgeman Images; 48 (LO), David S. Boyer/NGIC; 49 (UP), The Stapleton Collection/Bridgeman Images; 49 (LO LE), David S. Boyer/NGIC; 49 (LO RT), Everett Collection Inc/AL; **FROM SEA TO SHINING SEA:** 50-51, Universal History Archive/GI; 50 (A), Look and Learn/Bridgeman Images; 50 (B), Bettmann/GI; 50 (C), Everett Collection/SS; 50 (D), Bettmann/GI; 51 (A), PhotoQuest/GI; 51 (B), Painting by William Heine from Mrs. Mary C. Owens/George Mobley/NGIC; 51 (C), Adobe Stock; 51 (D), Art Collection 2/AL; 52, WHC/WHHA; 53 (UP), National Park Service Digital Image Archives; 53 (LO), Museum of the City of New York/Bridgeman Images; 54, WHC/WHHA; 55 (UP), Kean Collection/GI; 55 (LO), Archivac/AL; 56, WHC/WHHA; 57 (UP), Pierre Mion/NGIC; 57 (LO), Granger, All Rights Reserved; 58 (UP), Orhan Cam/SS; 58 (CTR), Granger, All Rights Reserved; 58 (LO), Bettmann/GI; 59 (UP LE), Carolyn Kaster/AP/SS; 59 (UP RT), Bettmann/GI; 59 (LO LE), Bettmann/GI; 59 (LO RT), The White House/Hulton Archive/GI; 60, WHC/WHHA; 61 (UP), World Archive/AL; 61 (LO), Everett Historical/SS; 62 (UP), The New York Public Library/Art Resource, NY; 62 (LO), LOC; 63 (UP), Bettmann/GI; 63 (LO LE), Library of Congress/GI; 63 (LO RT), LOC; 64 (UP), Peeradach Rattanakoses/SS; 64 (CTR), Bettman/GI; 64 (LO), Steve Schapiro/Corbis Historical/GI; 65 (UP LE), Bettmann/GI; 65 (UP RT), AP Images/North Wind Picture Archives; 65 (LO), AP Images/Denis Cook; 66, WHC/WHHA; 67 (UP), LOC; 67 (LO), Everett Collection Inc./AL; 68, WHC/WHHA; 69 (UP), Universal History Archive/GI; 69 (LO), Granger, All Rights Reserved; 70 (UP), holbox/SS; 70 (CTR LE), Vlad Kharitonov/NGIC; 70 (CTR RT), Vlad Kharitonov/NGIC; 70 (LO), MPI/GI; 71 (UP LE), North Wind Picture Archives/AL; 71 (UP RT), Bettmann/GI; 71 (CTR), Bettmann/GI; 71 (LO LE), The Frent Collection/GI; 71 (LO RT), Brown Brothers; 72, WHC/WHHA; 73 (UP), Pictures Now/AL; 73 (LO), Fotosearch/GI; 74, WHC/WHHA; 75 (UP), Art Reserve/AL; 75 (LO), Everett Historical/SS; **A NEW BIRTH OF FREEDOM:** 76-77, Peter Newark Military Pictures/Bridgeman Images; 76 (A), Peter Newark American Pictures/Bridgeman Images; 76 (B), Ed Vebell/GI; 76 (C), Bettmann/GI; 76 (D), Washington State Historical Society, Tacoma; 77 (A), Granger, All Rights Reserved; 77 (B), Granger, All Rights Reserved; 77 (C), LOC; 77 (D), William Lovelace/Express/Hulton Archive/GI; 78, WHC/WHHA; 79 (UP), Science History Images/AL; 79 (LO), Universal History Library/UIG via GI; 80 (LE), Stephen Jensen/Chicago History Museum/GI; 80 (RT), British Library/Science Source; 81 (UP), Bettmann/GI; 81 (LO), Pictures Now/AL; 82 (UP LE), LOC; 82 (UP RT), LOC; 82 (LO), Everett Collection Historical/AL; 83 (UP LE), LOC; 83 (UP RT), Everett Collection/SS; 83 (LO LE), Bettmann/GI; 83 (LO RT), Niday Picture Library/AL; 84, WHC/WHHA; 85 (UP), Granger Historical Picture Archive/AL; 85 (LO), LOC; 86 (UP), Orhan Cam/SS; 86 (LO), RBM Vintage Images/AL; 87 (UP LE), AP Images/Marty Lederhandler; 87 (UP RT), Pictures from History/Bridgeman Images; 87 (CTR), Bettmann/GI; 87 (LO), SS; 88, WHC/WHHA; 89 (UP), Bridgeman Images; 89 (LO), Old Paper Studios/AL; 90 (UP), LOC; 90 (LO), LOC; 91 (UP LE), Stock Montage/GI; 91 (UP RT), LOC; 91 (LO), LOC; 92, WHC/WHHA; 93, Rutherford B. Hayes Presidential Center; 94 (UP), Cosmonaut/iStockphoto/GI; 94 (LO LE), Minnesota Historical Society/Corbis/Corbis via GI; 94 (LO RT), MPI/GI; 95 (LE), Flip Schulke/Corbis/Corbis via GI; 95 (RT), Matthew Cavanaugh/EPA/SS; 96, WHC/WHHA; 97, Corbis via GI; 98, WHC/WHHA; 99 (UP), LOC; 99 (LO), LOC; 100, WHC/WHHA; 101, Library of Congress/GI; 102 (UP), Niday Picture Library/AL; 102 (LO), LOC; 103 (UP LE), LOC; 103 (UP RT), Roger Viollet Collection/GI; 103 (LO), Bettmann/GI; 104 (UP), Galyna Andrushko/SS; 104 (CTR RT), fotopak/Adobe Stock Photo; 104 (CTR LE), Corbis via GI; 104 (LO LE), Bettmann/GI; 104 (LO RT), Saul Loeb/AFP via GI; 106, WHC/WHHA; 107 (UP), LOC; 107 (LO), Bettmann/GI; **AMERICA TAKES CENTER STAGE:** 108-109, Apic/GI; 108 (A), LOC; 108 (B), Everett Historical/SS; 108 (C), LOC; 108 (D), Everett Collection/SS; 109 (A), Granger, All Rights Reserved; 109 (B), Bettmann/GI; 109 (C), Roger Viollet/GI; 109 (D), Niday Picture Library/AL; 110, WHC/WHHA; 111 (UP), LOC; 111 (LO), MPI/GI; 112 (UP), LOC; 112 (LO), Granger, All Rights Reserved; 113 (UP), LOC; 113 (LO), Bettmann/GI; 114, WHC/WHHA; 115 (UP), Robert Oakes/NGIC; 115 (LO), LOC; 116 (UP), Everett Historical/SS; 116 (LO LE), Popperfoto/GI; 116 (LO RT), Corbis via GI; 117 (UP LE), LOC; 117 (UP RT), LOC; 117 (LO), LOC; 118 (UP LE), Stock Montage/GI; 118 (LO), LOC; 118-119 (UP), Rex/SS; 119 (UP CTR), Alex Ross/WHC/WHHA; 119 (UP RT), LOC; 119 (CTR LE), The White House; 119 (CTR RT), National Archives; 119 (LO LE), Bettmann/GI; 119 (LO RT), John Rous/AP/SS; 120, WHC/WHHA; 121 (UP), Everett/SS; 121 (LO), Granger, All Rights Reserved; 122 (UP), Christopher Badzioch/iStockphoto/GI; 122 (CTR), Rudy Sulgan/The Image Bank/GI; 122 (LO), LOC; 123 (UP LE), Bettmann/GI; 123 (UP RT), Jim Watson/AFP/GI; 123 (LO), Fred Schilling, Supreme Court Curator's Office; 124, WHC/WHHA; 125 (UP), Punch/TopFoto.co.uk; 125 (LO), Chronicle/AL; 126 (UP LE), Peter Newark Military Pictures/Bridgeman Images; 126 (UP RT), Time Life Pictures/Mansell/The LIFE Picture Collection/GI; 126 (CTR), Hulton Archive/GI; 126 (LO), Bettmann/GI; 127 (UP), Buyenlarge Archive/UIG/Bridgeman Images; 127 (LO), LOC; 128 (UP), LOC; 128 (CTR LE), Mort Kunstler; 128 (CTR RT), Topical Press Agency/GI; 128 (LO), Kean Collection/GI; 129 (UP), Corbis/GI; 129 (CTR), Harry Todd/Fox Photos/GI; 129 (LO LE), Wally McNamee/Corbis/Corbis via GI; 129 (LO RT), Susan Walsh/AP/SS; 130, WHC/WHHA; 131, LOC; 132, WHC/WHHA; 133 (UP), Glasshouse Images/SS; 133 (LO), LOC; 134 (UP), Andrey Popov/SS; 134 (CTR), LOC; 134 (LO LE), LOC; 134 (LO CTR), LOC; 134 (LO RT), LOC; 135 (UP), The White House; 135 (LO), Everett Collection/SS; 136, WHC/WHHA; 137 (UP), Bettmann/GI; 137 (LO), NY Daily News Archive via GI; 138, WHC/WHHA; 139 (UP), Fotosearch/GI; 139 (LO), GL Archive/AL; 140 (UP LE), Bettmann/GI; 140 (LO LE), The U.S. National Archives and Records Administration; 140 (LO RT), LOC; 141 (UP LE), LOC; 141 (UP RT), FPG/GI; 141 (LO), Granger, All Rights Reserved; 142 (LE), Archive Photos/GI; 142 (RT), Glasshouse Images/SS; 143 (UP), Bettmann/GI; 143 (LO LE), Ed Clark/The LIFE Picture Collection via GI; 143 (LO RT), Sandra Baker/AL; 144 (UP), Bettmann/GI; 144 (CTR), WHC/WHHA; 144 (LO LE), Louis Glanzman/NGIC; 144 (LO RT), The New York Public Library, Astor, Lenox, and Tilden Foundations; 145 (A), Joe Bailey/NGIC; 145 (B), Patrick Semansky/AP/SS; 145 (C), Patrick T. Fallon/Bloomberg/GI; 145 (D), Olivier Douliery/Abaca Press/MCT/Newscom; 145 (E), Paul Schutzer/The LIFE Picture Collection via GI; 145 (F), Reuters/Adobe Stock; 145 (G), Keystone-France/Gamma-Rapho via GI; **SEEKING STABILITY IN THE ATOMIC AGE:** 146-147, Universal History Archive/GI; 146 (A), Everett Collection/SS; 146 (B), Bettmann/GI; 146 (C), Arthur Schatz/The LIFE Picture Collection via GI; 146 (D), Everett Collection Inc/AL; 147 (A), NASA; 147 (B), Paul Slade/Paris Match via GI; 147 (C), Cofiant Images/AL; 147 (D), Tom Stoddart/Reportage by GI; 148, WHC/WHHA; 149 (UP), Bettmann/GI; 149 (LO), Corbis via GI; 150 (UP), Bettmann/GI; 150 (LO LE), US Army; 150 (LO RT), FPG/GI; 151 (UP), Walter Sanders/The LIFE Picture Collection via GI; 151 (LO LE), Arthur Shilstone/NGIC; 151 (LO RT), Corbis via GI; 152 (UP), emarto/iStockphoto/GI; 152-153 (LO), AP Photo/Amy Sancetta; 153 (UP), Keystone/GI; 153 (LO RT), Jeffrey Greenberg/Universal Images Group via GI; 154, WHC/WHHA; 155 (UP), Glasshouse Images/SS; 155 (LO), FPG/Archive Photos/GI; 156 (UP LE), The U.S. National Archives and Records Administration; 156 (UP RT), Bettmann/GI; 156 (LO), Transcendental Graphics/GI; 157 (UP LE), Bettmann/GI; 157 (UP RT), Michael Rougier/The LIFE Picture Collection via GI; 157 (CTR), Dwight D. Eisenhower Presidential Library and Museum; 157 (LO), AP/Wide World Photos; 158, WHC/WHHA; 159 (UP), Corbis via GI; 159 (LO LE), John F. Kennedy Library/USN; 159 (LO RT), MPI/GI; 160 (UP LE), Corbis via GI; 160 (UP RT), Ed Clark/The LIFE Picture Collection via GI; 160 (LO LE), Keystone/GI; 160 (LO RT), Mediapunch/SS; 161 (UP LE), Hank Walker/The LIFE Picture Collection via GI; 161 (UP RT), AFP via GI; 161 (LO), Bettmann/GI; 162 (UP), Thomas Shanahan/iStockphoto/GI; 162 (CTR), James P. Blair/NGIC; 162 (LO LE), James P. Blair/NGIC; 162 (LO RT), John Frost Newspapers/AL; 163 (UP LE), LOC; 163 (UP CTR), Granger, All Rights Reserved; 163 (UP RT), John Frost Newspapers/AL; 163 (LO LE), Hulton Archive/GI; 163 (LO RT), Arlan Wiker/NGIC; 164, WHC/WHHA; 165 (UP), Everett Collection Inc/AL; 165 (LO), The U.S. National Archives and Records Administration; 166 (UP), George F. Mobley/NGIC; 166 (LO), Corbis via GI; 167 (UP LE), LOC; 167 (UP CTR), White House Photo/AL; 167 (UP RT), Dennis Brack/AL; 167 (LO LE), Universal History Archive/Universal Images Group via GI; 167 (LO RT), Bettmann/GI; 168, WHC/WHHA; 169 (UP), Fox Photos/GI; 169 (LO), Pictorial Press Ltd/AL; 170 (UP), Kenneth Garrett/NGIC; 170 (CTR), James L. Stanfield, NG Image Collection; 170 (LO), AP Photo; 171 (UP LE), Everett Collection Inc/AL; 171 (CTR), MPI/GI; 171 (UP RT), Joseph H. Bailey/NGIC; 171 (LO LE), Stephen St. John/NGIC; 172, WHC/WHHA; 173 (UP), UPI/AL; 173 (LO), Corbis via GI; 174, Vlad G/SS; 175, Newscom; 176, WHC/WHHA; 177 (UP), courtesy Jimmy Carter Library & Museum; 177 (LO), Anonymous/AP/SS; 178 (LE), Wilbur E. Garrett/NGIC; 178 (RT), Corbis/GI; 179 (UP LE), David Hume Kennerly/GI; 179 (UP RT), Alain Mingam/Gamma-Rapho via GI; 179 (LO), AP Photo/Bjoern Sigurdsoen/Pool; 180, WHC/WHHA; 181 (UP), SS; 181 (LO), Corbis via GI; 182 (UP LE), David Alan Harvey/NGIC; 182 (UP RT), Consolidated News Pictures/GI; 182 (CTR), AP Photo; 182 (LO), Hulton Archive/GI; 183 (UP LE), AP Photo/White House; 183 (UP RT), David Hume Kennerly/GI; 183 (LO), Stan Honda/AFP/GI; **PATHWAYS FOR A NEW MILLENNIUM:** 184-185, Sean Pavone/iStockphoto/GI; 184 (A), Josh Roberts/AFP via GI; 184 (B), Laperruque/AL; 184 (C), wachiwit/Adobe Stock; 184 (D), Spencer Platt/GI; 185 (A), AP Photo/John Miller; 185 (B), Paul Morigi/GI; 185 (C), Daniel Bockwoldt/picture alliance via GI; 185 (D), Peter Schreiber/Adobe Stock; 186, WHC/WHHA; 187 (UP), SS; 187 (LO), Everett Collection/SS; 188 (UP), Stephen R Brown/AP/SS; 188 (LO LE), Michel Gangne/AFP via GI; 188 (LO RT), Natalie Fobes/NGIC; 189 (UP LE), Newsmakers/Hulton Archive/GI; 189 (RT), Robert Daemmrich Photography Inc/Sygma via GI; 189 (LO LE), Brad Markel/Liaison/GI; 190 (UP), LOC; 190 (CTR), Kazuhiro Nogi/AFP/GI; 190 (LO LE), Donald Miralle/GI; 190 (LO RT), Evan Vucci/AP/SS; 191 (UP), White House Photo/AL; 191 (LO LE), Paul Morse/The White House; 191 (LO RT), Saul Loeb/AFP via GI; 192, WHC/WHHA; 193 (UP), Arnold Sachs/GI; 193 (LO), Larry Downing/Sygma/Sygma via GI; 194 (UP RT), Mark Reinstein/Corbis via GI; 194 (LE), Cynthia Johnson/The LIFE Images Collection/GI; 194 (LO RT), Arnie Sachs/Archive Photos/GI; 195 (UP LE), Jeff Swensen/GI; 195 (UP RT), George Widman-Pool/GI; 195 (LO), Porter Gifford/GI; 196, WHC/WHHA; 197 (UP), Hulton Archive/GI; 197 (LO), Robert Daemmrich Photography Inc/Corbis via GI; 198 (UP), The White House; 198 (CTR), Stringer/GI; 198 (LO LE), The White House; 198 (LO RT), The White House; 199 (UP), Eric Draper/White House/Getty Image; 199 (LO LE), Reuters/Larry Downing LSD/mk/Adobe Stock; 199 (LO RT), AP Photo/Tony Gutierrez; 200, Official White House Photo by Pete Souza; 201 (UP), Joe Wrinn/Harvard University/Corbis via GI; 201 (LO), White House Photo/AL; 202 (UP LE), Win McNamee/GI; 202 (UP RT), Pete Souza/The White House/GI; 202 (LO), AP Photo/Alex Brandon; 203 (UP LE), Ayhan Mehmet/Anadolu Agency/GI; 203 (RT), Drew Angerer/Bloomberg/GI; 203 (LO LE), Mark Wilson/GI; 204, Official White House Photo by Shealah Craighead; 205 (UP), Mathew Imaging/FilmMagic/GI; 205 (LO), Dennis Caruso/NY Daily News Archive/GI; 206 (LE), Matt York/AP/SS; 206 (RT), Josh Haner/The New York Times/Redux Pictures; 207 (UP LE), Chris Ratcliffe/Bloomberg via GI; 207 (UP RT), Jim Lo Scalzo/EPA-EFE/SS; 207 (LO), Chandan Khanna/AFP via GI; 208 (UP), 3dfoto/SS; 208 (CTR LE), Drew Angerer/GI; 208 (RT), Carolyn Kaster/AP/SS; 208 (LO LE), Spencer Platt/GI; 209 (UP), Jonathan Newton/The Washington Post via GI; 209 (LO LE), Carolyn Kaster/AP/SS; 209 (LO RT), SS; 210, Official White House Photo by David Lienemann; 211 (UP), Bettmann Archive/GI; 211 (LO), Jim Bourg/Reuters; 212 (UP), Sean Pavone/SS; 212 (CTR), North Wind Picture Archives/AL; 212 (LO LE), George Rinhart/Corbis/GI; 212 (LO RT), Adobe Stock; 213 (UP), Don Bartletti/Los Angeles Times via GI; 213 (LO), David Hume Kennerly/GI; **BACK MATTER:** 224, Jerry Driendl/GI

INDEX

For my sons, Jake and Sam, with love
—AB

Since 1888, the National Geographic Society has funded more than 12,000 research, exploration, and preservation projects around the world. The Society receives funds from National Geographic Partners, LLC, funded in part by your purchase. A portion of the proceeds from this book supports this vital work. To learn more, visit natgeo.com/info.

For more information, visit nationalgeographic.com, call 1-877-873-6846, or write to the following address:

National Geographic Partners, LLC
1145 17th Street N.W.
Washington, DC 20036-4688 U.S.A.

For librarians and teachers: nationalgeographic.com/books/librarians-and-educators/

More for kids from National Geographic: natgeokids.com

National Geographic Kids magazine inspires children to explore their world with fun yet educational articles on animals, science, nature, and more. Using fresh storytelling and amazing photography, *Nat Geo Kids* shows kids ages 6 to 14 the fascinating truth about the world—and why they should care.
kids.nationalgeographic.com/subscribe

For rights or permissions inquiries, please contact National Geographic Books Subsidiary Rights: bookrights@natgeo.com

Art directed by Amanda Larsen
Designed by Carol Norton

Hardcover ISBN: 978-1-4263-7199-8
Reinforced library binding ISBN: 978-1-4263-7200-1

Printed in the United States of America
20/WOR/1

The publisher gratefully acknowledges the kind assistance of presidential historian Michael Beschloss for his review of the first edition of this title in page proof form and Robert D. Johnston, professor of history and director of the Teaching of History Program at the University of Illinois at Chicago, for reviewing and commenting on all subsequent editions of the book, including this one. The publisher would also like to recognize the generous support of the late William B. Bushong, longtime staff historian for the White House Historical Association, who reviewed the first four editions of this title. Sincere thanks are likewise expressed to John Dickerson for writing this edition's foreword. The author extends special appreciation to the production team for this book, including Suzanne Fonda (project editor), Michaela Weglinski and Ariane Szu-Tu (project managers), Amanda Larsen (design director), Alix Inchausti (production editor), Anne LeongSon and Gus Tello (design production assistants), Michael McNey (maps), and Lori Epstein (photo director), and she offers enduring thanks to former art director Callie Broaddus and designer Carol Norton, who recently enlivened this book with a new design. Thank you, one and all.

Publisher's Note: The reporting presented on the 2020 election reflects the latest available information as of press time.

PAGE 1: The presidential seal was altered by President Harry S. Truman so that the eagle faced toward the olive branch, a symbol of peace, rather than toward the arrows of war.

PAGES 2-3: The arching columns of the South Portico were added to the White House in 1824. In 1948, at the suggestion of President Truman, workers added a second-floor balcony to the structure. The addition is called the Truman Balcony in his honor.

Presidential monuments to Abraham Lincoln (foreground) and George Washington punctuate the evening skyline in the nation's capital (with the U.S. Capitol Building shown behind). The Washington Monument was the tallest structure in the world when it was completed in 1884, measuring 555 feet 5⅛ inches high.